PACIFIC OCEAN

Equator

INDIAN OCEAN

THE

SAUVIGNON BLANC
& SÉMILLON

GRAPES

SAUVIGNON BLANC
AND SÉMILLON

Stephen Brook

Series editor: Harry Eyres

VIKING

VIKING

Published by the Penguin Group
Penguin Books Ltd, 27 Wrights Lane, London W8 5TZ, England
Penguin Books USA Inc., 375 Hudson Street, New York, New York 10014, USA
Penguin Books Australia Ltd, Ringwood, Victoria, Australia
Penguin Books Canada Ltd, 10 Alcorn Avenue, Toronto, Ontario,
Canada MV4 3B2
Penguin Books (NZ) Ltd, 182–190 Wairau Road, Auckland 10, New Zealand

Penguin Books Ltd, Registered Offices: Harmondsworth, Middlesex, England

First published 1992
1 3 5 7 9 10 8 6 4 2

Set in 9/12 point Linotron Janson Text 55 by Wyvern Typesetting Ltd, Bristol
Printed in Great Britain by Butler & Tanner Ltd, Frome and London

A CIP catalogue record for this book is available from the British Library

ISBN 0-670-82482-8

To Erik, Laura and Elliot

CONTENTS

MAPS

FOREWORD

Sancerre, Pouilly-Fumé, white Graves, Hunter Valley Sémillon, New Zealand Sauvignon Blanc: an interesting, at times outstanding, array of white wines, but what do they have in common? The truth is, not necessarily anything at all. These wines are made from two grape varieties, Sauvignon Blanc and Sémillon, which both originated in Bordeaux. Ampelographically, they are unrelated. When grown in the cool climates of New Zealand or Washington State, Sémillon can share the herbaceous, green leaf, gooseberry character of Sauvignon Blanc. But in Bordeaux the two varieties stand out as quite distinct: Sémillon rounder, more neutral, lower in acidity; Sauvignon sharper, almost tart, with a jejune fruitiness which provides attack but does not promise longevity.

So why are they treated together in this guide? The answer is that Sauvignon Blanc and Sémillon team up with magical effectiveness to make two of the world's great wines: the luscious sweet Sauternes, product of grapes affected with botrytis; and, made in tiny quantities, dry white Graves, aged and preferably fermented in oak, one of the few dry white wines with the ability to acquire fascinating new flavours with age.

Few people know Sauternes better than Stephen Brook, author of an authoritative work on the world's best sweet wines. Brook not only pays meticulous attention to the details of wine-making and, perhaps even more importantly, grape-picking; he also conveys the excitement of a region which has dramatically recovered from a long decline. White Graves is also enjoying a mini-renaissance, with wine like de Fieuzal and La Tour-Martillac challenging the long-established superstars, Laville Haut-Brion, Haut-Brion Blanc and Domaine de Chevalier. Sadly production at all these properties is insufficient for growing worldwide demand.

Overpopularity has for some time been a curse of those two wines from the upper Loire which show the Sauvignon Blanc at its freshest and grassiest: Sancerre and Pouilly-Fumé. Fashionable first in Paris and then a mainstay of the restaurant boom in Britain in the 1980s, this pair of one-time country bumpkins is now charging sophisticated metropolitan prices. In a field where the separation of sheep from goats (lazy producers who know they can get away with dull overcropped wines) is crucial, Stephen Brook can give expert guidance. But anyone who has tasted the magnificently pure, intensely flavoursome Cuvée Silex and Cuvée Pur Sang wines from the magus of Pouilly, Didier Dagueneau, will not resent his high prices, nor the opportunity for the pursuit of excellence which fashion has brought.

Ten years ago, when Sancerre and Pouilly-Fumé were beginning to be modish, no one could have guessed that a Sauvignon Blanc from the Southern Hemisphere would soon out-Sancerre Sancerre. But New Zealand's Cloudy Bay, brainchild of the astute Western Australian David Hohnen, became perhaps the ultimate cult wine of the 1980s. Not only is Cloudy Bay Sauvignon Blanc very, very good – perhaps the most intense and deliciously fruity expression of the grape yet achieved – but it has nurtured a generation of excellent competitors from New Zealand, some beginning to challenge Cloudy Bay for supremacy.

In other parts of the New World, Sauvignon Blanc, despite its fashionable status and growing demand, has performed disappointingly. Australia, apart from the odd corner such as Margaret River, does not seem to suit the variety: too hot, most likely. Results from California have been rather more interesting. The brilliant Robert Mondavi came up with his oaked Fumé Blanc, a successful wine undoubtedly, but one which has created no end of confusion by hijacking a name for a mythical style which certainly never existed in France. Now, lighter and less obviously oaked, or unoaked, California Sauvignons, such as those from Matanzas Creek and Frog's Leap, are offering a worthwhile half-way house between Sancerre and dry Graves.

Poor old Sémillon. This certainly cannot be called a fashionable grape: it has proved hard even for wine writers to capture its elusive flavours in words – indeed the grape is something of a chameleon, sometimes approximating closely to Sauvignon Blanc in grassy green flavours, sometimes veering off to the other extreme of soft melony roundness. But Sémillon, as Jancis Robinson argued in *Vines, Grapes and Wines*, has stronger claims to being considered a top-class grape variety than Sauvignon Blanc. Not only is Sémillon by far the more important partner in Sauternes (usually making up around 80 per cent of the blend), but at the other end of the world, in New South Wales's Hunter Valley, Sémillon without any assistance from oak makes some of the world's greatest, most sensationally long-lived dry white wines. When Lindemans was taken over by Penfolds in 1990 my main concern was whether Lindemans' commendable policy of storing classic older vintages for up to twenty years before release would be continued. It would be tragic indeed if wines like the 1970 Hunter Valley Sémillon Bin 3855, with its buttercup-yellow colour, its rich lanolin nose and its marvellous combination of freshness and fullness, ceased to be held back until they displayed the incomparable riches of maturity.

Harry Eyres

ACKNOWLEDGEMENTS

I owe a great debt to the national wine promotion organizations who helped me to organize trips to important wine regions and in some cases provided financial assistance to enable me to complete my researches. I wish to thank particularly the Wine Institute of California, and Food and Wine from France, where Catherine Manac'h and her colleagues helped me on many occasions. Fritz Ascher, of the Austrian Wine Marketing Board, arranged a splendid tasting for me in Vienna. Damjan Bulum of the Fond za Vino of Belgrade provided much useful information about Yugoslavia. I must also thank Sîtâ Garros in Bordeaux, who opened numerous doors in the Sauternes region. It is impossible to mention by name the innumerable proprietors who were generous with information, tastings and hospitality, but I must single out Mme Nicole Tari of Château Nairac and Florence and Denis Dubourdieu of Château Reynon, who invited me to stay with them in the Bordeaux region. Didier Dagueneau has devoted much time, effort and hospitality to increasing my understanding of the wines of Pouilly and Sancerre. Alois Lageder in Bolzano ensured that my knowledge of the Alto-Adige region was as complete as possible, and Bob Campbell in New Zealand and David Hohnen and Jane Adams in Australia were also generous with their help and suggestions. In California Rick Hanley of St Helena Wine Merchants allowed me to pick his brains and sample his wares. Andrew Henderson kindly arranged for me to taste a range of Chilean wines. Half the growers of St-Bris assembled one Saturday morning to present a thorough tasting of their appellation, which I greatly appreciated.

Many members of the wine trade have been helpful in organizing trips to countries such as Italy, where wine promotion does not appear to include assisting research. In London

David Gleave of Winecellars and Paul Merritt of Trestini, and in Chicago Seth Allen, assisted me greatly. The wine trade made tasting samples available and I wish to thank the following importers and merchants: John Armit, Avery's, Belloni, Bishopsmead, Deinhard, Peter Dominic, Michael Druitt, Ehrmann, Eldridge Pope, Enotria, Harvey's, Hedley Wright, Lawlers, Laytons McWilliam, Majestic, Oddbins, Penfolds, Rosemount, Tesco, Upper Crust and Waitrose. My thanks too to Catherine Scott.

Stephen Brook

INTRODUCTION

Ever since it was decided that certain grape varieties were noble and others not, Sauvignon Blanc and Sémillon have had a rough ride. While it is universally acknowledged that the two varieties, when allowed to succumb to botrytis (noble rot) and blended after vinification, can produce one of the great wines of the world – the sweet wines of Sauternes – few have made such claims for either variety when vinified dry. Jancis Robinson, in her *Vines, Grapes and Wines*, shows little enthusiasm for Sauvignon: 'The varietal has not proved . . . that unassisted it can produce wines for the future, and longevity is surely a component of greatness in wine.' The Australian winemaker Brian Croser is even more emphatic: 'It's a trivial wine to be drunk the year of the harvest . . . I've never seen a varietal Sauvignon Blanc that has taken age successfully. That's the case in California, Australia and New Zealand.' Such assertions are greeted with scorn by the likes of Didier Dagueneau in the Loire, who is convinced that Sauvignon is capable of a maturation and evolution in bottle comparable to the more fashionable Chardonnay.

As for Sémillon, the great French oenologist Émile Peynaud is dismissive. In an interview in the *Wine Spectator* (August 1989) he declared: 'Sémillon does not produce good dry white wines anywhere in the world.' Yet anyone who has tasted a top-quality twenty-year-old Sémillon from Australia's Hunter Valley has the evidence to contradict Peynaud's haughty judgment.

The reason why so many authorities are disdainful is that the majority of wines now being made from these grapes are, in varying combinations, dull, poorly made or even faulty, and produced with commercially inspired cynicism. In large areas of France they are regarded as workhorse grapes, and you cannot make noble wine if you treat your grapes as serfs. One only has to taste a dry white wine from a top Graves estate, a Sancerre from Lucien Crochet, a racy New Zealand Sauvignon, a Hunter Valley Sémillon, and the great sweet wines made from these varieties in the New World as well as in Sauternes, to know that, when treated with respect, they are capable of making great wine.

To the assertion that the general qualitative level of most Chardonnay seems, overall, considerably higher than that of most Sauvignon, Didier Dagueneau's reply is that Sauvignon is a more difficult grape with which to succeed, just as it is harder to make a great Pinot Noir than a great Cabernet Sauvignon. Yet nobody, he would argue, would claim that red burgundy is a lesser wine than claret on the grounds that it is more difficult to find great bottles of the former than of the latter.

Moreover, the Sauvignon enthusiasts argue, the question of yield is crucial. It has long been assumed of Sauvignon that large crops are compatible with good-quality wine; no conscientious Burgundian would seek to make Chardonnay employing the kinds of yields that have been commonplace in the Loire. With low yields, both Sauvignon and Sémillon are capable of producing wines that have precisely the concentration and structure that make them capable of the longevity and evolution that some critics have found lacking.

Sauvignon Blanc, when consumed young, is, or should be, an aromatic wine with considerable freshness, even raciness, of flavour. It can often display a grassy, herbaceous character, reminiscent of gooseberries or even passion fruit, that many consumers find attractive, others distracting. At its worst this grassy character can seem distinctly vegetal, akin to tinned peas or asparagus, not an aroma or flavour that most people wish to encounter in a glass. Sauvignon, especially when picked early, has high acidity that can, in a poorly made wine vinified from overcropped grapes, be tart and attenuated; that same acidity, in a well-made Sauvignon, is refreshing and elegant. Its aroma and flavours are modified by wood-ageing, and here too the acceptability of such alterations is a matter of taste.

The majority of Sauvignons from the Loire, from New

Zealand and from Chile are vinified in neutral containers such as stainless steel or enamel, and the wine is bottled young to preserve its freshness. In Bordeaux, especially in the Graves district, and in California and Australia, the wines tend to lack the aromatic qualities common in grapes grown in cooler regions, so they are often oak-aged. At best, wood-ageing gives wines of richness, complexity and longevity; but a combination of mediocre fruit and clumsy use of oak casks can result in wines that are dull and ungainly. Wood-aged Sauvignon is often blended with Sémillon. Although the Graves style at its best can be profoundly impressive, there is, I suspect, an almost snob-bish, knee-jerk resistance in Australia and California to the refreshing simplicity and verve of unoaked Sauvignon. If it isn't oaked, the assumption goes, it can't be very good.

Sémillon has a very different character. Its thin skin makes it susceptible not only to the desirable noble rot but to the dreaded grey rot. It lacks the aromatic flair of Sauvignon. It appears to have an intrinsic roundness and even heaviness of flavour and texture that earn it, especially in its youth, the apt description 'waxy'. Sémillon is more prolific than Sauvignon, and thus the danger of high yields is even greater, and the consequences equally distressing: dull, flat wines of no discern-ible character, such as used to be routine until a decade ago in most Bordeaux Blanc and Bergerac Sec.

Sémillon also differs from Sauvignon in its lack of acidity. Its very blandness, especially in youth, gives it a kind of blotting-paper character, so that it absorbs the qualities present in the soil more readily than Sauvignon. It does not share the instantly recognizable aromatic character of Sauvignon, Riesling or Muscat. Despite this tendency to blandness and low acidity, Sémillon can age extremely well. With oak-ageing it rapidly acquires a richness of flavour reminiscent of Chardonnay, and a propensity towards flabbiness. Yet in certain parts of the world, notably Australia's Hunter Valley, Sémillon is so rich in natural extract that it matures superbly without any wood-ageing at all. When grown in cool climates in areas such as New Zealand, Washington State and Yarra Valley in Australia, it can display a herbaceous character easy to confuse with Sauvignon.

Both varieties are susceptible to botrytis. This so-called 'noble rot' effects chemical transformations that concentrate the grape's sweetness and acidity; this process will be described in greater detail later. Botrytis is desirable, even essential, for sweet wines, but is the last thing that producers of dry wines wish to find in their vineyards. It is the greater susceptibility of Sémillon to botrytis that disposes some Bordeaux growers to prefer Sauvignon.

Wines made from botrytis-affected grapes are rich in extract, in glycerol, in acidity and, of course, in residual sugar. The art of making great sweet wine is not in attaining sweetness alone, which is easily done with overripe grapes, but in balancing these various elements to produce a wine that is harmonious as well as sweet, elegant as well as lush.

The majority of sweet Bordeaux wines from Sémillon and Sauvignon are Sémillon-dominated. Commercial factors have long played a part in the gradual displacement of Sauvignon in the region. Peter Vinding-Diers, however, a pioneer of modern vinification for white Graves, is a convinced supporter of Sémillon on qualitative grounds. In his view, Sauvignon grown in Bordeaux is excessively grassy and simply uninteresting, though he does not deny that Sauvignon-based wines are capable of long ageing in bottle. The problem with Sémillon, he believes, was that until recently nobody knew how to vinify it so as to get the best out of the grapes. Cool fermentation, in particular, has enabled winemakers to find a previously unsuspected finesse in Sémillon.

None the less, as far as Bordeaux is concerned the historical evidence, for what it's worth, supports the claims of Sauvignon. As long ago as 1801, Chaptal, in his *Traité sur la culture de la vigne*, was complaining that Sauvignon used to be much more widely planted in France; he attributed its unpopularity to the fairly low productivity of the vines. Cocks too, in his standard work on Bordeaux published in 1850, wrote: 'It is generally recognized today that Sauvignon is the mainstay of the best white wines, and that the leading *cru* of this region, Yquem, owes its superiority principally to the exclusive cultivation of this grape variety. This can be corroborated by the recent success of the proprietor of Château La Tour-Blanche who, over the last thirty years, has replanted almost his entire estate with this variety, with the consequence that his wine is now a serious rival to Yquem.' (My translation.)

Today Sauvignon represents no more than 20 per cent of the plantation at both Yquem and La Tour-Blanche. For this reversal there are many explanations. Because Sauvignon grapes grow in tight bunches, they are less prone than Sémillon to the ravages of botrytis. Sauvignon is also more susceptible to less welcome diseases and, if overcropped, the lifespan of the vine is considerably shorter than that of Sémillon. Frequent replanting entails loss of production as well as considerable labour and expense. In Bordeaux especially, Sémillon began to replace Sauvignon after the scourge of phylloxera in the late nineteenth century. Growers needed wine in a hurry, and Sémillon matched this purpose. Not that Sémillon is unsuited to Bordeaux, for as one grower put it to me: 'Les grands terroirs ont pardonné le Sémillon.' The best soils have forgiven the interloper Sémillon.

With very few exceptions, Sémillon in Bordeaux is most successful when blended with Sauvignon, for dry white wine as well as sweet wine. Sauvignon provides the acidity and that lively edginess the French call *nervosité*; Sémillon provides alcohol, richness and roundness.

To look only at Bordeaux, however, is to give a misleading impression of the status of the two varieties within France. According to figures published in 1990 in *La Journée Viticole*, in 1968 Sémillon was the second most widely planted white grape in France. But from 85,300 acres in 1968, the area planted had shrunk by 1988 to 50,000 acres and had been overtaken in second place by the more chic Chardonnay. Ugni Blanc, with over 250,000 acres planted, remained unchallenged as the most popular grape despite, or perhaps because of, its lack of distinction. Sauvignon, however, has had a remarkable success, boosted by new plantations in Touraine and southern France. From 22,160 acres in 1968, the area has risen to 30,000 acres, pushing the grape up into fourth-equal place with Grenache Blanc. The relative decline of Sémillon and the renaissance of

Sauvignon may largely be attributed to the vogue for fresh, youthful, aromatic wines at the expense of more richly structured, and more costly to produce, *vins de garde* for which Sémillon may be more appropriate.

Geographical Distribution

Long popular in Bordeaux, Sauvignon has also become a major crop elsewhere in France. In the Loire, especially in the appellations of Sancerre and Pouilly-Fumé, it reigns supreme. Sauvignon also flourishes in lesser appellations such as Haut-Poitou and Cheverny and is widely planted in the Touraine. Just west of the Chablis district lies the small appellation of Sauvignon de St-Bris. The pungency of Sauvignon from northern France must partly be derived from the cooler climate, but also from the fact that it is often planted on limestone or flint soils, whereas in the Bordeaux region the vines thrive on more alluvial soils.

Sauvignon is also planted widely in south-west France: in Bergerac, Monbazillac, Côtes de Buzet, Côtes de Duras and Montravel, as well as in more obscure appellations. It has also been gaining in popularity in southern France, where growers in the Coteaux d'Aix are planting Sauvignon to give a little freshness to white wines formerly dominated by Ugni Blanc, Clairette and Grenache Blanc.

Sémillon shares vineyard space with the dominant Sauvignon in Bordeaux and throughout south-west France, but it is absent from the Loire and very rare in Provence. It makes a major contribution to the sweet white wines of appellations such as Bergerac, Monbazillac, Montravel and Saussignac, as well as Sauternes, Loupiac, Ste-Croix-du-Mont, Cérons and Cadillac.

There is considerable clonal variation among both Sauvignon and Sémillon vines. Clonal selection is based on the analysis of vines in order to establish and propagate the most desirable characteristics and eliminate the least desirable. The merits and faults of specific clones are the subject of constant debate, but careful planting of the appropriate clone, using an appropriate rootstock, on the appropriate soil can give vines that are not only productive but have other important qualities such as longevity, regularity of yields and resistance to disease. Advocates of specific clones happily contrast the irregular production of earlier selections with the steady production of the latest clones which, they insist, can be achieved without any discernible loss of quality. Even a fanatic for quality such as Didier Dagueneau has planted a selection of clones (eleven, to be exact) and used a number of different rootstocks.

In Italy the desire of leading estates to be competitive in the international marketplace has led not only to the planting of Cabernet Sauvignon and Chardonnay but to tentative plantings of Sauvignon Blanc. The grapes flourish better in regions where there is a tradition of white wine production – Alto-Adige and Friuli – than in areas such as Tuscany. Sauvignon, still widely regarded as an almost experimental variety, is vinified in numerous styles, and the results are variable. Sémillon is virtually unknown.

Sauvignon is also an important variety in eastern Europe, especially in Yugoslavia, Hungary and Bulgaria. Although there is no reason to suppose that certain regions of, for example, Slovenia should not be capable of making world-class Sauvignon, wine production in eastern Europe has been dominated by cooperatives that only make wine of broadly acceptable commercial quality. The economic reforms of the 1990s, however, should lead to marked improvements in quality. Sémillon is found, sporadically, in Yugoslavia, Hungary and the Crimea.

Sauvignon is absent from Germany, but small quantities are planted in Austria and Czechoslovakia. In Spain, too, it has found increasing favour, notably in Penedès and Rueda. Sémillon is almost totally absent from all these countries.

In the United States Sauvignon Blanc is an important variety not only in California but also in states such as Texas and Washington. Excellent Sauvignons have emerged from

Washington State, but an increasing number of Californian oenologists and winemakers are taking the grape seriously. The mediocrity of many California Sauvignons is a consequence of planting the vines in rich and hence overproductive soils and in regions too hot for this variety. The cooler climate of Washington is thus proving more suitable, giving wines of dashing acidity. Sémillon in California is often catastrophic, though there are some successful, if commercially disastrous, Graves-style blends of Sémillon and Sauvignon. Sémillon fares best in California as the basis for very rich dessert wines. Again, Washington seems better suited to Sémillon, and these under-rated wines can age splendidly.

Both Sauvignon and Sémillon are widely planted in South America, and Chile in particular produces large quantities. Sémillon is abundantly planted, with 87,500 acres under vine, almost twice the quantity grown in all of France. Argentina, too, has plenty of Sémillon (13,750 acres). There is much discussion about the true identity of some of the South American vines, which appear to have been happily mutating for decades. Chilean Sauvignon Blanc, apparently descended from Bordeaux cuttings, can suffer from an excessive herbaceous quality and blandness.

In the New World the great success story for Sauvignon Blanc has been in New Zealand, where Hawke's Bay and Marlborough vineyards have produced racy wines very much in the Loire style. Their overall quality level is higher than their French counterparts', and individual wines can rival and even surpass the best that Sancerre or Pouilly have to offer. In Australia Sauvignon fares less well, sharing the faults typical of California Sauvignons. As in California, routine oak-ageing often obscures their varietal origin and has the unfortunate consequence of turning them into less interesting cousins of the more fashionable Chardonnay. Sémillon, however, has produced some magnificent wines, not only from the Hunter Valley, where three quarters of the country's 7,500 acres are planted, but also from newer wine regions such as Margaret River in Western Australia. It has also proved an excellent grape for sweet botrytized wines.

Viticulture and Vinification

The cultivation of Sauvignon has recently been the subject of intensive study by viticulturalists. Even the grape variety's most ardent admirers are fully aware that Sauvignon sometimes exhibits a strident grassiness and vegetal quality that few find enjoyable. When I have asked Loire growers why the 1985 vintage, for example, so often tastes vegetal, nobody has had a neat explanation. Consequently, viticulturalists have been studying ways to alter traditional cultivation of Sauvignon so as to avoid this strongly herbaceous character. Some attribute this aroma and flavour to overcropping, others to underripe or overripe grapes, yet others to careless viticultural and harvesting practices that allow vegetative matter such as leaves to find its way into the tanks.

A distinction has been made between fruit ripeness and aromatic ripeness. Sauvignon growers in warm climates such as California's Napa Valley have long been scratching their heads. Keen to vinify only grapes that are fully ripe, they find themselves picking ripe grapes with such high sugar content that, when fermented to dryness, they attain alcoholic levels of up to 14 degrees. At such levels, there is a strong possibility of a loss of aromatic quality and acidity, not to mention a lack of harmony and balance. This is why many California Sauvignons are, essentially, hot and heavy.

On the other hand, if the grapes are picked before they are fully ripe it is easier to conserve their aromatic quality, but a different risk is run: a taste of unripe grapes, a harsh weedy flavour, astringency. The trick, then, is to pick grapes that are fully ripe without having squandered their aromatic liveliness and their acidity. To achieve this, the excessive vigour of the Sauvignon vine must be controlled, and the vines trained so as to ensure that plenty of sunlight reaches the bunches during the maturation process. Current thinking advocates splitting the canopy of leaves over the rows of vines to allow greater penetration of sunlight. Other growers adopt the simpler method of thinning the canopy during the summer to achieve more even maturation. The point of opening up the canopy is to achieve the desired maturity at lower rather than higher sugar levels; it also tones down potentially vegetal aromas and flavours. The drawback is cost, since the method requires more wires and supports along each row. Yet the proven success of the method in New Zealand has persuaded growers in many other regions – including California and Bordeaux – to experiment with split canopies. A commercial justification for the practice is the hope that split canopies will increase yield without jeopardizing quality.

Not everybody shares the enthusiasm for canopy management. In the view of Tony Soter, a leading Napa Valley winemaker, canopy management is essentially remedial work that can be avoided by stopping your vines from growing at the right time. Splitting the canopy is, he argues, an admission that one has failed to control that growth and is thus an attempt to fool the vine. In his view, splitting the canopy is no more than fine tuning.

Both Sauvignon and Sémillon can easily taste dilute if yields are not kept within sensible limits. In poor vintages, yields are kept low by rain and rot, neither of which enhances quality, while in outstanding vintages, healthy vines can give a good crop without affecting quality. So generalizations about yields can be misleading. In the Graves, the best estates try to keep yields between 2.5 and 3 tons per acre; less scrupulous properties will aim for 3–4. Yields of 4 tons per acre are routine in the Loire, and in the fertile Napa Valley yields of up to 6 tons per acre are not unusual.

Harvesting is also a controversial subject, and opinions are deeply divided over, for example, the efficacy of picking by machine. Proponents of machine-picking argue that the technique gives them far greater flexibility in the vineyard; employing a team of pickers means that it can be too costly to delay picking those rows where the grapes may not be fully ripe. With a machine, it is far easier to pick at the correct moment. Advocates of machines also applaud the speed with which grapes can be picked and transported to the winery, minimizing the oxidation that many regard as the major enemy of white wine vinification. Opponents of the practice, such as Alphonse Mellot in Sancerre, argue that human pickers can be far more selective, that machines often damage the vines, that juice sprayed over the vines can lead to bacterial infections and rot, and that machines chuck too much vegetative matter into the bins.

I suspect that recent technological improvements have made it possible to machine-pick certain grapes, including these two varieties, without jeopardizing quality. In the Loire and New Zealand most of the harvesting is mechanical, often with impressive results. It is not possible, however, to make sweet wines of any quality from machine-picked grapes, since the machine cannot make the kind of selection that is essential to their production. Not all rot, after all, is noble rot; nor is it usual for rot, noble or otherwise, to be evenly spread throughout a vineyard.

One method of ensuring that grapes are picked at precisely the right moment is to pick more than once, a method known in France as *triage*. Ultra-scrupulous producers such as the Domaine de Chevalier in the Graves or Didier Dagueneau in the Loire send their pickers through the vineyards two or three times over a period that can be as long as a month. Grapes ripen unevenly, and the only way to ensure perfect fruit quality, they argue, is to remove rotten bunches and pick only the fully ripe ones. *Triage* is essential for making sweet wines because of the erratic, highly localized presence of botrytis in the vineyard. Moreover, Sauternes and similar wines are made from two or even three grape varieties (the third being the aromatic Muscadelle) which ripen at different times. The obvious drawback of *triage* is cost. Consumers expect a great Sauternes to be expensive, but they are far more cost-conscious when it comes to purchasing dry white wines. It is no accident that both Domaine de Chevalier and Dagueneau produce some of the most expensive wines in their appellations.

Once the grapes for a dry white wine – I shall discuss sweet wines when dealing with Sauternes – have been picked, the winemaker has two basic options. If he (and the use of this pronoun is not intended to exclude the numerous excellent female winemakers, especially in California) is primarily concerned to preserve aroma, freshness and acidity, he will press the grapes as soon as they reach the winery, ferment them in a neutral container such as stainless steel at a fairly low temperature, and after completing certain treatments such as fining and filtration and stabilization, bottle the wine young for early sales and early consumption. This would be a standard method in, for example, the Loire.

On the other hand, he may wish to make a wine of greater complexity, a wine capable of exhibiting with age a whole range of aromas and flavours never present in a very young wine. To achieve this he may use a number of methods, including maceration (which means allowing the grapes to soak for a while before being pressed, encouraging the extraction of chemical compounds from the skins), fermentation in small oak casks, and ageing in casks for anything from a few months to two years. This would be a typical method of vinification at a top-quality Graves estate.

Until about ten years ago maceration was frowned upon because of the risk of oxidation. Barrel-fermentation was practised at only a few estates, both because of its expense and because it is simpler, especially with temperature-controlled tanks, to control fermentation in steel than in barrels. Some estates, even in the Graves, never aged their white wines in wood, either out of stinginess or because they did not wish the wines to acquire woody flavours that would detract from the wine's fruitiness.

The arrival on the Bordeaux scene of young, innovative winemakers such as Peter Vinding-Diers and Denis Dubourdieu changed all that. Dubourdieu in particular, and his father Pierre of Château Doisy-Daëne, have helped bring about a revolution in the vinification of Sauvignon and Sémillon. Denis Dubourdieu is a professor of oenology at Bordeaux. He also owns a large estate near Cadillac, Château Reynon, and a small Graves property called Clos Floridène. He therefore practises what he preaches, and his own wines, especially Clos Floridène, are outstanding. He acts as a consultant to numerous

estates in the Graves, and has played a major part in transform-
ing some of them, such as Château de Fieuzal, into producers of
superb white wines. His influence has spread far beyond the
boundaries of Bordeaux, and Didier Dagueneau, the perfec-
tionist of Pouilly, willingly acknowledges his debt to
Dubourdieu's ideas.

Dubourdieu argues that the process of extraction entails
extracting both good and bad constituents from the raw
material at hand and good winemaking is knowing how to
control that process. In the case of white wines, the solids are
parted from the must before fermentation as, unlike red wines,
white wines are not fermented on the skins. Consequently,
most extraction has to take place before fermentation even
begins. With red wines, maceration often continues for up to a
month or more; with those white grapes that are pressed on
arrival at the winery this crucial process is bypassed altogether.
Thus for white wines, the stages that take place before fermentation – picking, pressing, clarifying the juice and so forth – are
of paramount importance.

Sweet white wines are a special case, as the action of
botrytis is in itself a kind of maceration, extracting compounds
and prompting chemical transformations. Thus, Dubourdieu
argues, the maceration process for Sauternes and similar wines
is completed before the grape is even picked. The vinification is
a piece of cake, once you have ensured that the grapes are
picked in the desired condition (which is not always possible).
To summarize, the extraction process for sweet wines takes
place before picking, for red wines during and after fermentation, but for white wines between picking and fermentation.
So with white wines the crucial choices are: when and how to
pick the grapes; whether to macerate those grapes; whether to
remove the stalks; how and when to press the grapes.
Dubourdieu compares white winemaking to taking a photograph. Once the picture has been snapped, the lab can play
around while developing the pictures, affecting shade and
nuance, but it can no longer alter the basic image.

Dubourdieu has established that it is essential, when making
wine from Sauvignon and Sémillon, to have healthy and mature

grapes. He insists that there is no excuse in the Bordeaux region not to have grapes in such condition, since even in appalling years such as 1972 white grapes reached maturity here. The lasting aromas one seeks are only present, he maintains, in mature grapes, which have a higher proportion of non-volatile aromas – by definition more durable than 'free' aromas. *Macération préfermentaire* – or skin contact, as English-speaking winemakers term the process – allows the extraction of these aromatic compounds as well as other chemicals from the skins.

There is nothing revolutionary about skin contact. Until about twenty years ago it was common practice for pickers to deliver grapes to the winery in, say, the early evening, and the grapes would sit overnight before being pressed. Delay, in other words, was a kind of maceration, admittedly under deplorably unhygienic conditions, for mixed in with the grapes were leaves and perhaps some rotten bunches and a few dead snails. The results were usually appalling, since maceration will extract unwelcome compounds if they are present. So in 1987, for example, even so ardent a proponent of skin contact as Didier Dagueneau avoided the procedure because the basic quality of the grapes was inadequate.

Nowadays, not only is the quality of the grapes monitored, but maceration takes place under a blanket of inert gas, thus avoiding any risk of oxidation. The grapes are always de-stalked. After maceration the next stage is *débourbage*, the settling of the must, allowing the heavier solids to sink to the bottom of the tank, whence they can be removed before fermentation. The extent of the *débourbage* affects the turbidity of the wine. Sometimes the process takes place before pressing, more usually after pressing. Dubourdieu's vinification method involves not only skin contact, but leaving the wine on the lees after fermentation, principally to continue the aromatic extraction. If the must is too turbid, that process of ageing on the lees will be problematic, even impossible; on the other hand, if the must has been excessively clarified, then the fermentation could be very slow or incomplete. Dubourdieu has devised an instrument that measures turbidity, so the process is not left to chance.

Two kinds of mechanical press are routinely employed. The horizontal press squeezes the grapes between metal plates, allowing the juice to dribble through slats in the plates as the press slowly revolves. Many properties are now switching to pneumatic presses, which exert pressure by means of a slowly inflating rubber bag. Winemakers love the gentleness of the pneumatic press, which minimizes the possibility of extracting harsh tannins and other undesirable elements. In the New World, where many wineries have been established from scratch, pneumatic presses are far more common, despite their expense. A very few properties still use old vertical (or hydraulic) presses, which are cumbersome and slow but share with pneumatic presses the advantage of great gentleness and give clear juice, which aids the fermentation process. Some Sauternes estates, Yquem included, still press their grapes this way.

After pressing, fermentation may begin, though, if desired, it is easy to prolong the *débourbage* and thus delay fermentation by keeping the must at a very low temperature. Fermentation unlocks the non-volatile aromas; it reveals what has hitherto been concealed. Yeasts, which transform the natural sugar of the grape into alcohol, play a crucial part in all this. At Château Reynon and at Serge Dagueneau's estate in Pouilly I have tasted two wines, vinified in the identical manner from the same batch of grapes, the sole difference being the yeast employed. The difference was considerable, especially at the aromatic level. Peter Vinding-Diers, an expert on yeasts, adamantly opposes the use of cultivated commercial yeasts, which can have the effect of standardizing white wines. He believes growers and winemakers must do all they can to isolate and cultivate the indigenous yeasts in their vineyards, so as to inculcate the specific local character of the wine.

The temperature of fermentation is another crucial factor. A decade ago there was a fad for fermentation at temperatures below 15 degrees Centigrade. The results were undeniably fresh and exhilarating, but the wines often tasted identical, making it difficult to identify the grape variety, let alone soil or regional characteristics. Moreover, fermenting at low temperatures increases the risk of a stopped fermentation, which is every winemaker's nightmare. To avoid this possibility, very powerful yeasts were added to the wine, which in itself promotes standardized flavours.

Nowadays, winemakers tend to favour a fermentation temperature of 18–19 °C. If you ferment in small oak barrels, it is almost impossible to avoid a higher temperature, about 21 °C. Dubourdieu, who favours barrel fermentation, admits that the fermentation aromas generated at this higher temperature are less pronounced than with cooler tank fermentations, but he argues that the non-volatile aromatic extraction is more complete, thus ensuring a better long-term evolution for the wine. Some winemakers, especially in California, ferment in tank – a no-risk procedure – and then age in oak. Others oppose this compromise, arguing that you are more likely to end up with heavily woody flavours if you wood-age a tank-fermented wine.

One could write a book-length essay on the fine points of oak-ageing, and I do not propose to do so. There are many variables among small oak barrels (*barriques*): the age of the barrel (after about four years the oaky flavours diminish and contribute little to the wine), the provenance of the oak, the way the wood is dried and toasted, the methods employed by the barrel-maker, the conditions in which the barrels are stored. All these variables will contribute different nuances. Some winemakers prefer new oak to one- or two-year-old oak; others have the opposite preference. Some prefer light toastings to heavy ones; and vice versa. There are no formulas. Those who employ small oak barrels may do so because they believe that wood maturation is an essential component of the flavour of wine, white or red, especially if that wine is intended to evolve in bottle. Others may simply be responding to a commercial demand for oaky wines.

If grapes fail to reach maturity their sugar content will be low and so will their eventual alcoholic level. A solution is to chaptalize the wine by adding sugar during fermentation. This sugar, converted into alcohol by the yeasts, boosts the alcohol level of the wine. In hot climates grapes almost always ripen sufficiently for chaptalization to be unnecessary. In cool climates, however, unripe grapes are a recurrent problem. In some cases chaptalization has become a matter of routine. Why leave the grapes on the vine for another week or two to attain full maturity, and thereby risk losing the entire crop to unexpected rain and rot, when you can pick early and sugar the must? I was astonished to learn that in the very warm and early-ripening Bordeaux vintage of 1989 a majority of classified growths decided to chaptalize their *red* wines.

Dubourdieu believes that there is hardly ever a justification for chaptalizing Sauvignon and Sémillon in Bordeaux, except in poorer vintages, when judicious sugaring can add about half a degree of alcohol, giving additional body to the finished wine. In 1987 in the Loire, the potential alcohol levels of grapes were no more than 9 or 10 degrees, insufficient to give well-balanced wine. In such circumstances chaptalization is essential. Chaptalization is more controversial in the Sauternes region, where much of the flavour of the wine is derived from residual sugar. There is, critics of chaptalization maintain, a difference between sugar added to the vat by the sackload and natural grape sugar, and chaptalized wines will always have a coarser flavour. I sympathize with this view, and occasionally feel I can detect a chaptalized Sauternes on the palate, although it is difficult to prove that there is a gustatory and qualitative difference between chaptalized and unchaptalized Sauternes.

After the alcoholic fermentation, a further fermentation process may or may not take place: malolactic fermentation, which converts hard malic acid into lactic acid. One consequence of malolactic fermentation is a reduction of overall acidity. In simpler Sauvignons, such as unwooded Sancerres, a fairly high level of acidity is desirable, so malolactic fermentation is avoided, often by chilling the must and killing off the yeasts. A few producers in the Loire favour malolactic fermentation, but to my mind the wines taste excessively rounded, even flabby. In Bordeaux, malolactic fermentation for white wines is more common.

The fermentation process, when completed, leaves residues in the wine known as lees, mostly composed of dead yeasts.

Some winemakers draw off (rack) the wine from the lees, so as to give a reasonably clear and clean product from the outset. The current conventional wisdom, inspired by Dubourdieu and the many oenologists who share his views, is to leave the wine on the lees for as long as possible. They are speaking of fine lees, of course, not the so-called gross lees, which could include leaves and other extraneous matter; the wine will have been decanted from the gross lees during *débourbage*. The justification for keeping the wine on the lees, either in tank or in barrel, is that enzymes present in those lees continue to extract aroma from the wine, as well as enriching the wine and giving it a more rounded texture. It is also believed that the lees reduce the woodiness of the flavour imparted by new oak. Dubourdieu points out that maturing the wine *sur lie* is only effective if the *macération préfermentaire* has been performed correctly. If unpleasant aromas have been extracted from the skins, then maturation on the lees will only accentuate them. Lees contact is intensified by *bâtonnage*, which is simply stirring up the lees regularly so as to keep the solids in suspension.

Some winemakers are wary of leaving the wine *sur lie*. Peter Vinding-Diers, for example, only does so in modest vintages, believing that in excellent vintages maturation *sur lie* gives the wine a fat, buttery taste he dislikes in Sauvignon and Sémillon. The method also requires intense care. The whole point of racking the wine off the lees is to prevent the wine picking up undesirable flavours and to minimize the risk of bacterial infection. Winemakers who leave their wine *sur lie* must be extremely vigilant.

Once the winemaker judges that the wine is ready for bottling, he will probably follow certain procedures to clean it. These include fining – which involves adding compounds to the wine which attract particles in suspension and precipitate them out – filtration, and chilling to extreme temperatures to encourage the formation of tartrate crystals which can then be removed. This last procedure is much criticized, since it is only done for cosmetic reasons. American consumers in particular regard deposits in bottled white wines as unacceptable, although they are totally harmless. Every major producer of

Sauvignon and Sémillon has tales of returned consignments or even lawsuits on the grounds that the wine contains 'glass'.

Fining and filtration are different issues, as the vast majority of consumers, with good reason, want a white wine to be limpid. Particles that remain in suspension detract from a wine's aesthetic appeal. Some winemakers fine with substances such as bentonite or egg white, not only to polish the wine before bottling but to remove protein from the must before fermentation, a procedure that in their view assists the vinification process. Others find that ageing and racking have the effect of cleaning the wine naturally, and that only a very light filtration before bottling is necessary. But most white wines are filtered with varying degrees of severity, especially those intended to be drunk young. These wines will not have undergone malolactic fermentation, and filtration prevents any possibility of secondary fermentation, which can be prompted by the presence of dormant yeasts resuscitated by, for example, changes in temperature.

I have dealt with Dubourdieu's theories in some detail because many top French winemakers model their winemaking on them. I have also gone into considerable detail because other winemakers are adamantly opposed to skin contact for these grape varieties. In California, for example, skin contact is frowned upon. There was a time when it was widely practised, but the results were deemed unsatisfactory. Winemakers such as Craig Williams of Phelps believe that since the grapes are grown in a different climate and often have thicker skins, maceration can extract not only aromatic compounds but tannins that give unattractive flavours. With such tannins in the wine, it is then necessary to fine or filter heavily, which, as the critics of these procedures rightly observe, will diminish the wine's flavour and complexity. Wines with high tannin, according to the winemaker David Ramey, require high acidity, which is precisely what many California Sauvignons lack. Lower tannin thus allows lower acidity, without, in Ramey's view, diminishing the crispness and balance of the wine. When Californians used skin contact on Chardonnay, they often found that the wine did not age well, and Ramey believes the same would be true of Sauvignon. Another danger of skin contact, according to the veteran Californian oenologist Vernon Singleton, is that it can broaden and coarsen the wine and lead to a loss of acidity, which may be acceptable in Sancerre or the Graves, but is undesirable in most parts of California.

Although these techniques are finding increasing favour in the Graves, not all proprietors have jumped on the bandwagon. Olivier Bernard, the owner of Domaine de Chevalier, which produces a most glorious white wine, claims never to have seen a great wine made by skin contact. He argues that if your viticultural practices are good, there should be no need for such measures. In brief, he regards skin contact as an attempt to improve mediocre grapes, a view utterly rejected by Didier Dagueneau, who argues that skin contact should only be used with good-quality grapes. Bernard is also critical of *bâtonnage*. He does not dispute that it gives an exuberant extraction of aromas, but he is making a different style of wine, a traditional white Graves that only reveals its aromatic and gustatory complexity after a long evolution in bottle. He does not want a wine that shows all its glory in its youth, and fears, like David Ramey, that wines made with skin contact will not age well.

Sweet Wines

To most grape-growers, the great enemy is rot. But some rot is less desirable than other rot, and in the Sauternes region it became apparent two centuries ago that a particular infection known as *Botrytis cinerea*, or noble rot, induced changes in the grapes' physical and chemical structure that actually improved the wine's quality. The region is bordered by two rivers, the mighty Garonne, a warm tidal river, and the much smaller, spring-fed Ciron which empties into it. In the autumn the confluence of cold and warm waters helps to generate fogs, which lie like a blanket over the low undulating vineyards on either side of the Ciron and across the other side of the Garonne. In the morning the fog burns off and, in good years, sunshine resumes.

It is the alternation of misty humidity and warmth that activates botrytis, or noble rot. If there is too much of one or the other, the results will be unsatisfactory. An excess of humidity and a lack of sunshine can prompt the development of *pourriture grise*, or grey rot, which is ruinous. Too much sunshine, on the other hand, can inhibit the botrytis spores from attacking the grapes. It is possible, indeed excessively common, to make sweet wines from Sauvignon and Sémillon even if the grapes have not been botrytis-affected, but the results can never be as complex as from nobly rotten grapes. Botrytis changes the grapes' chemical composition. The spores, feeding off sugar and tartaric acid, shrivel the skins, changing their colour to an unsightly brown and purple. Warm sunshine then speeds up the dehydration process, thus reducing the water content within the grape and concentrating the remaining sugar. A fully ripened Sémillon grape, before infection, may have a potential alcohol reading of about 13°. By the time the spores have completed their work, the potential alcohol will have risen to 17°, or more – the great estate of Yquem seeks to pick only botrytis-affected grapes with a potential alcohol of between 19° and 21°. Botrytis also transforms tartaric acid into gluconic acid and glycerol, which gives Sauternes its viscosity. There are also aromatic transformations, bringing to botrytized wines their somewhat honeyed aroma and opulence.

The dedicated Sauternes producer must have a masochistic streak. For there are certain years, such as 1978, when botrytis fails to strike. All the grower can do is pick overripe grapes that will give a rich sweet wine of no particular distinction. In other years, botrytis will munch away happily at grape skins in one part of the vineyard, but not in another. Sauvignon may find itself more susceptible to noble rot than Sémillon, or vice versa. Even on a single vine some parts of the bunch will be more profoundly affected than others. This is why *triage* is a routine procedure at all worthwhile Sauternes estates. Local propaganda would have us believe that the pickers select each grape individually before clipping it, to ensure that only fully botrytized fruit is used. In some circumstances the most conscientious estates will go to such lengths, but they are the exception rather than the rule.

When to pick is the perplexing question. Pick too early, and you may gather merely overripe fruit or only lightly botrytized grapes. But pick too late, and your entire crop may be wiped out by rain or grey rot. Great Sauternes, perhaps more than any other wine, is made in the vineyard. Yquem is not the finest wine of Sauternes because it uses only new oak, although that is a powerful contributing factor. It makes the best wine because its vineyards are on subtly different soils and expositions and because it is prepared to ensure that only the most suitable fruit is picked. There are years such as 1972 when the Yquem teams made eleven *passages* through the vineyards. Even so, *triage* alone cannot guarantee quality, and in 1972 the entire crop was declassified.

Triage and the courage to leave grapes on the vine as late as possible permit the best estates to make good Sauternes in years that the majority of producers regard as hopeless. Even in 1984, a fairly dismal year on the whole, patience and the willingness to be highly selective allowed a handful of estates to make good wine with real botrytis character. In 1985, a very dry year, botrytis remained absent until late October and November, by which time most growers had lost their nerve and picked. At Yquem, however, the pickers were still at work until the week before Christmas, and were rewarded with botrytized grapes. Often the greatest years are the easiest years: years such as 1990, when botrytis attacked the grapes quite early.

The selection process continues in the winery. The top estates are ruthless in weeding out barrels of insufficiently high quality. In 1978 Yquem rejected 85 per cent of their wine and sold it as generic Sauternes to wholesalers. In 1987 a number of properties sold off their entire crop in this way. So it is not surprising that Sauternes is an expensive wine. The yields are very low, with Yquem claiming the lowest average yield at just over half a ton per acre, and other properties varying from half a ton to 1.5, depending on the vintage. (The maximum permitted yield is less than 2 tons per acre.) Picking can take up to two months, which also adds to the cost. Although quite a few of these estates also produce dry white wine, either from young vines or as a kind of insurance policy in years when botrytis fails to appear, proprietors must assume that there will be vintages when it will not be possible to market any Sauternes at all.

Vinification methods vary. The best estates press and ferment each lot separately, keeping apart the different grape varieties, different *tries* and different vineyards. At some châteaux there can be up to thirty different lots, which allows unsatisfactory wines to be declassified. The grapes are usually, but not always, crushed before pressing. After *débourbage* the must is fermented, either in a tank or in *barriques*. Since the grapes are often picked quite late in the autumn, the cellar temperature is cool and the fermentation protracted. Six weeks, even two months, is not unusual. Some estates claim that their wine finds its natural balance of alcohol and sugar without interference from the winemaker. The alcohol generated by the action of the yeasts acts as a brake on fermentation; so, according to some winemakers, does a mysterious substance called botrycine, an antibiotic present in botrytized grapes, which supplements the activities of the alcohol by inhibiting the yeasts. It is rare for yeasts to remain active after they have generated 15° of alcohol. By picking grapes with a specific potential alcohol, it should be possible to achieve naturally a desirable balance of alcohol and residual sugar in the finished wine. At Yquem, for example, an ideal must would have a potential alcohol of 21°, which would result in a wine with 14.5° alcohol and 6.5° residual sugar. Other lots might vary slightly, but differences would be ironed out at the blending stage to give a perfectly balanced wine.

Many winemakers intervene to stop fermentation when they believe the balance is correct. In the bad old days a huge dose of sulphur dioxide did the trick, but conscientious winemakers are now making a long overdue effort to minimize its use. Chilling will also kill off the yeasts, and so will an expensive piece of equipment called the centrifuge. A combination of sulphur dioxide and chilling is commonly used.

It is difficult to make good Sauternes if the potential alcohol of the grapes is below 16°, which might give a finished wine with 13° alcohol (the legal minimum for the appellation) and 3° residual sugar. Growers unwilling to take the risk of leaving grapes on the vine long enough to ensure either *surmaturité* or full-blown botrytis infection may well find themselves picking at a potential alcohol of, say, 14.5°. At such levels chaptalization is unavoidable, and the final results are rarely impressive. Chaptalization, permitted up to two degrees, cushions the indolent winemaker against the consequences of his laziness and lack of courage. Except in poor years, such as 1972 and 1984, there can be little excuse for heavy chaptalization of sweet wines, especially since by definition some of that sugar will remain in an unconverted form in the finished wine.

After fermentation the wine will be racked and begin its rearing, its *élevage*. Less well-heeled properties still use tanks, claiming that they do not want their wines to have a woody flavour. But the real reason is likely to be cost. I have often compared the same wine ageing in tank with another batch ageing in barrel, and the wood-aged wine invariably displays greater complexity. As in the case of white Graves, estates have personal preferences for woods of different types and different ages. Only a handful can afford 100 per cent new oak (Yquem, Raymond-Lafon, Fargues, La Tour-Blanche since 1989), and not all winemakers are enamoured of the often strident vanilla flavour imparted by new oak. The wine remains in wood for between eighteen and thirty-six months before being bottled. Fining and filtration are common but by no means ubiquitous.

A new technique has proved controversial. There is nothing more irritating for growers than to have perfectly botrytized grapes rendered unusable by steady rain. To pick sodden grapes is to invite dilution of the must, which no conscientious grower will countenance. A certain Monsieur Chauvet invented a technique called cryo-extraction. This involves placing wet grapes in a 'cold chamber' which is chilled for up to twenty hours. Guiraud, in 1985, was the first estate to use the technique, but when Yquem followed suit in 1986 and 1987, controversy was inevitable, as though drying grapes was a form of cheating.

Comte Alexandre de Lur-Saluces, Yquem's owner, insists that cryo-extraction does no more than get rid of the moisture on the outside of the grape. It does not, he says, affect the chemical structure of the must.

The advocates of cryo-extraction regard it as a way to rescue a portion of the crop that would otherwise have to be sacrificed. Some oenologists and winemakers believe that the process does affect the quality of the must, and for the better. Experiments at Guiraud suggest that cryo-extraction gives deeper colour, better extraction, fatter wine and more developed aromas. Although most Sauternes winemakers only use the technique in problematic years – hardly anybody used cryo-extraction in 1988 – Denis Dubourdieu bucks the trend by claiming that it works more effectively in good years. In 1989, he told me, he used it at Château Doisy-Daëne where the chilling process, by removing moisture from the grape, increased the must weight, the potential alcohol of the grape, from 19° to 21°. He detects no change in aroma. Some producers have declined to jump on to this particular bandwagon. The Lurtons of Climens and Doisy-Dubroca point out that cryo-extraction is extremely costly and only useful in ameliorating poor vintages that are difficult to sell anyway.

For decades Sauternes, and sweet wines in general, were unfashionable. With the exception of Yquem, prices were low, in many cases far lower than the cost of production. Even Yquem was relatively underpriced, since its yields were about one quarter those of a *premier grand cru* estate in the Médoc. The consequences were dire. Producers cut corners and even highly reputable estates began producing wines of scandalously poor quality. Low prices inhibited new investment, and a combination of neglect in the vineyard and a failure to renew equipment in the winery accelerated the downward spiral. A renewal of interest in Sauternes in the 1980s has led to a swift rise in prices. Fortunately the majority of proprietors have used the profits to invest in their estates. Many properties that made lousy wine fifteen years ago are now producing Sauternes of superb quality.

Unfortunately, the lesser sweet wine appellations – Cérons,

Loupiac, Cadillac, Ste-Croix-du-Mont – have only recently begun to benefit by clinging to the coat-tails of Sauternes. Prices remain too low for most proprietors to be able to afford improvements in quality, especially in unfashionable appellations such as Monbazillac, Saussignac and Montravel. It remains sadly true that most wine from these appellations is appalling: the wines lack botrytis, sulphur dioxide levels are too high, chaptalization is all too evident even in good vintages, *barriques* are rarely used and the wines lack distinction and elegance. Climate has something to do with it. There are parts of Loupiac, for instance, where fogs are infrequent and botrytis is scarce. But there are large parts of that appellation, and of Cérons and Monbazillac, where the microclimate is ideal for the production of great sweet wine, and the failure to do so has everything to do with the attitude, and relative poverty, of the proprietors.

New World winemakers, by applying first principles and refusing to cut corners, have made some splendid Sauternes-style wines, usually from Sémillon. It is hard to distinguish some of them from Sauternes itself, although it remains to be seen whether Australian botrytized Sémillon, for example, will have the same kind of longevity as Sauternes.

Longevity

Botrytized Sauvignon and Sémillon are capable of a long and splendid evolution in bottle. Quite apart from the concentration of flavour and extract achieved by low yields, the natural constituents of the wine are certain to ensure long life, if not necessarily a fruitful evolution. With an alcoholic content of around 14.5°, a residual sugar content equivalent to about 4.5° or 5° alcohol, and fairly high acidity, the wine is built to last. I have drunk Sauternes from the nineteenth century that was still lush and intense in flavour, and sweet wines from lesser appellations on the other side of the Garonne, including Monbazillac, that were sixty years old and going strong. An old sweet wine in the Sauternes style exhibits secondary aromas and flavours that not all consumers will find pleasing: flavours such as burnt sugar and caramel, marmalade and butterscotch come to mind, all suggesting a light oxidation in the wine. I enjoy old wine flavours, despite their occasional lack of vigour, but many other drinkers prefer a good Sauternes at perhaps twenty years of age, while it still retains a measure of freshness. These wines will only age well if they were well made in the first place and the fruits of vintages that were not disastrous.

White Graves can also age superbly. Château Laville Haut-Brion is legendary for its ability to age, and I have drunk a forty-year-old Château La Tour-Martillac that tasted honeyed, fat and spicy, and had retained excellent acidity and length. This was, however, from the excellent 1949 vintage, and thus probably atypical. Thirty-year-old bottles from Domaine de Chevalier have also been superb, even from less exalted vintages. It has to be said that in the case of many white Graves, including Château Laville Haut-Brion, the wine's evolution was retarded by the excessive use of sulphur dioxide. This chemical, essentially an antioxidant, is used in many aspect of winemaking, from harvesting to disinfecting barrels to bottling. Because of its unpleasant aroma and harshness on the throat, conscientious winemakers have been reducing sulphur levels over the past decade, but older examples of white Graves (and some modern ones too) have clearly been drenched in sulphur dioxide. It can take years for its effects to dissipate, and when it finally does so the wine revealed beneath that cloak of sulphur is not necessarily glorious. Since sulphur dioxide delays the evolution of the wine, one wonders whether wines that unexpectedly become splendid in their extreme old age are not in fact recovering from a case of retarded development.

Few wine lovers think of undiluted Sauvignon as a suitable candidate for ageing. In my experience this expectation is correct, and even a first-rate New Zealand Sauvignon is usually past its best after three years. I have tasted Loire Sauvignons still in reasonable condition after six or more years in a good

cellar, but far more frequently such wines have lost their freshness and have developed either a vegetal or an oxidized flavour.
Yet old wine lists once offered Loire Sauvignons for sale that
were six or ten years old, and at prices comparable to fine claret.
This proves, argues Didier Dagueneau, that both the reputation and the quality of wines such as Sancerre and Pouilly-
Fumé have declined. Earlier this century a combination of good
vineyard practices, low yields and cask maturation would have
given richer, well-structured wines that positively required
some bottle-ageing before reaching their peak.

Synonyms and Nomenclature

Sauvignon goes by a number of other names in France, but it is
highly unlikely that you will ever encounter any of them on a
bottled wine. The one important synonym is Muskat-Silvaner,
the German and Austrian name for Sauvignon, although
Austrians are increasingly using the internationally understood
name of Sauvignon Blanc.

In the New World some Sauvignons are labelled as Fumé
Blanc. This invention dates from the mid-1960s when Robert
Mondavi, the pioneering Napa Valley winemaker, wanted to
exploit the vogue for Pouilly-Fumé. To counter the unpopular
herbaceous character of California Sauvignon at the time, he
oak-aged the wine and labelled it Fumé Blanc. It was so successful that innumerable other producers, initially in California but
then around the world, adopted the term. Unfortunately, it has
no definable meaning. Some wineries produce two Sauvignons,
one heavily oaked, the other very lightly oaked, and they are
then labelled either Sauvignon Blanc or Fumé Blanc according
to the whim of the winemaker or marketing manager. A Fumé
Blanc is often oaked – but not necessarily. In Australia,
moreover, there is no legal obligation for a wine labelled Fumé
Blanc to contain any Sauvignon at all.

As in the case of Sauvignon, Sémillon has a number of French synonyms, of which Chevrier has some significance, since it has been incorporated into the name of certain California Sauvignon–Sémillon blends, such as Vichon's Chevrignon and Kendall-Jackson's now defunct Chevriot. In South Africa, Sémillon goes under the wonderfully simple name Greengrape; and some older Hunter Valley Sémillons from Australia were known, confusingly, as Riesling. In Victoria, the grape known as Barnawartha Pinot is in fact Sémillon.

Sauvignon, Sémillon and Food

With two grape varieties capable of producing many different styles of wine, it is next to impossible to generalize about suitable accompaniments. The least complex Sauvignons, such as good Bergerac or Cheverny, are pleasant summer aperitifs, undemanding but refreshing. The raciness of unoaked pure Sauvignon – Sancerre type – goes well with certain first courses often regarded as difficult to match with wine. Gravadlax, even smoked salmon, and asparagus, go well with Sauvignon. Fish and chicken and veal, the standard white wine foods, are matched by Sauvignon and Sémillon as much as by Riesling or Trebbiano. Rich shellfish sauces need the weight of, say, a white Graves rather than a more racy Sauvignon. It is commonly supposed that cheeses are best accompanied by red wines, but this is not always the case. Roquefort and Sauternes is becoming quite a famous combination, and with fresh goat's cheese an unwooded Loire Sauvignon is the perfect accompaniment.

The final choice must be dictated by the style of the dish. The richer the sauce, the more likely it is that Sémillon or an oaked Sauvignon or Graves will be an appropriate match. It is arguable that some of these wines, especially very oaky Australian Sémillons, are, like rich New World Chardonnays, too overpowering to be satisfactory food wines. I find them enjoyable none the less. I would be wary of matching game, except for the more innocuous birds such as guinea fowl, with these wines. The richer the wine, the higher the temperature at which it should be served. Thus the only dry wines that should be served really cold are the simpler, more zippy Sauvignons.

The French like to drink lighter Sauternes, and sweet wines such as Ste-Croix-du-Mont or Loupiac, as an aperitif. Rather, they say they do, a half-fiction promoted as a marketing ploy to give a boost to sagging sales during the lean years of the 1970s. Personally, I prefer wines with a dry or even bitter finish with which to precede a meal. A glass of Sauternes-style wine, with over 14° alcohol, high glycerol content and a sweet finish, can be a trifle overwhelming at the start of a meal. On the other hand, such wines are an ideal accompaniment for foie gras and the richer pâtés.

Since foie gras rarely comes my way, Sauternes are more usually relegated to the end of the meal. I like to sip them on their own after the dessert dishes have been cleared, without any distractions in the form of fruit tarts, rice puddings or raspberry coulis, let alone marquis de chocolat or mango ice cream. Very occasionally one encounters desserts – such as plain raspberries, or peaches, or summer puddings – which can safely be accompanied by a rich sweet wine, but for the most part all that sugar, not to mention the high acidity of many fruits, is an enemy to good wine. I prefer to think of a glass of Sauternes as a kind of supplementary pudding, sufficiently rich and complex to be savoured on its own.

GAZETTEER

KEY TO RATING SYSTEM

Quality

🍇 indifferent

🍇🍇 average

🍇🍇🍇 good

🍇🍇🍇🍇 very good

🍇🍇🍇🍇🍇 outstanding

Price

★ cheap

★★ average

★★★ expensive

★★★★ very expensive

★★★★★ luxury

AUSTRALIA

Sauvignon Blanc does not appear to thrive in Australia. Figures that may not be up to date report that 2,200 acres of Sauvignon are planted, a substantial proportion of them in South Australia. It succeeds best when planted in cool regions such as Coonawarra and Padthaway. It is dangerous to generalize, but Australian Sauvignons tend to lack pronounced varietal character. The routine wizardries of Australian hi-tech winemaking produce fruity acceptable wines, but many of them merely hint at their varietal origin. Many are produced in an oaky Fumé Blanc style that is rarely satisfactory, especially since the term does not oblige a winemaker to include any Sauvignon whatsoever in the blend. Few Australian winemakers seem particularly interested in the variety, and Brian Croser's dismissive remarks have already been quoted in the Introduction.

Sémillon, on the other hand, is a great Australian triumph. It is much more plentiful than Sauvignon, with 6,700 acres under vine, representing almost 15 per cent of all white grape plantations. The celebrated cleanness of Australian vinification means that their Sémillon is largely free of the overdoses of sulphur dioxide that can mar white Bordeaux and Bergerac. Australian Sémillons can, however, be spoilt by high alcohol, as this grape variety easily attains exuberant must weights. Sémillon is, of course, a most impressionable variety, easily registering peculiarities of soil and mineral content, so where the variety is planted can determine the character of the wine.

Sémillon has been present in Australian vineyards more or less from their foundation. Most of it is found in New South Wales, about half of it in the Hunter Valley, where it attains its greatest distinction on the valley's volcanic soil. Young Hunter Sémillon can taste oddly neutral, but after ten years in bottle the transformation can be remarkable. Between its fruity youth

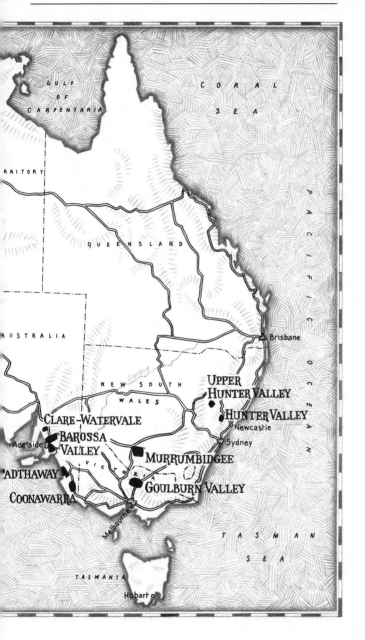

and its nutty, complex old age, the wine often goes through an ungainly, drab period, rather like Chenin from the Loire. Once mature, the wine will have become unctuous, toasty and rich, with chewy mineral nuances and that indefinable complexity characteristic of great wine. Although the Hunter Valley can be very hot and Sémillon is in any case known for its low acidity, wines from good vintages can have astonishing longevity. Skin contact is rare and the wines tend to be fermented at low temperatures and bottled young.

More commercial Sémillons are produced in South Australia's Barossa Valley and in other parts of New South Wales, notably the high-yielding Murrumbidgee Irrigation Area. Here the grape is often blended with other varieties such as Chardonnay, Chenin or Verdelho, and the results are less bizarre than the procedure suggests. Some very fine Sémillon is also being produced in the Margaret River region of Western Australia, a maritime area peculiarly susceptible to cool weather and severe frosts; it gives intensely flavoured fruit and wines with excellent balance. Margaret River Sémillon has a more herbaceous, racy character than its Hunter Valley counterpart, and a more modern crispness and aromatic freshness. Whether Margaret River Sémillons will age as well as those from the Hunter Valley it is too early to say, though personally I doubt it.

Winemakers have discovered that the richness, if not the complexity, of old Sémillon can be injected into young, more neutral Sémillon by the simple expedient of oak-ageing. This is commercially handy too. Traditional Hunter Valley Sémillon is not oaked, which is one reason why its evolution in bottle is so prolonged. Some purists are unhappy about wood-ageing Sémillon, but in my experience much of it is extremely attractive if you like full-blown oaky wines. Some producers, such as Moss Wood in Western Australia, have marketed oaked and unoaked versions of the same wine. Some unoaked versions are given a spell of skin contact, giving the young wine an aromatic appeal not normally found in youthful Sémillon.

Many assumptions that would be unquestioned in France are ignored in Australia. Irrigation is commonly practised, and yields tend to be far higher than those admitted to by the French. Chaptalization is forbidden, and is in any case unnecessary, but acidification can often prove a rival irritant, since added acidity is often detectable on the palate. If there is a fault in Australian wines, it is their very absence of faults. There are too many standardized elements in Australian viticulture and vinification: cold-temperature fermentation, centrifuging, injecting the must with cultivated yeasts, routine oak-ageing and so forth. No one could quarrel with the wines' overall quality; the danger is that they tend to taste much the same, whatever their provenance, whoever the winemaker. The fascination of Hunter Valley Sémillon is that in its traditional form it is a relatively untreated wine, allowing soil content and grape quality to speak out.

As for vintages, few are truly dire. For Hunter Valley Sémillon 1976 was good, 1979 great, 1983 excellent, 1984 average, 1985 good but not great, 1986 superb; 1987 was a late harvest of fine quality; despite rain, 1988 was very good too; but rain almost wrecked the 1989 and 1990 vintages. 1991 will be excellent. In Western Australia good whites were made in 1984; 1985 and 1986 were excellent, 1987 average. 1985, 1987 and 1988 were very good years for South Australian whites, though most will have been drunk long ago; 1989 was average. 1991 looks more promising overall.

The customary difficulty in assessing the quality of individual New World wineries is particularly acute in Australia. There is no local tradition, other than in the Hunter Valley, to determine the style of the wines. Each winemaker is free to shape and fashion wines at will. A winemaker may begin by making, say, simple but classically structured unoaked Sémillon, but then discover that the market, or his winery's marketing manager, wants a wine more accessible in its youth, so he switches to a fatter, oakier style. A few years later fashion changes again, when wine writers complain that such wines are too overpowering for food. So he slims down the style, retaining some use of oak but aiming for lower alcohol levels and less buttery richness.

Moreover, in Australia the number of wineries producing

wines from these two varieties is very large. Considerations of space forbid detailed consideration of them all, so some wineries are mentioned more briefly here.

Allanmere (NSW). Producers of a full-bodied oaky Hunter Valley Sémillon from bought-in grapes; spicy and intense and with good length.

Amberley (WA). An ambitious range of three different styles of Sauvignon and Sémillon, all well crafted.

Coldstream Hills (Victoria). Wine writer turned winemaker James Halliday (a dangerous precedent) made a first venture into sweet botrytized Sémillon in 1988, achieving a glorious ripe, peachy version with fine acidity.

Fleurieu Heritage (McLaren Vale, SA). A clever attempt by French winemaker Jacques Lurton to produce a Graves-style blend. The 1990 vintage was impressive but expensive.

Hanging Rock (Victoria). A new winery, its cold-fermented but *barrique*-aged Sémillon is rich and spicy and concentrated, and should age well.

Henschke (SA). In 1989 the winery, best known for superb Shiraz, produced a delicious *barrique*-aged Sémillon.

Hunter Estate (NSW). Hunter produce a Fumé Blanc that is leaner and racier than most Australian examples, piquantly oaky yet clean and fresh, and rich, spicy Sémillon.

Peter Lehmann (SA). An immense Barossa winery, producing a Fumé Blanc from Sémillon and Chenin Blanc; a dry Sémillon; and a fresh, sweetish blend of mostly Chardonnay and Sémillon. I like the latter; the other wines are dull.

Mildara (Victoria). Makers of a wide range of Sauvignons, some labelled Victoria, others Coonawarra, others 'Flower Label', for immediate consumption. The Sauvignons are fresh but often a touch raw, the Fumé a bizarre and broad-flavoured blend of Sauvignon with Chardonnay and Palomino.

Montrose (NSW). Some enjoyably spicy Sémillons and oaky and somewhat brutal Sémillon–Chardonnay blends.

Normans (SA). A somewhat anonymous Fumé blend, first made in 1989, shows less impressively than a varietally distinctive Sauvignon Blanc, which is crisp and vigorous.

Quelltaler (SA). An obituary notice of a Clare Valley winery (now owned by Wolf Blass) to honour some truly sumptuous wood-aged Sémillons.

Seppelt (SA). This well-known winery has produced inconsistent Sémillon–Chardonnay blends made from grapes from Barossa and Barooga. They range from the lush and fruity to the vegetal and flabby.

Sutherland (NSW). The winery produces big, melony, Hunter Valley Sémillon with good varietal character but a tendency towards blowsiness.

Tisdall (Victoria). The Sauvignon–Sémillon blends are sweetish and cloying, but the cool-climate Mt Helen Sauvignon Blanc is clean, lively and well balanced.

Yalumba (SA). Producers of rich, smoky, *barrique*-aged Botrytis Sémillon in 1987 and 1991.

BROWN BROTHERS

Victoria

Milawa, VIC 3678
Quality: 🍇🍇🍇   Price: ★★

Brown Brothers, founded in 1885 and still family run, regularly produce one of Australia's heftiest, fattest, oaked Sémillons, although it is only aged for a few months in a combination of new *barriques* and large oak casks. This burly style does not appeal to everyone, but I enjoy its frank opulence. Its lushness, sometimes dangerously close to blowsiness, suggests that this is a wine to be drunk fairly young, but it can age for up to ten years. The wine might be even more enjoyable if the alcohol level, usually about 14°, were slightly diminished.

The Sauvignon is equally blunt and oaky, and varietal character is absent. Its spiciness and overt oakiness make it quite distinct from the Graves-style wine on which it may have been modelled. It lacks finesse, but nobody can say the wine lacks character.

CAPE MENTELLE

Margaret River, Western Australia

> PO Box 110, Margaret River, WA 6285
> Vineyard: 25 acres of Sémillon
> SÉMILLON–SAUVIGNON
> Quality: 🍇🍇🍇   Price: ★★★

This Western Australian estate, only founded in 1976, has a deserved reputation for its delightful Sémillon–Sauvignon blend. That Cape Mentelle should excel at this style of wine is not surprising, since the estate is managed by David Hohnen, who later established Cloudy Bay winery in New Zealand. The grapes for this wine – roughly 60 per cent Sémillon, 30 per cent Sauvignon, 10 per cent Chenin Blanc – are machine-picked and about one third of the must is barrel-fermented in new *barriques* and aged in oak for up to six months. (The 1989 was simply half Sauvignon, half Sémillon.) Oaked and tank wines are blended in August before bottling, and the wine is usually released in January. The aromas are quite floral and often more marked than the palate by new oak. The blend combines freshness with rounded rich fruit, but recent vintages have shown a slight dose of residual sugar that is a touch overdone.

CHÂTEAU TAHBILK

Victoria

> Tabilk, VIC 3607
> Vineyard: 18 acres (60 per cent Sauvignon, 40 per cent Sémillon)
> Quality: 🍇🍇🍇   Price: ★★

This ancient estate has a fine reputation – by Australian standards, at any rate – for old-fashioned and long-lived reds, but it also produces some interesting white wines. The Sémillon–Sauvignon blend is lightly oaked, with only half the Sauvignon aged in new French oak for a year, and there is no malolactic fermentation. The 1987, tasted in 1990, was still undeveloped, but the acidity was lively and the nose more developed than when tasted a year earlier. Evidently this is a wine for the long haul, but it appears to have all the ingredients for an interesting life.

CULLEN

Margaret River, Western Australia

PO Box 17, Cowaramup, WA

Vineyard: 10 acres (60 per cent Sauvignon, 40 per cent Sémillon)

SAUVIGNON

Quality: 🍇🍇🍇   Price: ★★★

Cullen's organically treated Willyabrup vineyards were laid out in 1971 on granitic soils over a clay base. The Sauvignon, planted on gravelly loam in Margaret River, is picked twice: the first *trie* is aimed at conserving acidity, the second at gathering in fruit of maximum ripeness. The wine is *barrique*-fermented and partly aged in a mixture of Nevers and German oak. An oak-fermented Sémillon is also produced, though Cullen have discontinued their blend of the two varieties. The Sauvignon is certainly one of the most characterful and carefully made examples in Australia, combining ripeness with delicacy and using the oak to give a hint of spice and structure rather than to overwhelm the wine with vanilla flavours and tannin. Made in an austere style with plenty of acidity, these wines are designed to improve in bottle, although some vintages have developed vegetal aromas and flavours with time.

*

DE BORTOLI

Riverina, New South Wales

De Bortoli Road, Bilbul, NSW 2680

BOTRYTIS SÉMILLON

Quality: 🍇🍇🍇🍇   Price: ★★★★

De Bortoli are based in the fertile Murrumbidgee Irrigation Area and supplement their own production with bought-in grapes. In 1982 they made a stunning golden botrytized Sémillon that I and other tasters have mistaken for good Sauternes. In 1983 they modified the lusciousness by including 20 per cent Sauvignon in the blend. These remarkable wines are viscous, very intense, peachy, with a clear botrytis character and good length. Lower in alcohol than Sauternes, they have between 6.5° and 7.5° residual sugar. The only worrying aspect of the wine is that it seems so complete in its infancy, with its lush, forward fruit. There is nothing at all wrong with producing a wine in this accessible style, but it seems unlikely that it will develop much complexity with further ageing. Fortunately the microclimate seems to favour the production of a botrytized wine every vintage.

De Bortoli have also made a Dry Botrytis Sémillon that, in a very different way, is highly impressive, though I cannot help wondering about the circumstances in which one would actually want to drink a bottle of this rich, oaky, creamy wine.

GARRETT, ANDREW

South Australia

Kangarilla Road, McLaren Vale, SA 5171

SAUVIGNON–SÉMILLON

Quality: 🍇🍇🍇   Price: ★★

FUMÉ BLANC
Quality: 🍇   Price: ★★

The grapes are bought in from a variety of locations, mostly from McLaren Vale and from the Adelaide Plains. The Sauvignon–Sémillon blend contains 55 per cent Sauvignon, which is oak-fermented, blended with the Sémillon and matured in new *barriques*. With skin contact to boost its aromatic qualities, this wine is, not surprisingly, quite like Graves in style. Another wine, marketed as a Fumé Blanc, contains the same blend of grapes, but the Sauvignon is tank-fermented and the Sémillon barrel-fermented; after blending the wine is aged in new and one-year-old French and American oak. In this case the oak seems excessive in relation to the fruit.

HARDY (THOMAS) & SONS

South Australia

Reynell Road, Reynella, SA 5161
Production: 1.2 million bottles
FUMÉ BLANC
Quality: 🍇   Price: ★★

I am not sure what style the immense Hardy group is aiming for with their Hardy Collection Fumé Blanc, but I have always enjoyed its broad, spicy, assertive flavours. A blend of Sémillon and Sauvignon from Padthaway is less successful and lacks vigour. A Clare Valley Sémillon is marketed under the Leasingham Sémillon label, and a less expensive Sauvignon is sold under the Hutt Creek label.

HILL-SMITH

South Australia

> Yalumba, PO Box 10, Angaston, SA 5353
> Quality: 🍇🍇 Price: ★★
> BOTRYTIS SÉMILLON
> Quality: 🍇🍇🍇🍇 Price: ★★★★

Hill-Smith produce a full range of wines from these two grape varieties, both grown in the Barossa Valley. The Sauvignon Blanc (labelled Fumé Blanc until 1989) is a good wine, but lacks varietal character; its rounded oaky tones obscure the fruit and the sweet, ripe fruitiness can become cloying. Nor is the Sémillon, which receives some skin contact, much better: big, rich, oaky, not overpowering, yet essentially bland and leaden. Hill-Smith also produce a Sémillon–Chenin blend. There is little stylishness in these wines. The Botrytis Sémillon, however, is a copybook example of the style: bright gold in colour, a lively, sweet, sumptuous wine balanced with vigorous acidity. The wine is aged in French *barriques* for six months or so, which rounds out its sharp edges without imparting oak flavours.

HOUGHTON

Western Australia

> Dale Road, Middle Swan, WA 6056
> GOLD RESERVE SAUVIGNON BLANC
> Quality: 🍇🍇🍇 Price: ★★

Houghton, founded in the 1850s but now owned by Thomas Hardy, produce a Gold Reserve Sauvignon that is one of the fresher, more invigorating, Australian treatments of the variety. As a blend of different wines from various Western Australian vineyards, the components vary according to the vintage.

Although oak-fermented and full-flavoured, it has a hint of gooseberry character and quite good length. The wine does not go through malolactic fermentation and remains on the lees for about four months. The Wildflower Ridge Sémillon is a more commercial style of wine with a hint of sweetness; it is not intended to be aged. Sometimes these Western Australian Sémillons can be mistaken for Sauvignon because of their herbaceous flavours.

KIES

Barossa Valley, South Australia

Hoffnungsthal Road, Lyndoch, SA 5351

Quality: ▓▓▓   Price: ★★

This old winery changed its name from Karrawirra in 1983. Brian Fletcher is the able winemaker. The Sémillon–Sauvignon blend is an excellent example: spicy and lemony on the nose, and packed with fruit, powerfully oaked and stylish.

KNAPPSTEIN

Clare Valley, South Australia

PO Box 334, Clare, SA 5453

Vineyard: 25 acres (80 per cent Sauvignon, 20 per cent Sémillon)

Production: 96,000 bottles of Fumé Blanc; 6,000 bottles of Sémillon

FUMÉ BLANC

Quality: ▓   Price: ★★★

Best vintages: 1984, 1987, 1989

Until 1986 this winery was known as Enterprise Wines. Tim Knappstein was a pioneer of the Fumé Blanc style in Australia, which he first made in 1978. But the style has been repeatedly altered over the years. In 1987 Knappstein began to add Sémillon from bought-in grapes; by the late 1980s the style settled down into a blend of tank-fermented wines, mostly Sémillon, given skin contact and aged in new French and German oak for a few months. The Fumé Blanc lacks concentration, and has a hint of sweetness that may be commercially attractive but is ultimately cloying on the palate. The wine is unlikely to benefit from prolonged ageing in bottle.

KRONDORF

South Australia

Krondorf Road, Tanunda, SA 5352
Quality: 🍇–🍇🍇   Price: ★★

Nick Walker produces two Sauvignons at Krondorf. One comes from local grapes in the Barossa Valley; the other, a more generalized blend of McLaren Vale and Barossa Valley grapes, is labelled as South Australian. The grapes receive six hours of skin contact and in recent years a small proportion of the must has been barrel-fermented. The wine is only aged in oak for one month. I find these Sauvignons variable in quality. At their best they have an attractive piquancy and fruitiness, but in certain vintages the wines appear lean and angular, and in others sweetish and confected.

The Barossa Valley Sémillon, partly aged in French oak, is a decent, unambitious wine, sweetish and flavoury but lacking in intensity and elegance.

LINDEMANS

Hunter Valley, New South Wales

McDonalds Road, Pokolbin, NSW 2321
OLD HUNTER VALLEY SÉMILLON
Quality: 🍇🍇🍇🍇🍇   Price: ★★★★★
OTHERS
Quality: 🍇🍇–🍇🍇🍇   Price: ★★

A star among Sémillon producers, Lindemans (now owned by Penfolds) are still releasing minute stocks of older wines from the 1960s and 1970s. Many of them demonstrate what Hunter Valley Sémillon is all about. Some are fading, most are not. These Classic wines are unoaked, but their aromatic power and vigorous spiciness are astonishing. The wines are labelled with bin numbers – a tiresome Australian habit, since they are impossible to memorize. (What is more, some are labelled White Burgundy, Chablis or Riesling even though they are pure Sémillon. Australian wine marketing was more improvisational thirty years ago.) From 1970, for instance, I have tasted two Sémillons, Bin 3855 and Bin 3870, and the latter is holding up better. More recently, Lindemans have expanded their range with some delightful, well-balanced Sémillon–Chardonnay blends, with a gorgeous New South Wales Botrytis Sémillon and a number of Sauvignons. I have often found the acclaimed Padthaway Sauvignons disappointingly tart and undernourished, but the oak-aged Bin 95 bottlings (80 per cent Sauvignon from north-west Victoria, 20 per cent Chardonnay) have good body and retain a healthy acidity.

But it is the old Sémillons, with a complexity that many an old white Burgundy would envy, that are the glory of Lindemans. Made without the razzle-dazzle of French oak, they represent a triumph of grape and soil that illustrates what great white wine is all about.

McWILLIAM

Hunter Valley, New South Wales

Marrowbone Road, Pokolbin, NSW 2321
Quality: 🍇🍇–🍇🍇🍇 (Hunter Valley Sémillon 🍇🍇–🍇🍇🍇🍇)
Price: ★★–★★★

McWilliam make a sometimes bewildering range of wines from the Hunter Valley and from Hanwood in the Murrumbidgee Irrigation Area, but as at Lindemans, the glory of the white range is the Hunter Valley Sémillons. These come in a variety of bottlings, some called Mt Pleasant Elizabeth Riesling, others simply Hunter Sémillon. The quality is strangely variable. The grapes are grown on sandy loam in the Pokolbin district. They need at least five years in bottle before they show their paces. After three separate tastings of the rich, toasty, 1983 Mt Pleasant Sémillon, it is hard to believe that so complex and concentrated a wine is both unoaked and a mere 11° alcohol. I have conflicting notes on the Mt Pleasant and Hanwood Sémillon–Chardonnay blends: some have been anonymous wines, while others have had a rich oaky sweetness and a worrying lack of acidity. Hanwood Sauvignons have been straightforward, with a touch of appealing earthiness.

MERRILL, GEOFF

South Australia

Pimpala Road, Reynella, SA 5161
Quality: 🍇🍇🍇   Price: ★★

In the early 1980s Merrill, former winemaker at Château Reynella, made some gorgeous wines under his own label that seemed imbued with his own exuberant personality. The Sémillon that dominated the wine came from the Barossa Valley, while the Sauvignon came from the Adelaide Plains. The must was partly barrel-fermented, and aged in new French and American oak for six months. The wines were creamily textured, nutty but elegant, rich but delicate – complex indeed. Unfortunately, Merrill has dropped these stylish Sémillons from his current winemaking programme.

Under a second label, Mt Hurtle, Merrill has made some delicious McLaren Vale Sauvignon that tastes oaky but, Merrill assured me, is not.

MITCHELTON

Victoria

Mitchellstown Road, Nagambie, VIC 3608

SÉMILLON

Quality: 🍇🍇🍇   Price: ★

SÉMILLON–CHARDONNAY

Quality: 🍇🍇   Price: ★

Best vintages: 1986, 1988, 1990

Mitchelton have for some years been producing good solid examples of oak-aged Sémillon; half of the fruit is bought from growers in the Goulburn Valley. The wines are cool-fermented, then aged for a year in American oak, which gives them a strong vanilla flavour that blends well enough with Sémillon's broad, waxy flavours. Nobody could call these wines elegant, but they are plump and fruity and seem to retain their vigour after a few years in bottle. Outstanding vintages are aged at the winery for five years or more before release under the Classic Release label. The Mitchelton Sémillon–Chardonnay blends are rounded but less interesting. The fruity Fumé Blanc, oak-aged for three months, blends Sauvignon and Sémillon.

Fumé and Sémillon–Chardonnay styles for immediate drinking have been produced under the Thomas Mitchell label.

MOSS WOOD

Margaret River, Western Australia

Metricup Road, Willyabrup, WA 6284
Vineyard: 5 acres of Sémillon
Quality: 🍇🍇–🍇🍇🍇   Price: ★★★

Founded in 1969, Moss Wood is one of the few Australian wineries not to employ irrigation. The winemaker and present-day owner, Keith Mugford, has for some time been producing both wood-matured and unwooded versions of Sémillon. The unwooded wine is very different from Hunter Valley examples: it is lighter, with fresh and direct melony fruit, a wine of considerable charm. The wood-matured versions are far more complex, and benefit in terms of structure from the spell in oak. Attractive in their youth because of their richness and balance, they develop very slowly, and a 1985 in 1990 was still fresh and pungent despite the oaky foundations.

PENFOLDS

New South Wales

726 Princes Highway, Tempe, NSW 2038
Production: 480,000 bottles of Sémillon–Chardonnay
SÉMILLON–CHARDONNAY
Quality: 🍇🍇–🍇🍇🍇   Price: ★★
FUMÉ BLANC
Quality: 🍇   Price: ★★

It is always astonishing that so large a winery can consistently produce a range of wines of outstanding quality and often astonishing value. Penfolds are better known for their red wines, but their Sémillon–Chardonnay is an opulent example of the oaky style of Sémillon. The grapes come from Barossa and

Barooga, and the wine is aged in French and American *barriques*. The balance is exemplary, and although the wine is drinkable on release it should become more harmonious after a couple of years in bottle. The less expensive Koonunga Hill range from Barossa Valley includes a delicious Sémillon–Chardonnay made in a forward, creamy, oaky style.

Penfolds' Fumé Blanc is less exciting: plump, rounded and gently oaky, it lacks varietal character and length of flavour.

PETERSONS

Hunter Valley, New South Wales

Mount View Road, Mount View, NSW 2325

Quality: 🍇🍇🍇   Price: ★★

Petersons have produced some fine, waxy, Hunter Valley Sémillons, medium-bodied but intense. Reticent in their youth, these discreetly oaked wines will undoubtedly improve with time.

ROBSON, MURRAY

Hunter Valley, New South Wales

De Beyers Road, Pokolbin, NSW 2321

Vineyard: 25 acres of Sémillon

Production: Early Harvest Sémillon, 9,600 bottles; Sémillon, 6,000 bottles

EARLY HARVEST SÉMILLON

Quality: 🍇🍇   Price: ★★★

SÉMILLON

Quality: 🍇🍇🍇   Price: ★★★

Murray Robson usually produces two bottlings of single-variety Sémillon from twenty-year-old vines. Yields are exceptionally low. The Early Harvest Sémillon has good fruit and the citric acidity of early-picked grapes, but for my taste this is not what Sémillon is all about. I greatly prefer the regular bottling, although it is far more austere and closed when young and clearly needs bottle-age before showing at its best. Both wines are unwooded.

A little Sauvignon is made, for sale in Australia only.

ROSEMOUNT

Upper Hunter Valley, New South Wales

Rosemount Road, Denman, NSW 2328

WOOD-MATURED SÉMILLON

Quality: 🍇🍇 Price: ★★

FUMÉ BLANC, SHOW RESERVE SÉMILLON

Quality: 🍇🍇🍇 Price: ★★

BOTRYTIS SÉMILLON

Quality: 🍇🍇🍇 Price: ★★★★

It was Rosemount that first brought Australian wines to the attention of many non-Antipodean wine lovers. Phil Shaw produces a fine range of wines from Hunter Valley grapes. More impressive than the inexpensive Diamond white, a Sémillon–Sauvignon blend, are the Hunter Valley Fumé and Wood-matured Sémillon, and the Show Reserve Sémillon. The Hunter Fumé is given a touch of French oak-ageing and I have always enjoyed this spicy, fruity, vigorous wine. It may lack complexity but it is invariably delicious. The Wood-matured Sémillon has sometimes been clumsy, and I greatly prefer the richer Show Reserve bottlings. These are powerfully flavoured wines, and in certain vintages such as 1988 can taste overripe and brutal, with excessive residual sugar. None the less, the Show Reserve is an impressive example of wooded Hunter

Sémillon. Rosemount complete their range with an unctuous Botrytis Sémillon.

ROTHBURY ESTATE

Hunter Valley, New South Wales

Broke Road, Pokolbin, NSW 2321

HUNTER VALLEY SÉMILLON

Quality: 🍇🍇🍇🍇   Price: ★★–★★★

Best vintages: 1974, 1979, 1984, 1989, 1991

Rothbury was founded in 1971 by Len Evans, a leading guru of Australian wine and food. By the early 1990s Rothbury hopes to be self-sufficient and grapes will no longer be bought in. The estate, under winemakers David Lowe and Peter Hall, continues to make classic unoaked Lower Hunter Valley Sémillon from a soil of sandy clay and volcanic basalt. It rarely shows well in its stern youth, although its aromatic quality seems to develop more rapidly than its complexity on the palate. The wine requires patience, but in most vintages it is impeccably constructed. Vintages from the 1970s are still showing well, though current vintages are intended to be accessible when young. The zippy Len Evans Selection Sémillon–Chardonnay blend is less impressive. Unfortunately, some special Sémillon bottlings are unavailable outside Australia.

SALTRAM

South Australia

Angaston Road, Angaston, SA 5353
Quality: 🍇🍇   Price: ★

In recent years Saltram, now part of the Seagram empire, have made some very enjoyable Sémillons from Barossa Valley grapes. Made in a full-bodied oaky style, they can be a bit overpowering and alcoholic, but I defy anyone to dislike their sheer richness of fruit.

SHAW & SMITH

South Australia

248 Flinders Street, Adelaide 5000
Quality: 🍇🍇   Price: ★★★

This newcomer, which buys in all its grapes, released its first vintage in 1990. Martin Shaw used to work with Brian Croser at Petaluma, and Michael Hill-Smith, Australia's first Master of Wine, comes from a well-known winemaking family. Their Sauvignon in 1990 came from Geoff Hardy's Range Vineyard in the Adelaide Hills. They deliberately aim for a more pure style than is usually found in Australian Sauvignons. The wine is unoaked, allowing the excellent fruit to emerge; the acidity is vigorous and the wine has very good texture and length. The 1991 is even more vibrant.

TALTARNI

Victoria

> Moonambel, VIC 3478
> Vineyard: 57 acres of Sauvignon
> Production: 70,000–100,000 bottles of Fumé Blanc
> Quality: 🍇🍇🍇 Price: ★★
> Best vintages: 1982, 1984, 1988, 1990

The vineyards, first planted in 1969, are located close to the gentle hills of the Victorian Pyrenees north-west of Melbourne. Perhaps it is the presence since 1976 of a French winemaker, Dominique Portet, that gives the Fumé Blanc its distinction. The grapes are grown on poor gravelly soils, and yields are modest. Portet dispenses with skin contact and chaptalization and malolactic fermentation. Aged for about six weeks in new Nevers *barriques*, the sweetish Sauvignon fruit comes shining through, and the wine, moderate in alcohol and quite high in acidity, is beautifully balanced. It is best drunk within four years of release. Taltarni's straight Sauvignon Blanc is less complex, and sometimes tastes tart.

TYRRELL

Hunter Valley, New South Wales

> Broke Road, Pokolbin, NSW 2321
> Quality: 🍇🍇🍇 Price: ★★

Tyrrell, who take Sémillon very seriously indeed, make a fine, robust, traditional Hunter Valley Sémillon using indigenous yeasts, as well as a Sémillon-dominated blend with Sauvignon. This blend is unoaked, and is fresh, clean and vigorous. It has no great complexity, but is in a sharply differentiated style from the more austere and earthy but grandiose Sémillon, which is made from grapes grown in non-irrigated vineyards. The wine is fermented in old *barriques* and aged for a year in bottle before release. So is the inexpensive Long Flat White, which contains a high proportion of Sémillon.

AUSTRIA

Eighty-three per cent of Austria's vineyards are planted with white grape varieties, dominated by the local Grüner Veltliner. A small quantity (a mere 300 acres) of Sauvignon Blanc is grown, sometimes under the German name of Muskat-Silvaner. About half the vineyards are in southern Styria (Süd-Steiermark), and most of the rest are in the Burgenland in eastern Austria. Until the early 1980s the wine was vinified in a sweet style, but the growing fashion for French-style wines and the reaction to the 1985 wine scandal persuaded most producers to change to a dry style. The very varied limestone soils of the Süd-Steiermark are well suited to Sauvignon, and many of the best and most aromatic wines come from here; the Burgenland, with its generally warmer climate, produces richer but less refined styles.

A combination of good soils, low yields (about 2–3 tons per acre) and exemplary vinification means that the general standard of Austrian Sauvignon is extremely high, and constantly improving. In a tasting in Vienna late in 1990 of thirty Sauvignons from 1973 to 1989, most of the best wines came from 1989, partly because of the quality of the vintage but also because of the winemakers' growing confidence and skill. Many of the finest producers deserve a detailed listing, but unfortunately most of these wines are almost impossible to find, except in top Austrian restaurants. Production is tiny, demand and prices high. The best recent vintages have been 1985, 1986, 1989, the ultra-ripe 1990 and the leaner 1991.

From the Süd-Steiermark, top producers of Sauvignon include Baur and Sattler of Gamlitz, Hirschmugl of St-Andrä, Tement of Berghausen and Polz of Grassmitzberg. In the Burgenland, Georg Stiegelmar makes the most powerful and rich Sauvignon I have found in Austria; high acidity saves it from flabbiness. Other good Burgenland producers include Anton Kollwentz of Grosshöflein and Hans Feiler of Rust. The Viennese *négociant* Niedermayer makes an excellent Sauvignon too.

With their fullness of flavour and, in good vintages, the powerful ripe acidity that is highly characteristic of Austrian white wines, these Sauvignons can be among the very best in Europe.

CHILE

Nobody knows how much Sauvignon Blanc and Sémillon are planted in Chile, but informed estimates suggest that there are 7,500–10,000 acres of Sémillon and 5,000 acres of Sauvignon under vine. Most of these vines are ungrafted, since phylloxera has never ravaged Chile. Indeed, the vines tend to be remarkably free from disease. But the situation is complicated by the presence of another variety known as Sauvignonasse or Sauvignon Vert. According to some authorities, Sauvignonasse is not Sauvignon at all but a variety closer to the Italian Tocai Friulano. Others believe Sauvignonasse to be simply an inferior clone adopted by many Chilean vineyards. Whatever the nature of the beast, it gives wine of considerably less interest than true Sauvignon. Yet in terms of acreage under vine, Sauvignonasse swamps true Sauvignon, with 31,000 acres planted.

Sauvignon is often blended with Sémillon, which given the local preference for big oily whites is probably not a felicitous combination in this instance. Indeed, the kind of white wine that Chileans find agreeable does not find favour in Europe. Until the early 1980s most vinification took place in large neutral oak casks: stainless steel tanks and new wood only began to be introduced into Chilean wineries in about 1990. Consequently, many Chilean white wines have a tendency to be big and flat, full-flavoured but lacking in the raciness and elegance of the best European Sauvignons. Nor have I encountered any examples of Sauvignon–Sémillon blends that come close in quality or style to good white Graves. It seems probable that most Chilean vineyards, despite the cool nights of the Andes foothills, are simply too hot to give copybook Sauvignon. Moreover, yields are high enough to make even the most cynical Italian growers blush. For Sémillon, yields can be as high as 45 tons per acre.

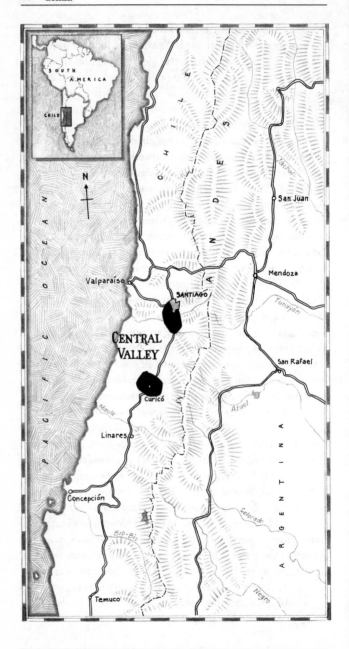

Many of the largest Chilean wineries are well equipped and produce clean, efficiently made Sauvignons that are agreeable white wines of no great character. Most production is handled by large cooperatives, so even privately owned wineries end up purchasing a large proportion of their needs from the coops, either as grapes or as wine. Nevertheless, many wineries grow at least some of their own Sauvignon. Errázuriz Panquehue has planted 70 acres of Sauvignon. For their export-only Caliterra label, the outcome of a joint venture with Franciscan Vineyards of California, some 98 acres of Sauvignon and 25 of Sémillon have been planted. Another export-only label is Montes, a range produced from 210 acres (20 of Sauvignon) in the Curicó Valley by Aurelio Montes. Early vintages were disappointing, but in 1990 Montes produced a fresh, clean, grassy, unwooded Sauvignon, and a fatter Fumé wine that had spent two months in American oak and ended up lacking in zest and freshness. In style, the unwooded wine is not unlike a good-quality Bergerac Sec. Santa Rita also succeeded with Sauvignon in 1990 by keeping yields down to European levels.

Other wineries, even the well-known Concha y Toro and Viña San Pedro with its range of Gato Blanco and Llave d'Oro Sauvignons, turned out a succession of dull, vegetal, souped-up wines, often with excessive sulphur dioxide. San Pedro owns extensive vineyards: 400 acres of Sauvignon and 25 of Sémillon. (The lean and lively 1989 indicates that San Pedro is beginning to produce crisper wines more suited to European, and probably North American, tastes.) Undurraga have planted 150 acres with Sauvignon in the Maipo Valley; unfortunately, I have yet to taste one I found enjoyable. Only Torres, a Spanish house based in the southern region of Curicó with its relatively cool climate, has managed to produce wines of interest. Domaine Caperana is also producing characterful Sauvignon from Maipo. The Los Vascos winery, with 135 acres of Sauvignon planted in Careten Valley, is a joint venture between the Lafite Rothschilds and the Eyzaguirre family, so this estate too will be worth keeping an eye on. Its fresh, sweetish wines are sold only on the export market.

*

TORRES, MIGUEL

Panamericana Sur Km 195, Curicó

Production: 46,000 bottles of Bellaterra Sauvignon Blanc

Quality: 🍇 Price: ★–★★

In 1979 this excellent Spanish house acquired over 350 acres of mature vineyards south of Santiago and established a modern winery with imported equipment. Two Sauvignons are produced. Curicó, also called Santa Digna, is cold-fermented in tanks and sees no wood. The Bellaterra blends 60 per cent barrel-fermented in American oak with 40 per cent tank-fermented wine. The barrel-fermented portion is matured in oak for about five months before being blended. The unwooded wine is clean and crisp but lacks concentration of flavour. The markedly oaky Bellaterra is much richer and retains good acidity.

FRANCE

Bergerac and Monbazillac

Since Monbazillac is an enclave within the large Bergerac region east of Bordeaux, it is appropriate to consider these two areas together, especially since most of the estates producing Monbazillac also produce Bergerac. The Bergerac vineyards are planted on the plains and hills on either side of the Dordogne river; those of Monbazillac lie south of the river, close to the town of Bergerac itself. The white grapes planted are the familiar Bordeaux varieties: Sémillon, Sauvignon Blanc and Muscadelle. Bergerac is produced in a number of styles; Monbazillac is always sweet.

The Bergerac region is vast, with 25,500 acres under vine. About 45 per cent of the production is of white wine, with Sémillon the leading white grape, accounting for 75 per cent of the plantations. Not long ago it was difficult to find any dry white Bergerac of more than humdrum quality, but a determined campaign is under way, led by many young growers of greater sophistication than their elders, to improve quality. Prices have been low for both Bergerac and Monbazillac, and the only way for conscientious estates to remain profitable is to raise prices, a move only tolerated by consumers if there is a noticeable amelioration in quality. One way to improve standards is to lower yields. Not long ago maximum official yields for Bergerac Sec were as high as 80 hectolitres per hectare (5.3 tons per acre). They were then reduced to 72 hectolitres per hectare, and since 1988 have been reduced further to 66 (4.4 tons per acre).

In rural France wine estates and the skills required to run them are still handed down from father to son. Making wine is

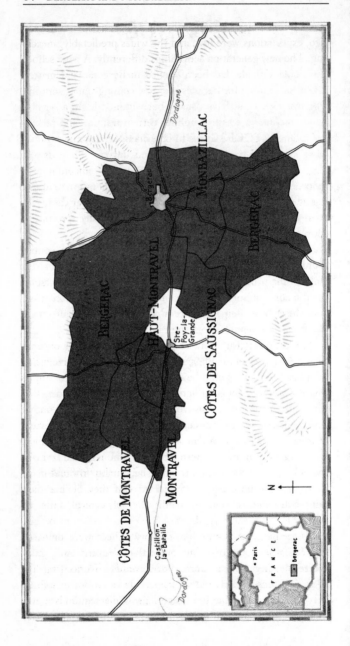

just another way of earning a living. Until about twenty years ago, expectations were low, and the wines predictably unexciting. The new generation sees things differently. A wine school, the École Viticole, has been opened in Bergerac and matters taken for granted for decades are now coming under scrutiny. For instance, vines have usually been trained high, a sensible economic measure as it simplifies certain training and picking procedures. Yet there seems to be evidence that grapes trained high lose their typicity of aroma and flavour. There is also much discussion about the use of clones – uncommon in Bergerac – and the density of foliage. In other words, all the issues hotly debated in the major Sauvignon regions of the world – the Graves, the Loire, New Zealand – are now on the agenda in Bergerac too.

Some young growers are experimenting with skin contact and barrel-fermentation. The results have been mixed, often, it seems to me, because the quality of the fruit is not yet sufficiently concentrated to survive an onslaught of oak. Nevertheless, the trend is welcome since it reflects an intention to make the best wine possible from the raw materials available.

The prospects for Monbazillac, a sweet wine that once rivalled Sauternes in richness and complexity, are less promising. Monbazillac is, or should be, made in exactly the same way as Sauternes from grapes afflicted by the botrytis that develops after autumnal fogs roll in from the river. But, as in Loupiac and Ste-Croix-du-Mont, standards slipped to such an extent that prices plummeted, and nowadays very few growers can make the commitment of resources and time required to make fine sweet wine. Standards are often lamentably low and many producers are unbearably complacent – if they believe their wines are as good as they say – or insufferably cynical, if they do not.

Monbazillac has a very long history. There were monastic vineyards here in 1080, but no major planting until 1511. Curiously, the vineyards face northwards, overlooking the Dordogne valley. There are considerable variations in soil: up on the plateau there is a limestone subsoil; maturation is slower and yields less abundant than down on the plain, where clay dominates. The best Monbazillac tends to come from the plateau, the best Bergerac Sec from the plain.

The area used to be dominated by great estates, but by 1986 there were 429 growers farming over 6,000 acres. 144 growers belong to the cooperative. Five communes are entitled to the appellation: in descending order of size they are Monbazillac itself, Pomport, St-Laurent-des-Vignes, Colombier and Rouffignac. The maximum yields are 40 hectolitres per hectare (2.7 tons per acre) and chaptalization is permitted to 2 degrees of alcohol. Because the minimum alcohol level is 11°, growers are encouraged to pick grapes at much lower must weights than would be contemplated in Sauternes.

If you were to read and believe all the brochures put out by the CIVRB, the body responsible, among other matters, for promoting the region's wines, you would imagine that at harvest time the vineyards are filled with pickers selecting only the most perfect botrytized grapes. This is far from the truth. Bernard Ginestet's book on Bergerac and Monbazillac has a splendid colour photograph of a harvesting machine happily at work in front of the region's showpiece, Château Monbazillac. The CIVRB was aghast, but the photograph merely reflects the truth. The only growers who pick by hand are those who do so for quirky reasons of their own or those whose vineyards are too steep or too tiny for machine-picking to be practicable. Similarly, hardly any growers practise *triage*. Those that do usually confine their first *passage* to weeding out rotten grapes or obviously excessive production, and the second *passage* to picking everything that is left. Consequently, the vast majority of wine sold as Monbazillac is a mildly sweet, vapid concoction with no trace of botrytis.

There are some other appellations bordering Bergerac where wines, mostly sweet, are made from the same grape varieties. Within Bergerac itself one finds Bergerac Moelleux and the less sweet Bergerac Demi-Sec, unpretentious wines usually made from overripe Sémillon. To the west of Bergerac, not far from St-Émilion, are the fourteen communes of Montravel, where some 3,000 acres generate, confusingly, three separate wines: Montravel itself, a dry white grown on thin alluvial soil close to the Dordogne; Côtes de Montravel, a sweet wine grown on the slopes just north of the river; and Haut-Montravel, a slightly sweeter wine made on slopes with higher limestone content. Vines are trained high and over half the crop is machine-harvested. The sweet wines are mostly of miserable quality, and only constitute about 20 per cent of the region's production. Yields can be as high as 4 tons per acre, botrytis is rare and the maximum amount of residual sugar in the wine is restricted to 54 grams per litre, so the wines can never be unctuous. Finally, to the west of the Monbazillac area lies Saussignac, another sweet wine area. Much of its production is in fact sold as Côtes de Bergerac Moelleux instead. It makes little difference, since in a blind tasting it would be difficult to distinguish between these various appellations.

In addition to the properties listed below there are some good wines to be found at the following estates. Château Truffière-Thibaut used to offer for sale some very old vintages of Monbazillac; recent vintages have been less impressive. Domaine La Truffière-Tirecul, on the slopes of Monbazillac, makes a pure dry Sémillon as well as a Bergerac Sec with 60 per cent Sauvignon. (The real curiosity here is a Monbazillac called Tirecul, made entirely from Muscadelle.) One of the larger proprietors of the region, Jean-Pierre Martrenchard of Château Le Mayne, makes very commercial wines, but his Bergerac Sec Cuvée Réservée is aged *sur lie* and has more complexity than his other dry wines.

The best estates of Haut-Montravel are Domaine de Libarde at Nastringues and Château de Masburel at Fougueyrolles, but that is not saying a great deal.

CAVE COOPÉRATIVE DE MONBAZILLAC

AC Monbazillac

Monbazillac, 24240 Sigoulès
Production: 2 million bottles
Quality: 🍇–🍇🍇   Price: ★–★★

Best vintages: 1962, 1964, 1966, 1970, 1975, 1976, 1981, 1985, 1989

Founded in 1941, this cooperative now has 150 members who own about 2,500 acres, one third of which is AC Monbazillac. The cooperative only buys grapes – 80 per cent Sémillon, 10 per cent Sauvignon, 10 per cent Muscadelle – and is strict about rejecting those of poor quality. Its own wines are mediocre, and the single-estate wines are definitely superior. All grapes are machine-picked, and there is no *triage* except at Château Monbazillac. Yields approach 2 tons per acre. Vinification is technically exhaustive, with centrifuging and at least three filtrations.

The single-estate wines are those of Château Monbazillac (q.v.), the sixteenth-century château owned by the cooperative, Château Septy (50,000 bottles), Château La Brie (70,000 bottles), Château Pion (32 acres giving 45,000 bottles), Château Marsalet (54 acres leased by the cooperative and producing 55,000 bottles) and Château Les Saintes at Rouffignac. La Brie has a reputation for finesse rather than lushness, while Château Septy tends to be slightly richer.

CHÂTEAU BELINGARD-CHAYNE

AC Bergerac Sec, Bergerac Moelleux, Monbazillac

Pomport, 24240 Sigoulès

Vineyard: 98 acres (60 per cent Sémillon, 30 per cent Sauvignon, 10 per cent Muscadelle)

Production: 100,000 bottles

BERGERAC SEC

Quality: 🍇🍇🍇   Price: ★

BLANCHE DE BOSREDON

Quality: 🍇🍇🍇   Price: ★★

This well-run estate in lovely hilly country is owned by the Comte de Bosredon. For Bergerac Sec, the grapes are machine-picked, and both Sauvignon and Muscadelle receive between twelve and eighteen hours of skin contact if the grapes are perfectly healthy. Each variety is fermented separately then left *sur lie* for up to a month. In 1987 Blanche de Bosredon was made for the first time, a wine made from old vines, half Sémillon, half Sauvignon, fermented in new Allier *barriques* and left on the lees for seven months. This first vintage was mediocre, but the following vintages were much better, with plenty of silky, oaky fruit.

The Bergerac Sec is fresh and lively with ample fruitiness, and is released under the Château du Chayne label. At present the production of Blanche de Bosredon is limited to a few thousand bottles, but there are plans to increase production. The Monbazillac, picked with a must weight of at least 16° (17° in 1988 and 1989), is bottled as Château Belingard and is unexciting. The wine is aged in tank for a year, then in 600-litre casks for up to eighteen months. Not even the Bosredons can work up any enthusiasm for their Bergerac Demi-Sec, produced almost solely for local British vacationers, who inexplicably love the gummy stuff.

CHÂTEAU COURT-LES-MUTS

AC Bergerac Sec, Saussignac

Razac-de-Saussignac, 24240 Sigoulès

Production: Bergerac Sec, 65,000 bottles; Saussignac, 10,000 bottles

BERGERAC SEC

Quality: 🍇🍇   Price: ★

SAUSSIGNAC

Quality: 🍇   Price: ★

An accomplished oenologist, Pierre Sadoux, runs this very well-maintained property with his wife. The Bergerac Sec is a blend of 70 per cent Sémillon and 30 per cent Sauvignon; the grapes are macerated overnight. This is a good fruity wine of some weight and richness. The Sadoux have become well known as almost the last defenders of Saussignac. I certainly know of no other good producers of this wine. It is made mostly from Sémillon, and is machine-harvested with average yields of 3 tons per acre. The wine is bottled about eighteen months after the harvest; fairly low in alcohol, it has about 40 grams per litre of residual sugar. I find it insipid and mild, with a certain melony Sémillon flavour.

CHÂTEAU GRINOU

AC Bergerac Sec

Monestier, 24240 Sigoulès

Vineyard: 20 acres (50 per cent Sémillon, 50 per cent Sauvignon)

Production: 120,000 bottles

Quality: 🍇   Price: ★

Guy Cuisset, who has run this family property since 1977, is a leading Young Turk of the Bergerac region. Few of his elders will have sought out and tasted, as he has, New World Sauvignons. He is a restless experimenter, trusting to his experience rather than to fad or formula. Since 1988 he has used skin contact, and leaves the wine on the fine lees until bottling in the winter.

Cuisset finds that these procedures increase the longevity of his wine. Yields are fairly high at 4 tons per acre, and the grapes are picked mechanically. I tasted his 1989s, a difficult vintage, and had some doubts, but this is certainly an estate to keep an eye on.

CHÂTEAU HAUT-BERNASSE

AC Bergerac Sec, Monbazillac

24240 Monbazillac

Vineyard: 15 acres (75 per cent Sémillon, 15 per cent Sauvignon, 10 per cent Muscadelle)

Production: 20,000–25,000 bottles of Bergerac Sec; 10,000 bottles of Monbazillac

MONBAZILLAC

Quality: 🍇   Price: ★★

BERGERAC SEC

Quality: 🍇   Price: ★

Jacques Blais, the cello-playing proprietor, acquired the estate in 1977, and is essentially self-taught. He has developed a peculiar system of getting two crops from the same vines. In September he picks grapes for the dry wine, leaving outer bunches to develop over-maturity or, with luck, botrytis. They are then hand-picked in late October and used to make Monbazillac. Yields for Monbazillac are about 1 ton per acre.

The sweet wine is aged in old Sauternes *barriques* for twelve to fourteen months. The vines are young and the wines lack some excitement, but they have a tangerine freshness that is appealing. The 1986 and 1988 vintages are promising, and Blais is evidently keen to make wines of high quality.

CHÂTEAU LA JAUBERTIE

AC Bergerac Sec

24560 Colombier

Vineyard: 70 acres

Production: 220,000 bottles; 5,200 bottles of Réserve Mirabelle

Quality: 🍇🍇🍇   Price: ★★

This grand property became famous after its purchase in 1973 by Henry (Nick) Ryman. Assisted by his Australian-trained son Hugh, his fresh racy wines captivated the English market in particular. The vines are high-trained because all cultivation and harvesting is mechanical; yields are quite high, yet the Jaubertie wines are often outstanding. Ryman believes that his wines eclipse those of his neighbours, 'because they don't know how to make wine and I employ people who do'.

Since 1988 the winemaker has been Charles Martin, who also had plenty of New World winemaking experience. If the grapes are healthy they receive some skin contact before passing through a pneumatic press. The must is cold-fermented at about 13 °C, and the wine is bottled early.

There are a number of different *cuvées*. The Bergerac Sec (or Sémillon Sec) used to have 75 per cent Sémillon, but more recently has had as much as 95 per cent. The Cépage Sauvignon used to contain a large amount of Sémillon too, but now it is almost pure Sauvignon. There is also a luxury *cuvée* called Réserve Mirabelle, a blend of Sauvignon and Sémillon fermented in new Allier and German oak, and aged in wood for about three months.

The wines, once reasonably priced, are now considerably more expensive, but remain among the very best that Bergerac can offer. Ryman also buys in grapes to produce wines marketed under the Domaine de Grandchamp label. The style of the dry wines is fresh and assertive, with pungent aromas and crisp fruit of a delicate herbaceous flavour. Ryman has made excellent Monbazillac, but never in sufficient quantities to be marketed.

CHÂTEAU LES MIAUDOUX

AC Bergerac Sec

Saussignac, 24240 Sigoulès

Vineyard: 32 acres (85 per cent Sémillon, 10 per cent Sauvignon, 5 per cent Muscadelle)

Production: 90,000 bottles
Quality: 🍇   Price: ★

Gérard Cuisset is an innovative winemaker at present somewhat hampered by old-fashioned equipment. The vines are planted on the clay and limestone soil typical of the region, but the heavy clay content seems to dampen the spirits of the wines, which are fresh and well made but not yet distinguished.

CHÂTEAU MONBAZILLAC

AC Monbazillac

24240 Monbazillac
Vineyard: 54 acres
Production: 55,000 bottles
Quality: 🍇🍇   Price: ★★

This splendid Renaissance château dominates the Monbazillac plateau and is the region's major tourist attraction. Its wines are made by the cooperative. There is little *triage* other than a preliminary foray through the vineyard to eliminate inappropriate grapes. Yields are low at just over 1 ton per acre. The 1976 was a splendid wine, but some subsequent vintages have been disappointing. One hopes that the fine vintages of the late 1980s will show a return to former standards.

CHÂTEAU DU TREUIL-DE-NAILHAC

AC Bergerac Sec, Monbazillac

Monbazillac, 24240 Sigoulès
Vineyard: 25 acres, and 175 acres at other properties
Production: 44,000 bottles of Château du Treuil Monbazillac; 18,000 bottles of Château La Borderie Monbazillac

BERGERAC SEC

Quality: 👑👑👑   Price: ★

MONBAZILLAC

Quality: 👑👑👑   Price: ★★–★★★

Best vintages: 1952, 1955, 1957, 1959, 1962, 1967, 1975, 1979, 1981, 1986, 1988, 1989

Monsieur Vidal, the proprietor of this estate on the plateau of Monbazillac, also owns two other properties: La Borderie, down on the plain, and Fonrousse. Although the production from each property is vinified separately, the vinification methods are identical. Yields are relatively low, and Vidal has long been a practitioner of skin contact. The must is fermented at exceptionally low temperatures to give fresh, lively wines. From Château du Treuil Vidal produces a pure Sauvignon Bergerac, whereas from Château Fonrousse the wine is 100 per cent Sémillon. I much prefer the former. Château La Borderie gives light, fresh, unpretentious wines.

Vidal, aided by his son, makes one of the best Monbazillacs from his hand-picked vineyards at Château du Treuil, which are planted with 60 per cent Sémillon, 20 per cent Sauvignon and 20 per cent Muscadelle. After fermentation the wines are aged in tanks for a year, then in large old casks for about two years. Only the best wine is bottled under the estate name; sometimes as much as 80 per cent is sold to wholesalers.

The wine can be outstanding. In 1975 Vidal had wholly botrytized grapes with must weights of 22° and yields of only 7 hectolitres per hectare. That richness of fruit was surpassed only in 1989, which Vidal considers his best vintage since 1955. The best wine in *barriques* of the vintage has been aged.

CLOS FONTINDOULE

AC Monbazillac

24240 Monbazillac

Vineyard: 42 acres (60 per cent Sémillon, 20 per cent Sauvignon, 20 per cent Muscadelle)

Production: 50,000 bottles

Quality: 🍇   Price: ★★

Best vintages: 1942, 1943, 1947, 1949, 1955, 1959, 1964, 1967, 1970, 1976, 1980, 1982, 1983, 1985, 1986, 1988, 1989

This estate, located high on the Monbazillac plateau, is owned by Gilles Cros, a proprietor of the old school. Although there is no systematic *triage*, the grapes are picked by hand as late as possible in the year. The must is fermented in cement tanks, and aged in old wood for up to two years. Only the best years are bottled and marketed under the estate name. The cellars are filthy, yet the wines are rich and flavoury, which makes me speculate about how superb the wine could be if the vinification were improved. Certainly Cros obtains some excellent fruit. In 1988 he had average must weights of 19.6°, and in 1989 the average was 21.5°. Since his wines rarely exceed 13.5° alcohol, they are very sweet indeed. With age the wines become plump and raisiny, with strong barley-sugar and marmalade flavours. They lack freshness but have a chunky, baked fruitiness that is far closer to traditional Monbazillac than the anaemic wines of most other producers.

Bordeaux

Despite changes in the market that have prompted Bordeaux growers to shift from white wine production to red, about one

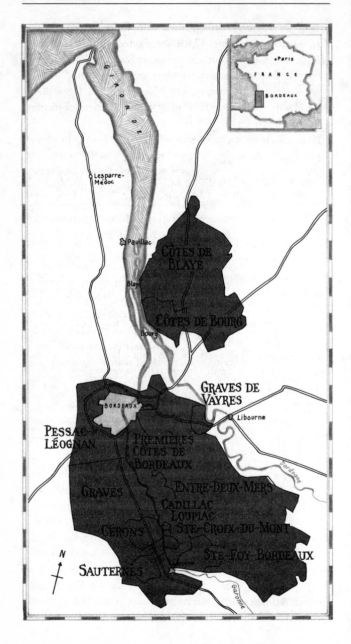

fifth of the region is still planted with white grapes. Of the 261,700 acres under vine, 47,840 are planted with white grapes. The great majority are either Sauvignon Blanc or Sémillon, but in the appellations where sweet wines are made, a small amount of Muscadelle is also found, and Muscadelle and Ugni Blanc and insignificant quantities of other white varieties are planted in Entre-Deux-Mers.

About 24,700 acres give wines entitled to be sold as Bordeaux Blanc. Entre-Deux-Mers white vines occupy 6,400 acres. The Graves (including the fairly new super-appellation of Pessac-Léognan) accounts for 6,500 acres, of which 47 per cent are planted with white grapes. The large Blaye region on the opposite bank of the Gironde from the Médoc is planted with 2,962 acres, its neighbour Côtes de Bourg Blanc with 222, and Graves de Vayres Blanc with 480.

Total plantations of grapes destined for the production of sweet white wine amount to 10,560 acres, the largest individual appellation being Sauternes itself with 3,500, though its neighbour Barsac, with 1,390 acres, is entitled to be sold as Sauternes. The large area on the other side of the Garonne, the Premières Côtes de Bordeaux, is the next largest producer of often insipid sweet white wine, much of which, confusingly, is sold under the Cadillac appellation; these regions are planted with 1,790 acres. In decreasing area of plantation, you will also encounter: Graves Supérieurs (1,160 acres), Ste-Croix-du-Mont (1,029), Loupiac (740), Bordeaux Supérieur (290), Ste-Foy Bordeaux Blanc (230), Cérons (220) and Côtes de Bordeaux St-Macaire (123).

Given the size of the region, it is not surprising that the range of styles is immense. Because of Bordeaux's alluvial soils, Sauvignon tends to be less pungent and aromatic than in northern France. Often it is blended with Sémillon, but since many consumers enjoy the freshness of undiluted Sauvignon, a considerable quantity of pure Sauvignon is marketed too. In general, the major merchants and producers are not keen to promote varietal wines, and prefer to maintain the French emphasis on appellation and *terroir*.

A mixture of complacency, low prices and ignorance meant

that until about ten years ago a disgracefully high proportion of white Bordeaux was of appalling quality, a liquefied form of sulphur dioxide. The unfavourable market for sweet white wines, which could hardly have been improved by the ghastly brews coming out of the Premières Côtes, led many growers to grub up their white vines and plant red grapes such as Merlot. However, since demand for well-made quaffable white wines at reasonable prices remains high, more far-sighted producers, notably the cooperatives, invested in technologically sophisticated equipment that allowed them to make fresh and fruity white wines. Young Bordeaux winemakers swallowed their pride and headed off to Australia for a season to work out why the Antipodes was so successful at satisfying the international market for well-made, characterful white wine at reasonable prices. By 1990 the overall standard had improved beyond recognition. Ambitious producers, aware of the splendours of top white Graves, have made efforts to produce more serious wines, using techniques such as skin contact and barrel-fermentation. Malolactic fermentation is the exception rather than the rule.

The top vintages for red Bordeaux are not necessarily equally good for white. Often the hot years which produce great clarets give white wines that can be heavy and blowsy. Thus 1962 was usually better for whites than the fabled 1961, and 1983 is superior to 1982. Although there are great variations between individual properties, some outstanding white Bordeaux were made in 1970, 1975, 1976, 1978, 1979, 1981, 1983, 1985, 1987, 1988 and 1989. Of current vintages, 1985 is rounded and ripe and forward, 1986 very variable in quality, but 1987 is surprisingly good and already attractive. 1988 is no heavyweight, but stylish and well balanced, while the best 1989s are wonderfully rich and powerfully structured. 1990 proved even hotter and drier than 1989, with dry whites of very mixed quality. In some wines the balance is unpromising, but the best 1990s should rival those of the previous year. The diminished crop of 1991 was picked too early, unripeness being a lesser evil than rot, and the wines will be mediocre at best.

GRAVES

From the suburbs of the city of Bordeaux, the Graves region spreads to the south-east, hugging the River Garonne for over thirty miles to just beyond Langon. To the north the vineyards have shrunk as the city suburbs spread: over the past century about 10,000 acres of vines have been gobbled up. Château Haut-Brion, for example, is almost entirely surrounded by conurbation. The best Graves vineyards are not along the river, but a mile or two inland, where the gravel outcrops from which the region derives its name rise to a modest height. The central Graves is dominated by the Sauternes vineyards and their neighbours, and these will be assessed separately. To the south and west of the Sauternais is a patchy area, of less complexity than the northern Graves. Forty-five per cent of Graves wine production is white.

In 1987 the best *terroirs* of the northern Graves were awarded their own appellation, Pessac-Léognan; 32 per cent of the wines are white. According to André Lurton, a leading proprietor in the appellation, the potential of white wines from Pessac-Léognan is extraordinary because of the complex geological structure of the soil, which can vary considerably within a single vineyard. Many Pessac-Léognan vineyards are on gently rolling slopes that have excellent drainage. The new appellation insists on lower yields and on at least 25 per cent of the white vines being Sauvignon, which seems hard on those who, rightly or wrongly, believe that a high proportion of Sémillon is desirable in a *vin de garde*.

Whether there really was a need to create yet another appellation is questionable, and good estates to the south of Pessac-Léognan may resent the implication that the new appellation is necessarily superior. Nevertheless all the region's classified growths are within the 2,200-acre Pessac-Léognan area. An official classification of the Graves was made in 1953, and revised in 1959 and 1960. Recent improvements in the quality of other estates, and a lack of improvement in some classified estates, means that the classifications should not be taken as gospel. The classified growths are: Bouscaut, Carbonnieux, Domaine de Chevalier, Couhins, Couhins-Lurton, Haut-Brion, La Tour-Martillac, Laville Haut-Brion, Malartic-Lagravière and Olivier. A revision was scheduled for 1984 but has not yet appeared.

In addition to the wines described in the section that follows, it is worth drawing the reader's attention to some other wines of good quality. Château Montalivet, made by Pierre Dubourdieu, the proprietor of the Sauternes estate of Doisy-Daëne, is a sound, reasonably priced Graves. Château Haut-Gardère has a growing reputation, but I have never encountered it. At Cérons, Olivier Lataste, the owner of the Grand Enclos au Château de Cérons, began in 1989 to produce a wine fermented in *barriques*, of which half are new. The first release, called the Cuvée de l'Enclos, was supple and judiciously oaked.

CHÂTEAU BOUSCAUT

AC Pessac-Léognan, *cru classé*

Cadaujac, 33140 Pont-de-la-Maye

Vineyard: 20 acres (52 per cent Sémillon, 48 per cent Sauvignon)

Production: 24,000 bottles

Quality: 🍇🍇   Price: ★★★

From 1968 to 1980 Bouscaut was American-owned, and the *régisseur* was Jean Delmas of Château Haut-Brion. In 1980 it was acquired by Lucien Lurton, who owns a number of Bordeaux properties. The soil at Bouscaut, the only important estate in Cadaujac, is unusual in that there is clay and sand as well as gravel over a limestone subsoil. The vines are old and the vinification meticulous. A pneumatic press is used, and although there is no skin contact the must receives a three-day *débourbage* at 6 °C. Since 1985 the wine has spent six months in new oak *sur lie*, with no racking, and since 1988 a third of the wine has been fermented in new *barriques*.

The second wine of Château Bouscaut is Château Valoux, a small proportion of which is aged in *barriques*.

Despite the efforts being made at Bouscaut, this remains an unexciting wine: firm, yet slightly coarse and lacking in character and vigour.

CHÂTEAU CABANNIEUX

AC Graves

33640 Portets

Vineyard: 15 acres (80 per cent Sémillon, 20 per cent Sauvignon)

Production: 40,000 bottles

Quality: 🍇   Price: ★★

Best vintages: 1983, 1986, 1988

Located on the highest land in Portets, the Cabannieux vineyards, on very deep gravel, have excellent ventilation and experience little rot. There are signs of renewed investment in this unpretentious estate. A pneumatic press is being installed, and since 1989 the grapes have been lightly macerated before pressing. After fermentation in stainless steel tanks the wine stays briefly on the fine lees before being racked. The wine is mostly aged in tank, but an increasing proportion is spending some months in *barriques*. Recent vintages have been characterized by a flowery nose of considerable charm, while on the palate the wine is rounded and slightly earthy. It can be drunk young or aged for six or seven years.

CHÂTEAU CARBONNIEUX

AC Pessac-Léognan, *cru classé*

33850 Léognan

Vineyard: 104 acres (65 per cent Sauvignon, 34 per cent Sémillon, 1 per cent Muscadelle)

Production: 200,000 bottles

Quality: 👑👑👑   Price: ★★★★

Best vintages: 1971, 1975, 1979, 1981, 1983, 1985, 1988, 1989

The largest white wine estate in the Graves, Carbonnieux has never enjoyed a particularly exalted reputation, but the owner, Antony Perrin, is determined to improve the quality.

The grapes, grown on pebbly and sandy soils, are hand-picked. Perrin practises *triage* if necessary, both in the vineyards and at the winery. The vinification reflects the influence of Denis Dubourdieu, a consultant here since the mid-1980s. Only 10 per cent of the grapes are given skin contact, but there is a long *débourbage* before fermentation. Fermentation begins in tank but is completed in well-toasted Limousin *barriques*, of which one third are renewed each year. The wine stays in barrels for ten months, remaining *sur lie*, and is stirred regularly. This method of vinification was begun tentatively in 1982 and was fully developed with the 1988 vintage. The second wine is Château Latour-Léognan.

Quality at this long-established estate has taken a quantum leap with the 1988 vintage. Perrin aspires to make wines that are rich, characterful and have good length, and he has the raw materials and commitment with which to succeed.

CHÂTEAU COUHINS-LURTON

AC Pessac-Léognan, *cru classé*

Villenave-d'Ornon

Vineyard: 15 acres (100 per cent Sauvignon)

Production: 25,000 bottles

Quality: 🍇🍇🍇   Price: ★★★★

Best vintages: 1983, 1986, 1988, 1989

This classified growth has been divided into two properties. I have never encountered Couhins, but Couhins-Lurton is widely available, since it is part of André Lurton's portfolio of important estates. (See Château La Louvière.) The subsoil here has quite a high clay content as well as gravel. Older vintages of Couhins-Lurton were not exciting, but since 1982 barrel-fermentation in new *barriques* has produced a very distinctive Sauvignon that goes from strength to strength. The 1988 vintage was a landmark year for this wine, which is fresh and aromatic, yet rich and weighty and with excellent length. Earlier vintages had been fairly short-lived; whether current vintages will attain the same longevity as the greatest white Graves remains to be seen.

CHÂTEAU DE CRUZEAU

AC Pessac-Léognan

St-Médard-d'Eyrans

Vineyard: 26 acres (90 per cent Sauvignon, 10 per cent Sémillon)

Production: 60,000 bottles

Quality: 🍇🍇   Price: ★★

This estate was acquired by André Lurton in 1974 and replanted in 1979. More woods have been cleared recently to increase the size of the vineyards. Lurton believes the quality of the deep gravel soil here is outstanding. The plantation reflects his preference for a preponderance of Sauvignon. Lurton, here as with his other Graves properties, is fermenting an increasing proportion of the wine in barrels; at the outset, Cruzeau saw no wood at all. On the few occasions I have tasted this wine, it has struck me as sound rather than brilliant. Only when the vines are older and the style more established will it be possible to decide whether the proprietor's expectations are being realized. At present it is a clean, well-made wine that should be drunk young.

CHÂTEAU DE FIEUZAL

AC Pessac-Léognan

33850 Léognan

Vineyards: 20 acres (50 per cent Sauvignon, 50 per cent Sémillon)

Production: 16,000 bottles

Quality: 🍷🍷🍷🍷   Price: ★★★★★

Best vintages: 1985, 1987, 1988, 1989

Owner Gérard Gribelin entrusts the winemaking at this exciting estate to the very able Michel Dupuy, who insists on *triage* at harvest time. Before 1984 the wine was unwooded, but in 1985 Denis Dubourdieu arrived as a consultant and introduced partial skin contact, fermentation in new *barriques*, and maturation and *bâtonnage* in oak for up to sixteen months.

Dupuy's aim is to make a white wine capable of ageing up to twenty years. He is a partisan of Sémillon, though Sauvignon aromas and flavours tend to dominate the wine in its youth. Recent vintages have been sumptuously oaky, but well balanced, supple and fruity. Fieuzal is clearly a rising star in the Graves, and the prices are rising as rapidly as its reputation.

CHÂTEAU HAUT-BRION

AC Pessac-Léognan, *cru classé*

33660 Pessac

Vineyard: 10 acres (50 per cent Sémillon, 50 per cent Sauvignon)

Production: 10,000 bottles

Quality: 🍇🍇🍇🍇🍇   Price: ★★★★★

Best vintages: 1966, 1970, 1975, 1976, 1978, 1981, 1982, 1985, 1988, 1989

The most famous red wine estate of the Graves also produces, under the watchful eyes of Jean Delmas and Jean Portal, a small quantity of sumptuous white wine that, while approachable young, needs many years in bottle to show its true quality. The average age of the vines is thirty years, and the soil has less clay content than its equally illustrious neighbour Laville Haut-Brion. Yields are between 2 and 3 tons per acre. There is no skin contact, as Haut-Brion believes the wine acquires enough tannin and richness from fermentation in *barriques*. The grapes are pressed in old vertical presses, and no cultivated yeasts are used. Since 1987 the wine has been fermented entirely in new oak, and remains in *barriques* for twelve to fourteen months.

The only criticism one can make of this splendid wine is its exceedingly high price, which does not prevent it from being sold out before it is even released. (The 1986 vintage was not released.)

CHÂTEAU LARRIVET HAUT-BRION

AC Pessac-Léognan

33859 Léognan

Vineyard: 4 acres (50 per cent Sauvignon, 50 per cent Sémillon)

Production: 7,500 bottles

Quality: 🍇🍇🍇🍇 Price: ★★★

The sale of this estate to the food company Andros in 1987 has unexpectedly led to an improvement in quality. Moreover, new plantations will soon increase the white vineyards to about 25 acres. Since 1987 the wines have been *barrique*-fermented in 70 per cent new oak to give a rich, full-bodied style of Graves.

CHÂTEAU LAVILLE HAUT-BRION

AC Pessac-Léognan, *cru classé*

33400 Talence

Vineyard: 8.5 acres (60 per cent Sémillon, 40 per cent Sauvignon)

Production: 5,000–14,000 bottles

Quality: 🍇🍇🍇🍇🍇 Price: ★★★★★

Best vintages: 1964, 1970, 1975, 1981, 1983, 1985, 1987, 1988, 1989

Laville is the white wine of Château La Mission Haut-Brion, which since 1983 has been under the same ownership and administration as Château Haut-Brion. The vines are slightly older than at Haut-Brion and yields are equally low.

1987 brought considerable changes: the old vertical press was replaced by a horizontal press, and a system was instituted of giving one third of the grapes some skin contact. Fermentation begins in tank and is completed in *barriques*. No cultivated yeasts are added. Since 1987 only new oak has been used; the wine remains in *barriques* for twelve to fourteen months. The old practice of bottling a separate Crème de Tête in outstanding years has been discontinued.

The wine, like Haut-Brion, is sold out before release, yet it requires even longer bottle-ageing than its neighbour. The price is astronomical, and production minute, especially since replanting has taken some vines temporarily out of production. Laville's longevity is legendary, although the oldest example I have tasted is the splendid 1964 Crème de Tête. Sulphur dioxide levels soared in the 1970s and early 1980s and some poor wines were made, but the new management has revived the true potential of the estate, adding a new elegance to a wine long celebrated for its richness and weight.

CHÂTEAU LA LOUVIÈRE

AC Pessac-Léognan

33850 Léognan

Vineyard: 25 acres (70 per cent Sauvignon, 30 per cent Sémillon)

Production: 80,000 bottles

Quality: ▼▼▼▼   Price: ★★★

Best vintages: 1967, 1970, 1975, 1978, 1982, 1983, 1985, 1988, 1989

This beautiful château is the flagship estate of the ubiquitous André Lurton, who bought the property in 1965. His other properties in the Graves are Couhins-Lurton, Cruzeau and Rochemorin.

Lurton is an admirer of Sauvignon, which he finds more expressive in its youth than Sémillon, and more capable of ageing than Sémillon enthusiasts are prepared to admit. When I tasted some barrel samples alongside Lurton, it was clear that he was less happy with the combination of oak and Sauvignon than with oak and Sémillon. The oldest La Louvière I have tasted is 1966, but Lurton assures me that some vintages from the late 1950s and 1960s are still drinking well.

In 1983 Lurton began to experiment with barrel-fermentation here, but it was not until 1987 that the entire crop was fermented in wood, most of it new. Perhaps because Lurton has not made up his mind about such matters as maceration, La

Louvière seems to lack a distinctive style. It certainly has finesse, and is improving from year to year. Enjoyable when young, the wine should age gracefully without difficulty.

Château Coucheroy is the estate's inexpensive and reliable second label.

CHÂTEAU MALARTIC-LAGRAVIÈRE

AC Pessac-Léognan, *cru classé*

| 33850 Léognan |
| Vineyard: 7.5 acres (100 per cent Sauvignon) |
| Production: 10,000–12,000 bottles |
| Quality: �   Price: ★★★ |

Jacques Marly-Ridoret was the owner of this estate from 1947 until its sale in 1990 to the champagne house Laurent-Perrier. Bruno Marly, one of his ten sons, has been the winemaker since 1979. The vines are planted in a single parcel, facing south and south-west. Beneath a layer of gravel and pebbles lies a rich bed of clay. It was on the oenologist Émile Peynaud's advice that Jacques Marly did not replant his Sémillon and Muscadelle vines. The average age of the vines is twenty-five years.

Triage is practised in the vineyard. Because Malartic-Lagravière like to pick their grapes early to preserve acidity, the wine is nearly always chaptalized. There is no skin contact, but since 1988 Marly has been experimenting with completing the fermentation in *barriques*. The wine is aged in *barriques*, of which 25 per cent are new, and the first few months are spent *sur lie*.

I find this wine disappointing – citric, yet lacking in vigour and complexity. There is a troubling lack of fruitiness and frequently an excess of sulphur dioxide. The chaptalization often gives a hot, coarse finish. The wine keeps quite well but does not appear to improve greatly with age.

CHÂTEAU DE MALLE

AC Graves

> Preignac, 33210 Langon
> Production: 7,000 bottles
> Quality: 🍇🍇🍇   Price: ★★

The *deuxième cru* Sauternes estate of Château de Malle also produces a very attractive white Graves from equal proportions of Sauvignon and Sémillon. The two varieties receive some skin contact and are then vinified together in *barriques*, of which half are new. The wine spends nine months in wood *sur lie*. It is a reasonably priced and very well-made modern Graves, which should be drunk within five years.

CHÂTEAU OLIVIER

AC Pessac-Léognan, *cru classé*

> 33850 Léognan
> Vineyard: 42 acres (65 per cent Sémillon, 30 per cent Sauvignon, 5 per cent Muscadelle)
> Production: 130,000 bottles
> Quality: 🍇   Price: ★★★

If only this wine were as lovely as the property's moated medieval château. The white vines, which on average are forty years old, are planted on low-lying ground with a considerable clay content. There is no skin contact and the wine is tank-fermented. Since 1985 one third of the wine has been aged for four months in new *barriques*, the remainder in tank. Sulphur dioxide is still used with a liberal hand, and the lack of more committed wood-ageing results in a rather dull, commercial wine, inoffensive but meagre, and lacking in sheer fruit, let alone elegance.

CHÂTEAU RAHOUL

AC Graves

> 33460 Portets
> Vineyard: 6 acres (100 per cent Sémillon)
> Production: 14,000 bottles
> Quality: 🍇🍇🍇 Price: ★★★★
> Best vintages: 1983, 1985, 1986, 1987

It was at this modest property that the Danish winemaker Peter Vinding-Diers made his reputation as an outstanding producer of white Graves. After many changes of ownership, Vinding-Diers left in the late 1980s and acquired Château de Landiras (see Domaine La Grave). Since 1986 Rahoul's proprietor has been Alain Thiénot, who also owns other Bordeaux properties and a champagne house. He plans to increase production, and one can only hope he will maintain the high standards of the previous regime, especially since Rahoul has always been a triumph of technique over raw materials.

The vineyards are now about fifteen years old. The grapes receive very little skin contact and are pressed in a pneumatic press. Thirty per cent of the must is fermented in new *barriques*, the remainder in temperature-controlled tanks at 16 °C. The wine is aged for six to eight months in new *barriques* and becomes complete and harmonious quite soon after bottling, with a rich, creamy, oaky flavour. It is probably best consumed within five years.

CHÂTEAU ROCHEMORIN

AC Pessac-Léognan

> 33650 Martillac
> Vineyard: 15 acres (80 per cent Sauvignon, 20 per cent Sémillon)

Production: 35,000 bottles

Quality: 👑👑👑 Price: ★★

Another of André Lurton's properties, Rochemorin was acquired in 1974 and replanted in 1979. The vineyards are well situated on a high ridge over gravel soil. The estate produces inexpensive wines that are extremely well made and offer good value, especially when you consider that new *barriques* have been used here since 1986. The wine is fresh and simple; lacking in concentration perhaps, but a lively and delicate Graves without pretensions.

CHÂTEAU SMITH-HAUT-LAFITTE

AC Pessac-Léognan

33650 Martillac

Vineyard: 25 acres (100 per cent Sauvignon)

Production: 50,000 bottles

Quality: 👑👑👑 Price: ★★★★

In 1990 the Cathiard family took over this grand property, which since 1958 had been owned by the Bordeaux merchants Eschenauer. Eschenauer's investment had been considerable, including planting all the Sauvignon vines, and the cellars are magnificent.

The vineyards surround the winery, and the soil consists of gravel, quartz pebbles and sand. The grapes receive no skin contact and fermentation begins in tank. The must is then transferred to *barriques*, of which half are new. Until 1984 no wood was used; today the wine spends up to eight months in *barriques*, but not on the lees.

Smith-Haut-Lafitte is a commercial, slightly overpriced wine without great complexity, but it is well made, fresh and elegant. Only a lack of concentration keeps it out of the top league. Before *barrique*-ageing was introduced, the wine was adequate but boring, but since 1984 the quality has improved substantially. Sometimes I detect a rasping edge, especially in hot vintages such as 1985 and 1988, and I often find the wine more successful in lesser vintages such as 1984 and 1987. The 1989 is delicious. The wines are best enjoyed young.

CHÂTEAU LA TOUR-MARTILLAC

AC Pessac Léognan, *cru classé*

33650 La Brède

Vineyard: 15 acres (60 per cent Sémillon, 35 per cent Sauvignon, 5 per cent Muscadelle)

Production: 25,000–36,000 bottles

Quality: 🍇🍇🍇🍇   Price: ★★★

Jean Kressmann, who still lives at the château, made his first vintage here in 1929, and the current winemaker is his son Loic. The average age of the vines is an impressive forty years, and some Sémillon planted in 1884 still contributes a few bunches. The long-range plan is gradually to double the production of white wine. Denis Dubourdieu acts as a consultant, though the Kressmanns insist they make the final decisions. They are wary of skin contact and only began to ferment all the must in Allier *barriques* in 1987; half these barrels are new. The wine remains *sur lie* for ten months and is stirred regularly.

I find this an excellent Graves, lively and spicy despite the high proportion of Sémillon. The oak contributes richness and creaminess rather than woody flavours, and the wine is full of fruit. It keeps very well, and a 1949 I drank at the château had exactly the qualities one hopes to find in mature Graves: a voluptuous honeyed nose, and on the palate rich, chewy flavours and the nutty complexity of full maturity.

CLOS FLORIDÈNE

AC Graves

Pujols

Vineyard: 10 acres (50 per cent Sauvignon, 40 per cent
 Sémillon, 10 per cent Muscadelle)

Production: 18,000 bottles

Quality: 🍇🍇🍇🍇   Price: ★★★

Owned by Florence and Denis Dubourdieu, as the name suggests, Clos Floridène demonstrates that the famous oenologist
is not all talk and no action. Dubourdieu renovated this small
estate in 1982, and many of the Sauvignon vines are still young.
The soil is a thin, clayey sand on a limestone subsoil. The wine
reflects Dubourdieu's favoured techniques, and is aged in new
barriques. A creamy, spicy wine that is very attractive in its
youth, it is too early to say how well it will evolve in bottle. I
find its lack of length slightly worrying, but this should be
remedied once the Sauvignon vines are older. The wine is
reasonably priced and consequently hard to find.

DOMAINE DE CHEVALIER

AC Pessac-Léognan, *cru classé*

33850 Léognan

Vineyard: 10 acres (70 per cent Sauvignon, 30 per cent
 Sémillon)

Production: 7,000–12,000 bottles of Domaine de Chevalier;
 3,000–6,000 bottles of Bâtard Chevalier

Quality: 🍇🍇🍇🍇🍇   Price: ★★★★★

Best vintages: 1964, 1966, 1970, 1978, 1979, 1980, 1981,
 1983, 1985, 1986, 1987, 1988, 1989

Anyone who wishes to make a case for the nobility of the Sauvignon grape should use this estate as a model. Utterly traditional, it produces superb white wines that are capable of developing in bottle for decades. Olivier Bernard, who has taken over the domaine's administration from Claude Ricard, is determined to maintain the standards Ricard set over many decades.

The grapes are only picked when fully mature, even in difficult vintages such as 1984. There can be up to five *tries* lasting three weeks, and the domaine claims to be the only Bordeaux estate that harvests grapes for dry white wine with such care. Skin contact is avoided and Bernard is content to continue using horizontal presses and to fine before fermentation in new oak. Every lot is preserved separately, so that no two *barriques* are identical. No cultivated yeasts are added. The wine spends five weeks on the lees, but is then racked and remains in *barriques*, of which a third are new, racked regularly, for eighteen months.

Frost in 1985 destroyed 2.5 acres of Sauvignon vines, temporarily upsetting the balance of the vineyard. To mop up the excess Sémillon, Bernard created a temporary second wine called Bâtard-Chevalier, vinified in the same way as the *grand vin*.

Domaine de Chevalier is characterized by tremendous concentration of flavour. A densely structured wine with good acidity, it needs eight years or more to show at its best. Its very high price is justified by the fact that it is a hand-crafted product. Although Laville Haut-Brion is often regarded as the finest white Graves, in my view the ultra-traditional Domaine de Chevalier is the greater wine – sleek, rich, oaky, sumptuous, powerful, intense – and thus one of the world's best white wines.

DOMAINE LA GRAVE

AC Graves

Landiras
Vineyard: 35 acres (100 per cent Sémillon)
Quality: 🍇🍇🍇   Price: ★★★

The history of this evolving estate is somewhat confusing. In the 1980s, during his spell as winemaker at Château Rahoul (q.v.), Peter Vinding-Diers also produced wines from his own property, Domaine La Grave, near Portets. With his purchase of Château de Landiras in the late 1980s, Vinding-Diers embarked on an ambitious planting programme, which will reach a maximum of 100 acres. Over the course of the 1990s the wine, labelled either as Domaine La Grave or Château de Landiras, will use more and more grapes from the château's vineyards, which are planted with every known clone of Sémillon on a variety of suitable rootstocks. Average yields are just over 2 tons per acre; the must is cold-fermented, then aged in *barriques* for up to ten months. The result is an oaky rounded wine, very appealing in its youth but capable of ageing in bottle for up to ten years.

Vinding-Diers has also leased acreage in the Premières Côtes to produce an inexpensive 100 per cent Sémillon wine first made in 1989 and labelled as Notre-Dame de Landiras (AC Bordeaux). Less concentrated than La Grave, this wine is unoaked, yet plump and rounded. Like La Grave, it offers outstanding value.

OTHER DRY WHITE BORDEAUX

Vast quantities of dry white wine are also made on the other side of the Garonne in Entre-Deux-Mers, where 6,400 acres are entitled to this appellation. (The reds from this region are

sold as Bordeaux or Bordeaux Supérieur.) Vineyards cover only
the most suitable slopes, the rest being filled with cow pastures,
forests, or vegetable and wheat fields. Compared to the essentially flat Graves and Médoc, Entre-Deux-Mers is a deeply
rural region of rolling hills and quiet villages. The soil around
Sauveterre and Targon, composed of a tough mixture of sand
and clay, is particularly well suited to white wine production.
Until quite recently the standard of winemaking was undistinguished: prices for grapes were lower than in other parts of
Bordeaux, and there was little incentive for proprietors to
reduce yields and to improve quality. That has now changed.
Some growers realize that the only way to achieve reasonable
prices for their wines is for them to improve the quality, and
some of the large cooperatives that dominate the region have
been pace-setters, with substantial investments in technology.

Dry white wines may use one of two appellations in Entre-
Deux-Mers. Entre-Deux-Mers itself requires a maximum yield
of 4.6 tons per acre (70 hectolitres per hectare), whereas
Bordeaux Sec is slightly higher at 5 tons per acre (75 hectolitres
per hectare). Certain minor grape varieties, such as Colombard,
Ugni Blanc and Merlot Blanc, are permitted in Entre-Deux-
Mers, but their contribution to the blend is limited to 30 per
cent. These minor varieties are beginning to disappear from the
region, and most quality-conscious growers are concentrating
their efforts on Sémillon, the dominant white variety,
Sauvignon and Muscadelle. At Château de l'Aubrade at
Rimons, for example, Jean-Pierre Lobre makes Bordeaux Sec
from Sémillon and Sauvignon, while the Entre-Deux-Mers also
contains Muscadelle. The wines are made in identical fashion
and sell for the same price. The difference is a matter of taste
rather than quality.

With a very few exceptions, a typical Entre-Deux-Mers, such
as Château de Launay, offers fresh, simple whites intended for
immediate consumption. With yields about 50 per cent higher
than in the Graves, and with machine-picking almost universal,
it is difficult to achieve the same quality of fruit that the great
Graves estates strive for. A few proprietors are adopting
fermentation in *barriques* and other techniques used to make

modern white Graves. Yet few of the resulting wines are satisfactory, and I suspect the explanation lies in the quality of the fruit. With higher yields than in the Graves and a less appropriate soil for structured white wines, oak can easily overwhelm the essentially dilute nature of the fruit.

A small quantity of dry white wine is also made by leading Sauternes estates. This tends to come from young vines not suitable for making botrytized wine, or from lots picked before botrytis appeared and rejected from the final blend, or, in a few cases, from vineyards that have no real connection with the estate under whose name they are marketed. With a few exceptions these wines are of modest quality, despite their provenance. They function as an insurance policy in years when the sweet wine production is negligible or, as at some estates in 1987, non-existent.

Among the Sauternes estates that produce a dry white wine are Châteaux Broustet, Caillou, Rayne-Vigneau (70 per cent Sauvignon; unwooded), Rieussec ('R') and La Tour-Blanche. Château Lafaurie-Peyraguey makes Brut de Lafaurie (4,000 bottles; 50 per cent Sauvignon; one third fermented in new *barriques*). The Sec de Doisy-Daëne is very well made and better value than many of these wines. The dry white from Doisy-Daëne called St-Martin spends a year on the fine lees and is thus a much more oaky style.

The Médoc is, of course, dominated by red grapes, but a few properties, such as Château Margaux, have, usually for obscure historical reasons, maintained a small production of white wine. Château Loudenne's sometimes herbaceous white wine is popular in Britain; made half from Sauvignon and half from Sémillon, it is tank-fermented and bottled in the spring following the harvest. Château Talbot produces the disappointing Talbot Blanc (50,000 bottles). One hundred per cent Sauvignon, the wine has since 1989 begun to feel a touch of oak. A barrel-fermented Blanc de Lynch-Bages (40 per cent Sauvignon, 40 per cent Sémillon, 20 per cent Muscadelle) was first produced in 1990.

In addition to small estates offering lively modern white Bordeaux (such as Château Roquefort and Château Tour de

Mirambeau's Cuvée Passion), some excellent wines are made as blends for some of the major Bordeaux merchants. One of the most successful is the oak-aged Numéro Un marketed by Dourthe, of which half a million bottles are produced annually. Interestingly, 60 per cent of the wine comes from Blaye. Almost as delicious is Peter Sichel's 100 per cent Sémillon barrel-fermented Sirius. The latest contenders are Maître d'Estournel and Alpha. Alpha is the brainchild of three leading Pomerol winemakers, who produce a blend from 37 acres in Entre-Deux-Mers planted with 52 per cent Sémillon, 46 per cent Sauvignon and 2 per cent Muscadelle. The vinification follows Dubourdieu's techniques. Maître d'Estournel, first released in 1990, is a blend of 60 per cent Sauvignon, 38 per cent Sémillon and 2 per cent Muscadelle. The wine is part of a range created by Bruno Prats of Château Cos d'Estournel.

Some cooperatives, equipped with the latest technology, have begun producing fresh, lively white wines. Univitis, for example, produces 10 per cent of all Bordeaux Blanc, including some up-market wines such as a Sauvignon matured *sur lie* and a wine aged in new oak. These wines are often superior to the branded wines marketed by the large Bordeaux merchants of which Mouton-Cadet is a well-known and exceedingly boring example.

CHÂTEAU BONNET

AC Entre-Deux-Mers

Grézillac, 33420 Branne

Vineyard: 100 acres (60 per cent Sémillon, 20 per cent Sauvignon, 20 per cent Muscadelle)

Production: 500,000 bottles

Quality: 🍇🍇🍇   Price: ★★

André Lurton (see Château La Louvière) actually lives at Château Bonnet, a late-eighteenth-century château which his grandfather purchased in 1897. This immense property lies south of St-Émilion. The cool-fermented white wine is light and fresh, and the winemaking here is exemplary. Even the 1989, a vintage in which maintaining acidity was difficult, was delicate and fruity and fragrant. Dining one night at Bordeaux's most highly regarded restaurant, the St-James, I ordered a menu in which wine, unspecified, was included. The white wine was Château Bonnet and I was more than pleased with the choice. It represents excellent value and is consistently reliable.

An oak-fermented and aged *cuvée* is now being produced, with the wood providing an additional spiciness rather than weight and structure.

CHÂTEAU GUIRAUD ('G')

AC Bordeaux

Sauternes

Vineyard: 17 acres (70 per cent Sauvignon, 30 per cent Sémillon)

Production: 6,000 bottles

Quality: 🍇   Price: ★★★

This Sauternes *premier cru* estate has for some time been producing a dry wine called, simply, 'G' from young vines planted on sandy gravel soil. In recent years the wine has been fermented in new *barriques* and aged in barrels for six to twelve months. It is a good wine, rounded from the oak-ageing, yet without much excitement, despite the high proportion of Sauvignon. The 1988 was the best of recent vintages.

CHÂTEAU MARGAUX (PAVILLON BLANC)

AC Bordeaux

33460 Margaux

Vineyard: 30 acres (100 per cent Sauvignon)

Production: 40,000–50,000 bottles

Quality: ♥♥♥♥   Price: ★★★★★

Best vintages: 1983, 1986, 1987, 1988, 1989

White wine has been made at Margaux since the 1920s, but it was given a boost in the late 1960s when the vineyard was replanted. Red grapes used to be planted in this section of the vineyard, but since it was prone to frost it was left fallow after the phylloxera outbreak in the late nineteenth century and subsequently reserved for white wines. The soil is gravelly and yields are low. On Émile Peynaud's advice only Sauvignon has been planted, so as to differentiate the wine from white Graves.

Margaux uses whole-cluster pressing and thus avoids skin contact. The grapes are picked when very mature, so the acidity tends to be relatively low. The wine is fermented in *barriques*, of which one third are new. There is no malolactic fermentation and the wine is aged in wood for eight months, and not released for a further two years.

I was not enamoured of Pavillon Blanc in the early 1980s, but since 1983 the quality has improved considerably. It is plump and peachy, occasionally with a hint of liquorice on the nose. The wine is made in a rich, powerful style, though it seems oddly lacking in vigour given that it is made entirely from Sauvignon. It ages gracefully, gaining complexity after about five years.

CHÂTEAU REYNON

AC Bordeaux

> Béguey, 33410 Cadillac
>
> Vineyard: 44 acres (50 per cent Sémillon, 45 per cent Sauvignon, 5 per cent Muscadelle)
>
> Production: 120,000 bottles
>
> Quality: 🍇🍇   Price: ★★

This château, the home of Denis Dubourdieu, is appropriately surrounded by vineyards. The white wine here is less distinguished than his Graves, Clos Floridène (q.v.), but it is well made and reliable. The soil is varied, with deep gravel over clay on a well-drained plateau, and slopes of the clay and limestone typical of the right bank of the Garonne. The grapes are given skin contact but fermented in temperature-controlled tanks, and the wine is often matured *sur lie* in tanks for up to nine months. Château Reynon also produces a fine Cuvée Vieilles Vignes, made from mostly Sauvignon vines that are more than twenty-five years old.

CHÂTEAU SÉNÉJAC

AC Bordeaux

> Le Pian-Médoc, 33290 Blanquefort
>
> Vineyard: 4 acres (100 per cent Sémillon)
>
> Production: 3,000 bottles
>
> Quality: 🍇🍇🍇   Price: ★★★
>
> Best vintages: 1985, 1988

Sénéjac is a real curiosity. White wine has been made at this small Haut-Médoc estate for ninety years, but a serious effort to make fine white wine only began in 1984. The winemaker here is Jenny Dobson, a New Zealander who once worked at

Rahoul. More vines have been planted, including some Sauvignon, so in the 1990s the meagre production will double. The soil is limestone with some iron content, and yields are about 2.5 tons per acre.

Until 1989 the grapes were partially de-stemmed. Now they are pressed whole in a pneumatic press without skin contact. The must is fermented in *barriques*, of which about half are new, and since 1987 the wine has been left *sur lie* and stirred. Malolactic fermentation is not discouraged.

Sénéjac is a ripe wine, with distinctive aromas of bananas and white peaches, and an attractive piquancy. A certain ungainly quality keeps the wine out of the very top rank of white Bordeaux.

CHÂTEAU THIEULEY

AC Bordeaux

La Sauve-Majeure, 33670 Créon

Vineyard: 54 acres (65 per cent Sauvignon, 35 per cent Sémillon)

Production: Sauvignon, 110,000 bottles; Cuvée Francis Courselle, 48,000 bottles

CHÂTEAU THIEULEY

Quality: 🍇🍇   Price: ★

CUVÉE FRANCIS COURSELLE

Quality: 🍇🍇🍇🍇   Price: ★★

The amiable man in shorts and a T-shirt hosing down the cellars didn't look like a professor of oenology, but that is Francis Courselle's profession. He is also a splendid winemaker. His vines are planted on the clay and limestone soil commonly found in Entre-Deux-Mers, but on the slopes there is much gravel too.

He makes two wines. Château Thieuley is made entirely from Sauvignon. The grapes are machine-picked, given twelve to eighteen hours' skin contact and fermented in tank at 18–20 °C. The wine is unashamedly commercial but of excellent quality: clean, fresh and nutty.

The second wine is Cuvée Francis Courselle, first made in 1986. The must, half Sauvignon, half Sémillon, is fermented in new *barriques* and aged for six months *sur lie*, with *bâtonnage*. This wine is absolutely delicious. The oak is pronounced but does not dominate the fruit, and on the palate the wine is plump and velvety and packed with ripe fruit. It is exceptional value, and should be consumed fairly young.

CHÂTEAU D'YQUEM ('Y')

AC Bordeaux

Sauternes, 33210 Langon

Blend: 50 per cent Sauvignon, 50 per cent Sémillon

Production: 3,000–25,000 bottles

Quality: 🍇🍇🍇🍇🍇   Price: ★★★★★

The first time I tasted this wine, blind, I was stumped. It smells like good Sauternes, I asserted, but it's completely dry. It was 'Ygrec', a most bizarre wine made at Yquem, usually only in vintages when it is difficult to make great Sauternes. The vines are no different from those used to make the *grand vin*. When the selection of lots is made, there may be some barrels that only attained 16° potential alcohol and also lack botrytis. Other lots will consist of wines of 12° made from grapes that never achieved sufficient maturity but were picked before rot set in.

These unsatisfactory lots will be blended to give a dry wine with about 14° alcohol, a potent brew indeed. This explains the botrytis aroma present in some vintages, since some of the richer lots will have been made from partly botrytized grapes. The wine is aged for eighteen months in new *barriques*.

The wine was made frequently in the uneven 1970s, and I have encountered the 1972, 1977, 1978, 1979 and 1980. Since

1980 the wine has only been made in 1985 and 1986, when a mere 3,000 bottles were produced. It has a big, waxy, lanolin nose, quite marked by Sémillon, and is lush and firm on the palate. Occasionally the high alcohol is evident. 'Y' ages well but unevenly. The 1960 and 1964, tasted in 1988, were fully mature but not tired, while the 1977 was showing signs of oxidation.

'Y' has had a mixed reception, but I count myself as an enthusiast. It has a unique character, great richness and power, and true individuality in an age when even good white wines can often taste all too similar.

UNION DES PRODUCTEURS DE RAUZAN

AC Entre-Deux-Mers

33420 Rauzan
Vineyard: 1,550 acres
Quality: 🍇🍇   Price: ★

This innovative cooperative, now sixty years old, is made up of 300 growers whose vineyards constitute 2 per cent of the entire Bordeaux region. They produce three white wines. Fleur de Rauzan is 70 per cent Sauvignon and 30 per cent Sémillon; Comte de Rudel is the reverse. Fleur is the more popular, a clean and perfectly acceptable version of simple aromatic Sauvignon; excellent aperitif wine. Comte de Rudel, which sells for the same price, is more rich and spicy, while avoiding the heaviness and oiliness that afflicts carelessly made Sémillon. The third wine is the Reserve called 'R', a Bordeaux Sec aged in new *barriques* for eight months. The grape blend varies from year to year. I have only tasted the 1988 'R', which was pure Sauvignon. I found it cloying in its oakiness and hence clumsy. Subsequent vintages may improve once the winemakers have learnt how to use new oak with a lighter touch.

SAUTERNES

Since the Sauternais is an enclave within the Graves, it is not surprising that its soil structure, gravel over a subsoil of clay, resembles that of the Graves in general. Of the five communes that make up the appellation, Sauternes, Bommes, Preignac and Fargues have this kind of soil, while the fifth and most northerly and flat commune, Barsac, has a higher proportion of alluvial deposits and clay over a chalky base. Sauternes and Bommes are gently undulating, offering a variety of exposures and excellent drainage. The wines from these two communes tend to be a bit richer and fatter than those from Barsac, but it is risky to generalize. There does seem to be a distinctive Barsac style, lighter in colour and with greater acidity and finesse than many plumper wines from the other communes. Rather confusingly, Barsac alone may be labelled either under its commune name or as Sauternes. (For information about how Sauternes is made, see the Introduction.)

Although Sémillon is much more widely planted than Sauvignon, it was not always thus. Sémillon is, however, more susceptible to noble rot than Sauvignon and has more body, which explains why it is favoured by most growers. Sauvignon vines are slightly more productive than Sémillon, so the percentage of Sauvignon in the finished wine is usually slightly higher than its presence in the vineyard suggests.

The origins of Sauternes are somewhat obscure, but by 1855 a classification was drawn up which remains essentially in force today, although a handful of estates have disappeared or been divided or swallowed up. As with the Médoc classification of *crus*, the authorities put great emphasis on the estate's *terroir*. Since 1855 the soil structure has not changed, but winemaking techniques have. The slump in fashion which affected the Sauternais in the postwar years and kept prices depressed meant that many *premiers crus* were producing wine of dreary quality. When the tide turned in the 1980s and growers could once again expect good prices, many proprietors made considerable and long overdue investments. At long last, most of the eleven *premiers crus* are producing wines worthy of their status.

Yquem stands alone as Sauternes's sole *premier grand cru classé*. Despite one or two lapses in the 1960s, its supreme status remains unchallenged. In certain vintages other wines may approach its monumental splendour, possibly equal it, but for sheer consistency no other estate can match Yquem. The *premiers crus* are, in alphabetical order: Climens (Barsac), Coutet (Barsac), Guiraud (Sauternes), Haut-Peyraguey (Bommes), Lafaurie-Peyraguey (Bommes), Rabaud-Promis (Bommes), Rayne-Vigneau (Bommes), Rieussec (Fargues), Sigalas-Rabaud (Bommes), Suduiraut (Preignac) and La Tour-Blanche (Bommes). The *deuxièmes crus* are: d'Arche (Sauternes), Broustet (Barsac), Caillou (Barsac), Doisy-Daëne (Barsac), Doisy-Dubroca (Barsac), Doisy-Védrines (Barsac), Filhot (Sauternes), Lamothe (Sauternes), Lamothe-Guignard (Sauternes), de Malle (Preignac), Nairac (Barsac), Romer-du-Hayot (Fargues) and Suau (Barsac).

The economic revival of Sauternes has been aided, without doubt, by a succession of very fine vintages in the 1980s. It was not always thus. 1961, 1962 and 1967 produced fine Sauternes, but the other vintages of the 1960s are best forgotten. The next decade began well with good 1970s and excellent 1971s, but the following three years were poor, though I have tasted some attractive Barsacs from these vintages. 1975 and 1976 were both superb, though in very different ways. Which vintage you prefer is a matter of personal taste: I find 1975 has a slight edge, since many of the luscious 1976s are maturing too rapidly. 1979 is an attractive vintage, perhaps a touch light, and 1980 has been underestimated. 1981 produced some excellent wines, but others seem ungainly and charmless. 1982 is very patchy, as rain interrupted picking; consequently the harvest dates proved even more crucial than usual. 1983 was a great year, the finest since 1976. 1985, with its hot dry weather, gave many sweet luscious wines marred only by a lack of botrytis. 1986 and 1988 are both superb, with 1988 showing greater elegance. 1989, an exceptionally hot dry year, was none the less blessed with botrytis and some exceptional and concentrated wines have been made; their extreme richness means that a few may prove unbalanced, but only time will tell. 1990 was another very hot year, but botrytis arrived surprisingly early and picking began in mid-September. Even Yquem had completed the harvest by 10 October. The wines are exceptionally sweet and unctuous. The 1991 harvest was exceptionally early and *tries* came to a halt in mid-October as noble rot became grey rot; quality is unlikely to be high.

There is no doubt that good Sauternes benefits enormously from long bottle-ageing. Young Sauternes from a good botrytis vintage, up to ten years old, has a rich flavour of peaches and apricots, supported by the honeyed nuances of noble rot. After fifteen or twenty years tastes of marmalade and barley sugar come to the fore, and become richer and more intense as time goes by. Colour gives very little indication of maturity, although a young wine coloured a very deep gold could give cause for concern. In 1976 both Rieussec and Guiraud were deeply coloured from the outset and have aged less gracefully than many other wines of that vintage. In a fifty-year-old wine, a mahogany colour may indicate a certain oxidation, but not necessarily. What is surprising is how often one encounters a little known wine from a supposedly mediocre year five decades ago, and discovers the wine to be still fresh and highly palatable. That combination of botrytis, residual sugar, acidity and alcohol can keep a Sauternes going almost indefinitely.

Good storage is essential. If you lack the facilities for long-term storage in stable conditions, it is better to seek out older vintages from reliable merchants and auction houses. With the enormous price increases of the late 1980s, vintages from, say, 1975 or 1976 are beginning to look like bargains – if you can find them. Sauternes should not be served too cold; cellar temperature is perfect.

CHÂTEAU D'ARCHE

AC Sauternes, *deuxième cru classé*

Sauternes, 33210 Langon

Vineyard: 74 acres (90 per cent Sémillon, 10 per cent Sauvignon)

Production: 36,000 bottles

Quality: 🍇🍇🍇   Price: ★★★★

This pretty estate, with the highest vineyards in Sauternes, has since 1981 been leased by Pierre Perromat, who is anxious to restore its reputation. Perromat keeps the yields low, and has been known to make ten *tries*. The average age of the vines is thirty-five years old. An old vertical press is still in use here, and the must is fermented in steel tanks at 18 °C. Thereafter half the wine spends up to two years in *barriques*, of which half are new, as Perromat is aiming for a rich, powerful style. The 1983 was impressive, but I have been less than amazed by subsequent vintages. On revisiting the winery in May 1990 I was astonished to find that some of the 1988 vintage was already bottled. But the 1990 finds d'Arche back on top form.

CHÂTEAU BASTOR-LAMONTAGNE

AC Sauternes

Preignac, 33210 Langon

Vineyard: 98 acres (78 per cent Sémillon, 17 per cent Sauvignon, 5 per cent Muscadelle)

Production: 90,000–120,000 bottles

Quality: 🍇🍇🍇   Price: ★★★–★★★★

A large estate owned by a major bank may not sound like a promising formula for good winemaking, but this is a well-maintained and reliable property. The winemaking is frankly commercial – yields are often close to the maximum, no pretence is made of picking individually botrytized grapes, and the wine is sometimes chaptalized – yet the results are more than satisfactory. The wine is aged in Limousin and Allier *barriques*, 25 per cent of which are new, for eighteen months.

Bastor-Lamontagne is not one of the great Sauternes. It usually lacks concentration, but it offers very good value. If it rarely excites, it equally rarely disappoints. It can usually be drunk young with pleasure, although the wine will keep. The 1989 and 1990 are outstanding.

CHÂTEAU BROUSTET

AC Sauternes, *deuxième cru classé*

Barsac, 33720 Podensac

Vineyard: 40 acres (63 per cent Sémillon, 25 per cent Sauvignon, 12 per cent Muscadelle)

Production: 30,000 bottles

Quality: 🍇 Price: ★★★★

Broustet is owned by Eric Fournier of the superb St-Émilion estate Château Canon. Despite his dedication I find this a difficult wine to like. Yields are low; many of the vines are old, especially the Muscadelle; the soil is complex. Yet the wine often strikes me as ungainly. The must is fermented in small stainless steel tanks then aged in *barriques*, 40 per cent of which are new, for up to two years.

Broustet is quite an alcoholic Barsac. This does not displease Fournier, who seeks plenty of alcohol and not too much residual sugar. And this, I suspect, is why Broustet often seems unbalanced. Moreover, Fournier, as an absentee proprietor, has had staff problems at the estate, but has apparently sorted them out and is seeking to improve the quality. The 1989 and 1990, tasted from cask, are a considerable improvement on earlier vintages.

CHÂTEAU CAILLOU

AC Sauternes, *deuxième cru classé*

Barsac, 33720 Langon

Vineyard: 32 acres (90 per cent Sémillon, 10 per cent Sauvignon)

Production: 48,000 bottles

Quality: 🍇   Price: ★★★

This family estate is run energetically by the Bravo family. Yields are high, and the wine is fermented in stainless steel before being aged in *barriques*, of which 25 per cent are new. The wine is high in alcohol and relatively low in residual sugar. Until 1976 the best lots from outstanding years were bottled separately as a Crème de Tête, and some of the older vintages of this *cuvée* were undoubtedly impressive, though often marred by volatility and excessive alcohol. The 1943 and 1947 were still showing well after over forty years. Since 1976 the Crème de Tête bottling has been replaced by something called Private Cuvée. I am opposed to these special bottlings, since the effect is to deprive the standard wine of the best lots, thus ensuring that the wine will disappoint in comparison with its rivals. I have often tasted Caillou blind and never rated it highly.

   None the less, a visit to Caillou is worthwhile. Not only is the château itself pretty, but the Bravos are hospitable and a number of vintages are usually available for tasting and purchase. When I last visited Caillou the 1921 vintage was still for sale – at a price.

CHÂTEAU CLIMENS

AC Sauternes, *premier cru classé*

Barsac, 33720 Podensac

Vineyard: 86 acres (98 per cent Sémillon, 2 per cent Sauvignon)

Production: 36,000 bottles
Quality: ♕♕♕♕♕   Price: ★★★★★

An unpretentious farmhouse on a gentle slope, among the highest in Barsac, produces a wine that many regard as the only major rival to Yquem itself. Climens was purchased by Lucien Lurton in 1971 and he has meticulously maintained its reputation. The must is barrel-fermented, and up to twenty-five lots of different *tries* and parcels are kept separately until January. There is a rigorous selection of barrels: after the rainy 1982 vintage, for example, two thirds of the crop was rejected.

Climens is an extremely discreet wine despite the almost complete absence of Sauvignon. In its youth, which is protracted, it always seems reined in. There is no shortage of lush ripe fruit, but the wine is less flashy than many of its rivals and marked by an apricot freshness, great concentration and a clean acidity, rather than by unctuousness or extreme oakiness. Only one third of the *barriques* at Climens are new, which is probably a sound policy given the nature of the wine. Its elegance and impeccable balance permit Climens to age superbly, and vintages from the 1970s are still youthful. One characteristic of Climens is its consistency in so-called poor vintages. Even 1972, 1973 and 1978 here are more than adequate.

Both 1975 and 1976 were superb, though Brigitte Lurton-Belondrade, who supervises Climens, believes both 1983 and 1985 are even better. In 1984 the wine, although delicious, was sold under a second label of Les Cypres de Climens. All the wines of the late 1980s are certainly among the top wines of those vintages.

CHÂTEAU COUTET

AC Sauternes, *premier cru classé*

Barsac, 33720 Podensac
Vineyard: 91 acres (80 per cent Sémillon, 20 per cent Sauvignon)

Production: 90,000 bottles

Quality: 🍇🍇🍇   Price: ★★★★

For some years Coutet has had an inflated reputation. Owned by Marcel Baly of Strasbourg, the ancient property has employed a number of different winemakers and the results have been troubling. Yet old bottles of Coutet confirm the *cru*'s potential.

The average age of the vines is thirty-five years, and the vinification is highly traditional. A vertical press is used, and the must is fermented in *barriques*, of which half are new. The lots are gradually blended after each racking. Coutet, a pale wine because of the soil, is never particularly unctuous. At its best it is elegant and refined, and it can age magnificently. In the finest years – 1970, 1971, 1975, 1976, 1988, 1989 – the best lots are bottled separately as Cuvée Madame. Only about 2,000 bottles are produced and the wine, which I have never tasted, is reputed to be marvellous. But perhaps Cuvée Madame deprives the regular wine of its richest components.

Nevertheless the 1971 was delicious here, as was the 1975. The 1981 was surprisingly good, but wines from the great 1983 vintage have been shockingly inconsistent. The arrival of a new winemaker, Jean-Luc Baldes, in the late 1980s heralds, one hopes, an amelioration of Coutet's quality and reliability. 1989 and 1990 are excellent.

CHÂTEAU DOISY-DAËNE

AC Sauternes, *deuxième cru classé*

Barsac, 33720 Podensac

Vineyard: 37 acres (70 per cent Sémillon, 20 per cent Sauvignon, 10 per cent Muscadelle)

Production: 50,000 bottles of Château Doisy-Daëne; 40,000 bottles of Château Cantegril

Quality: 🍇🍇🍇   Price: ★★★★

Pierre Dubourdieu, the proprietor of Doisy-Daëne, must be the only Sauternes winemaker who claims he doesn't much like the stuff. 'I don't make Sauternes,' he once told me. 'I make Doisy-Daëne.' Fortunately this affectation has no bearing on the wine's quality. Doisy-Daëne is very distinctive, and only Sémillon grapes are used for the Sauternes. Dubourdieu wants a wine that is relatively light, unchaptalized, attractive in youth but capable of long evolution in bottle.

The must is barrel-fermented, and when the desired balance of alcohol and residual sugar is achieved, he centrifuges to remove remaining yeasts. The wine is then aged in *barriques*, of which one third are new, returned to steel, and bottled about eighteen months after the harvest. Centrifuging and filtration do not, Dubourdieu insists, strip the wine of extract and flavour, but instead enhance its purity and finesse.

My experience of Doisy-Daëne is patchy, but the 1970 is excellent, and the 1982, 1983 and 1990 very good. The 1986 is rather dull, but the 1989 is unusually rich and unctuous. Clearly, by some oversight, Dubourdieu has made a Sauternes.

Doisy-Daëne is far from being a top Barsac, but it has personality, is impeccably made and is reasonably priced. Even more of a bargain is Dubourdieu's other Barsac property of Cantegril, in effect his second wine.

CHÂTEAU DOISY-DUBROCA

AC Sauternes, *deuxième cru classé*

Barsac, 33720 Podensac

Vineyard: 8 acres (80 per cent Sémillon, 20 per cent Sauvignon)

Production: 4,500 bottles

Quality: 🍇🍇🍇   Price: ★★★

When Lucien Lurton bought Château Climens in 1971 this tiny *cru* came as part of the package. The vines are on average about twenty-five years old, and the vinification here is identical to Climens and supervised by the same team under Christian Broustaut. The wine can be high in acidity and sometimes uncomfortably high in sulphur dioxide, so it repays keeping for quite a few years. Doisy-Dubroca is reasonably priced, and well worth looking out for.

CHÂTEAU DOISY-VÉDRINES

AC Sauternes, *deuxième cru classé*

Barsac, 33720 Podensac

Vineyard: 57 acres (80 per cent Sémillon, 20 per cent Sauvignon)

Production: 36,000 bottles

Quality: 🍇🍇🍇   Price: ★★★★

Since 1851 this estate has been owned by the Castéja family. The vineyards are relatively high, on a clay and limestone plateau exposed to the south-west. The wine is fermented in *barriques*, and aged in wood for eighteen to twenty-four months. Until the early 1980s this was often a dull, vapid wine, but a determined and successful effort is under way to improve the quality. From 1989 onwards, only new *barriques* have been used. The 1986 is rich, with ample botrytis and fine acidity. 1988 is concentrated and elegant, and 1989 outstanding.

CHÂTEAU DE FARGUES

AC Sauternes

Fargues, 33210 Langon

Vineyard: 33 acres (80 per cent Sémillon, 20 per cent Sauvignon)

Production: 12,000 bottles

Quality: 🍇🍇🍇🍇🍇   Price: ★★★★★

The Lur-Saluces family of Château d'Yquem have also owned the grand but ruinous Château de Fargues since 1472. Until the 1930s they made few efforts to develop its vineyards. Today the wine is made by the Yquem team in the same way as Yquem itself, except that not all the *barriques* are new. The microclimate differs from that at Yquem, and the grapes often ripen a week later, with the attendant risks of greater susceptibility to rain and cold. Only vines that are fifteen years old or more and that attain a potential alcohol of 20° are used. Yields, at 1 ton per acre, can be even lower than at Yquem. The two wines, somewhat unfairly, are invariably compared, since they come from the same stable. Fargues in its youth can be more attractive than Yquem, but is usually outpaced by the *premier grand cru* in the long run. Even so, Fargues is a sumptuous, deeply flavoured Sauternes, luxurious and, at exactly half the price of Yquem, still very expensive.

CHÂTEAU FILHOT

AC Sauternes, *deuxième cru classé*

Sauternes, 33210 Langon

Vineyard: 148 acres (55 per cent Sémillon, 40 per cent Sauvignon, 5 per cent Muscadelle)

Production: 150,000 bottles

Quality: 🍇   Price: ★★★★

The château and park here make up a splendid estate, and its owner, Comte Henri de Vaucelles, is immensely knowledgeable about the history of the region. One wishes, though, that more of this energy were directed towards improving the quality of the wine. In 1788 Thomas Jefferson thought Filhot the best Sauternes after Yquem. This is far from being the case today.

The microclimate delays the maturation of the Filhot grapes, and de Vaucelles is wary of leaving them too long on the vine for fear of frost damage. The must is fermented and aged in fibreglass vats.

When Henri de Vaucelles came to Filhot in 1974, the place was run down. No Sauternes had been bottled in 1963, 1964, 1965 and 1968. He succeeded in making a rich and succulent wine in 1976, but subsequent vintages have often been bland and feeble, in a lean, citric style. Premature oxidation has afflicted some wines, and after visiting the cellars I could see why. Vintages in the late 1980s have shown a distinct improvement, though it is too early to determine whether, like the 1976 wine, this is a freak occurrence or sign of a new concern for quality.

CHÂTEAU GILETTE

AC Sauternes

Preignac, 33210 Langon

Vineyard: 11 acres (94 per cent Sémillon, 4 per cent Sauvignon, 2 per cent Muscadelle)

Production: 5,000–10,000 bottles

Quality: 🍷🍷🍷–🍷🍷🍷🍷🍷   Price: ★★★★★

Best vintages: 1949, 1953, 1955, 1959, 1961 (all Crème de Tête)

Undoubtedly the most unusual property in the region. The cellars adjoin the pretty mansion in Preignac where the Médeville family lives. Here the old vintages are stored, in cement tanks and in 200,000 bottles. All vintages of Gilette are old vintages, for no wine is bottled until it is about twenty-five years old.

The soil at Gilette, sandy gravel over a subsoil of rock and clay, is warmer than elsewhere and thus the grapes are unusually precocious. Nevertheless yields are very low and the must, which is fermented in stainless steel, is never chaptalized. The wine is racked and filtered and, after ruthless selection, the remaining wine is left untouched in large vats, where it evolves very, very slowly until Médeville considers it is ready to be bottled. The current release is 1962. Of course not all vintages are considered worthy of this treatment. Moreover, the cost of conserving wines for a quarter of a century before releasing them is enormous, so Gilette is never cheap, but then neither is any thirty-year-old Sauternes.

Various categories of wine are made. Crème de Tête is made only in great years from selected grapes. Until 1958 a wine styled Demi-Doux was made in mediocre years. The regular Gilette is simply called Doux. The Gilette method does not sound like a formula for good winemaking, but the Crème de Tête wines are undeniably impressive; rich and honeyed, with flavours of banana, orange and butterscotch. Sometimes the power (and alcohol) are excessive, but the wine is so voluptuous and full-flavoured that one forgives the lack of finesse.

A mile away is the other Médeville property of Les Justices. It is twice the size and yields are twice as high. This is a more traditionally made Sauternes, which spends twelve to eighteen months in *barriques*. It is attractively styled and attractively priced.

CHÂTEAU GUIRAUD

AC Sauternes, *premier cru classé*

Sauternes, 33210 Langon

Vineyard: 215 acres (67 per cent Sémillon, 32 per cent Sauvignon, 1 per cent Muscadelle)

Production: 100,000 bottles

Quality: 🍾🍾🍾🍾   Price: ★★★★★

In 1981 a rich young Canadian, Hamilton Narby, bought this large, run-down estate. Narby's investment was colossal, and so was his ambition, which was to challenge the supremacy of Yquem. By 1990 Narby had left Guiraud, and the estate is now run by his able former manager, Xavier Planty. Narby was never satisfied with the high proportion of Sauvignon in the vineyard, and new plantations were of Sémillon. The excess Sauvignon is used to make the dry white 'G' (q.v.). Yields are low and the must is never chaptalized. Half the must is fermented and aged in *barriques*, of which one third are new, for over two years. The blending takes place gradually after each racking, and the wine is only filtered just before bottling.

Guiraud is one of the richer Sauternes, an unashamedly sumptuous mouthful of wine. Despite the poor condition of the cellars, good wines were made in 1962 and 1964, but the 1970s were disappointing, although the 1979 is surprisingly fruity and balanced. The 1983 is outstanding: lush, peachy, concentrated, toasty, but vigorous despite the richness. In 1985, as in 1983, Guiraud had an average must weight of 19.5°, and a good proportion of botrytized grapes. The 1986, 1989 and 1990 all look hugely promising. Guiraud is a top Sauternes charging top prices.

CHÂTEAU LAFAURIE-PEYRAGUEY

AC Sauternes, *premier cru classé*

Bommes, 33210 Langon

Vineyard: 74 acres (93 per cent Sémillon, 5 per cent Sauvignon, 2 per cent Muscadelle)

Production: 80,000 bottles

Quality: 🍷🍷🍷🍷🍷 (since 1983)   Price: ★★★★★

The ivy-covered château, surrounded by medieval walls, is one of the most picturesque in the region. Back in 1855 this was rated the third-best property in Sauternes, but only in recent years has it been possible to understand why. Between 1967 and 1977 the wine spent hardly any time in wood, and Lafaurie was deadly dull. Then the owners, the well-known firm of Cordier, decided to revert to more traditional forms of vinification in order to improve the quality.

With the 1981 and 1983 vintages one can discern an enormous leap in quality. Michel Laporte, the winemaker, has gone back to using vertical presses and to fermentation in *barriques*. Since 1985, 40 per cent of the barrels have been new. Laporte likes barrel-fermentation because the process is slow and there is less likelihood of a loss of aromas. Equal care is taken in the vineyard; in 1985, a difficult year, there were eight *tries* to ensure that only botrytized grapes were picked with an average must weight of 21°.

Of recent vintages, 1981 is good and 1983 excellent: oaky, and with very good concentration. The 1984 is a great success for the vintage, as is the 1985. 1986, 1988 and 1989 all show marvellous promise.

CHÂTEAU LAMOTHE

AC Sauternes, *deuxième cru classé*

Sauternes, 33210 Langon

Vineyard: 20 acres (70 per cent Sémillon, 20 per cent Sauvignon, 10 per cent Muscadelle)

Production: 15,000 bottles

Quality: 👁👁   Price: ★★★

The Lamothe estate was divided up in the early twentieth century, and this, the smaller portion, is owned by the Despujols family. It is rarely exported. The vines are planted on relatively steep south-west facing slopes, and the average age of the vines is about forty years. So there is a potential for good winemaking here. Recent vintages have been plump and peachy, showing good fruit but little finesse and concentration. A new generation took over the winemaking in 1989, so judgment should be deferred.

*

CHÂTEAU LAMOTHE-GUIGNARD

AC Sauternes, *deuxième cru classé*

Sauternes, 33210 Langon

Vineyard: 37 acres (90 per cent Sémillon, 5 per cent Sauvignon, 5 per cent Muscadelle)

Production: 36,000 bottles

Quality: 🍇🍇🍇   Price: ★★★★

This is the larger chunk of the Lamothe estate, which was split up earlier this century. Until 1980 the wine was made at Château d'Arche and the cellars had fallen into disrepair. Then the estate was bought by Philippe and Jacques Guignard, whose parents own Château de Rolland in Barsac. The vineyards here are in two sections: one on a gravelly plateau facing Sauternes, the other on clay and limestone soil facing north and north-west towards the Ciron. Most of the vines are between thirty and forty years old.

Four to six *tries* are not uncommon. The grapes are pressed in vertical presses and fermented slowly in small stainless steel tanks. In 1990 half the must was *barrique*-fermented. The wine is aged in *barriques*, of which 30 per cent are new, for a year. The Guignards have certainly turned this neglected property around, and apart from a disappointing 1986 I have been impressed by recent vintages, even the tricky 1987. Compared to other Sauternes, Lamothe-Guignard is fairly lean and racy, but the wine is intense, very fruity, and lively. In 1989 the grapes had a must weight of 22° and the wine was excellent, but possibly excelled by the creamy 1990. With prices still reasonable, this is a wine to look out for.

CHÂTEAU DE MALLE

AC Sauternes, *deuxième cru classé*

Preignac, 33210 Langon

Vineyard: 61 acres (80 per cent Sémillon, 19 per cent Sauvignon, 1 per cent Muscadelle)

Production: 40,000 bottles

Quality: 🍇🍇   Price: ★★★

Château de Malle, with its exquisite château and gardens, is the major tourist attraction of the Sauternes. For some reason the wine has never been in the front rank, even though since 1983 the youthful and enthusiastic Alain Pivonet has been the winemaker. The vines are thirty-five years old, and the must is fermented half in new oak, half in one-year-old barrels. The wine is then aged for a maximum of eighteen months in barrels, of which one third are new. The estate practises *triage*, yields seem modest, the winemaking is conscientious. Yet de Malle always seems little more than a pleasant, workmanlike Sauternes, adequate but never exciting. Even the fine 1986 vintage produced a soft, slightly flabby wine. The 1989 is fat and rounded and generous, but lacks, like most of de Malle's wines, the sheer concentration of flavour one expects from top Sauternes.

A second wine is marketed under the name Château de Ste-Hélène.

CHÂTEAU NAIRAC

AC Sauternes, *deuxième cru classé*

Barsac, 33720 Podensac

Vineyard: 40 acres (90 per cent Sémillon, 6 per cent Sauvignon, 4 per cent Muscadelle)

Production: 25,000 bottles

Quality: 🍇🍇🍇🍇   Price: ★★★

I have a soft spot for Nairac, having got to know the former owner, Tom Heeter, and having stayed at the lovely eighteenth-century château. The vines were planted in 1956, but the wine was never château-bottled until Heeter and his wife Nicole Tari bought Nairac in 1972. Despite problems with frost and floods, Heeter transformed a routine Barsac into a thoroughly exciting wine. *Triage* was often exhaustive – there were eleven pickings in the awful year 1974 – and in 1977, 1978 and 1984 no Nairac was bottled. The grapes are pressed in a vertical press, and fermented slowly in *barriques*, of which half are new. In some vintages, such as 1988, all the fermentation takes place in new oak, though the wine is aged in a mixture of old and new. The wine often remains in barrels for up to thirty-six months, and Nairac has always been heavily marked by oak flavours, which some wine lovers find excessive.

In 1987 Tom Heeter left Nairac, and Nicole Tari appointed Max Amirault as the new winemaker. Amirault has made few changes. Lots from different grape varieties and different *tries* remain separate until quite a late stage, so a tasting at Nairac is always fascinating and instructive.

Heeter made remarkable wines in the unpromising vintages from 1972 to 1974, but 1975 is the first great Nairac, a wine of real elegance and breed, superior to the 1976. 1979 and 1980 are a delicious pair, and the toasty, intense 1983 is still far from mature. 1986 seems less satisfactory, but both 1988 and the very concentrated 1989 and 1990 should be excellent.

CHÂTEAU RABAUD-PROMIS

AC Sauternes, *premier cru classé*

Bommes, 33210 Langon

Vineyard: 81 acres (80 per cent Sémillon, 18 per cent Sauvignon, 2 per cent Muscadelle)

Production: 60,000–100,000 bottles

Quality: 🍇🍇🍇🍇   Price: ★★★★

The Château Rabaud classified in 1855 was divided in 1903, but in 1929 the two parts were reunited, only to be split up again in 1952. Château Rabaud-Promis now includes the vineyards of former *deuxième cru* Château Pexoto, without having compromised its own first-growth status. There is little clay in the soil, and the wines are distinguished by their lightness and elegance.

In the 1970s Rabaud-Promis probably made grubbier wine than any other *premier cru*. Philippe Dejean, the skilful manager and winemaker since 1981, has made major changes. In 1988 a pneumatic press was acquired, and Rabaud's subterranean vats are now a thing of the past, with half the must being fermented in steel, half in new *barriques*. In 1990 Dejean began to ferment the entire crop in new oak.

Rabaud has quite a distinctive style, though this may alter along with the changes in winemaking techniques of the late 1980s. I find the wine sleek and lively, one of the least sumptuous but most elegant of Sauternes. The 1986 is excellent, the 1988 positively racy and impeccably balanced: a most delicious wine. The only criticism one can level is a slight lack of complexity. That is, however, a bearable price to pay for a wine as moreish as this.

CHÂTEAU RAYMOND-LAFON

AC Sauternes

Sauternes, 33210 Langon

Vineyard: 49 acres (80 per cent Sémillon, 20 per cent Sauvignon)

Production: 24,000 bottles

Quality: 🍇🍇🍇🍇🍇   Price: ★★★★★

This estate is the creation of Pierre Meslier, the former manager of Château d'Yquem. According to Meslier, the property was unclassified in 1855 because of the youth of its vines. Its location is certainly admirable, bordering both Yquem and Sigalas-Rabaud. When Meslier bought the property in 1972 only 8.5 acres were under vine, so the expansion has been considerable. As the Mesliers never cease pointing out, the wine is made in exactly the same way as Yquem, with fermentation in new *barriques*, where the young wine stays for three years.

The Mesliers' tireless self-promotion has earned them some enemies, but any dispassionate assessment of the wine has to conclude that it is very fine indeed. When young, it can seem closed and excessively oaky, but Raymond-Lafon is a wine of great depth and concentration, structured for the long haul. By having the courage to delay picking until as late in the year as possible, Meslier has made excellent wine even in difficult years such as 1981, 1984 and 1985. There are varying reports, however, of inconsistent bottlings of the 1983. So it is all the more regrettable that the Mesliers have succumbed to such snobbish marketing devices as numbered imperials, restricted allocations and prices exceeded only by Yquem and Fargues.

CHÂTEAU RAYNE-VIGNEAU

AC Sauternes, *premier cru classé*

> Bommes, 33210 Langon
>
> Vineyard: 178 acres (80 per cent Sémillon, 20 per cent Sauvignon)
>
> Production: 90,000 bottles
>
> Quality: 🍇🍇   Price: ★★★★

Rayne-Vigneau, which dominates one of the hillocks of the Sauternais, has been substantially renovated since its sale in 1971 to the company that owns Château Grand-Puy-Ducasse. The soil is unusually steep and stony, which ensures good drainage. The director, Patrick Emery, has brought the cellars up to date, with pneumatic presses since 1988, and 800 *barriques*, of which half are new. Until the late 1980s the must was fermented in stainless steel tanks, but from 1990 onwards Emery is fermenting one third of the crop in *barriques*. The wine spends up to twenty-four months in wood, half new, before bottling. The second label is Clos l'Abeilley.

It is not hard to detect the improvements at Rayne-Vigneau, but there is still quite a long way to go. Yields are fairly high, and a lack of richness in the wine suggests that grape selection is less rigorous than it should be. Commercial considerations still seem to take priority over a drive for the highest quality.

CHÂTEAU RIEUSSEC

AC Sauternes, *premier cru classé*

Fargues, 33210 Langon

Vineyard: 153 acres (80 per cent Sémillon, 18 per cent Sauvignon, 2 per cent Muscadelle)

Production: 100,000 bottles

Quality: 🍇🍇🍇–🍇🍇🍇🍇🍇   Price: ★★★★★

Rieussec remains a puzzle. It has everything going for it, yet until recently the wines were not as good as they should have been. Albert Vuillier, who bought and renovated Rieussec in 1971, sold a majority share in 1984 to the Domaines Barons de Rothschild, so there can be no shortage of investment in the property. The winery is set on a hill surrounded by vines planted on very varied soils. The grapes are pressed in horizontal presses and fermented in stainless steel. The wine is aged in *barriques*, of which half are new, for eighteen to twenty months. Rejected lots are usually sold as Clos Labère.

Old vintages such as 1959 have been quite marvellous, so there is no intrinsic reason why Rieussec should not produce superb wines. And occasionally it does so: the 1976, now getting long in the tooth, was rich and honeyed, the 1983 is magnificent, and the 1986 will also be splendid in time. Other vintages through the 1980s seem well made, attractive, medium-bodied, yet lacking in depth and stylishness. Often Rieussec does well in lesser vintages: both the 1984 and 1987 seem superior to the soapy 1985. Very different notes about the same wine tasted on different occasions suggest there may be bottle variations, a worrying sign; other tasters report similar experiences. It also seems that Rieussec is lazier than many other properties, preferring to make its selection from the best lots in the winery rather than by picking only the ripest and most botrytized grapes. Notwithstanding, it is hard to fault the elegant splendour of the vintages from 1988 to 1990.

CHÂTEAU ROMER-DU-HAYOT

AC Sauternes, *deuxième cru classé*

Bommes, 33210 Langon

Vineyard: 40 acres (70 per cent Sémillon, 25 per cent Sauvignon, 5 per cent Muscadelle)

Production: 25,000 bottles

Quality: 🍇   Price: ★★★

There is no longer a château at Romer-du-Hayot, since it was demolished to make way for the autoroute that bisects the vineyards of Sauternes. The wine is now made by the principal proprietor, André du Hayot, at Château Guiteronde in Barsac. I have only tasted two vintages, and found one of them, the 1982, considerably better than expected from a property with no international reputation.

CHÂTEAU ST-AMAND

AC Sauternes

Preignac, 33210 Langon

Vineyard: 50 acres (85 per cent Sémillon, 14 per cent Sauvignon, 1 per cent Muscadelle)

Production: 58,000 bottles

Quality: 🍇🍇   Price: ★★★

The lovely little château here is the centrepiece of one of the oldest properties in Sauternes. The vines are old and dispersed among four parcels, each with a different soil structure. Louis Ricard seeks to make a well-balanced wine combining botrytized and overripe grapes. He hardly ever chaptalizes and the must is fermented in tanks. The wine spends only four months in *barriques* and is bottled within two years of the harvest.

St-Amand borders Barsac, and to me the wine has the freshness of a good Barsac. Inexpensive yet reliable, it is often successful in lesser vintages such as 1984 and 1985. The 1983 was more concentrated than some of the preceding vintages. St-Amand lacks complexity, but has a neatness and elegance that make for a very attractive if undemanding glass of wine.

Somewhat confusingly, the wine is also sold under the label of Château de la Chartreuse.

CHÂTEAU SIGALAS-RABAUD

AC Sauternes, *premier cru classé*

Bommes, 33210 Langon

Vineyard: 33 acres (80 per cent Sémillon, 20 per cent Sauvignon)

Production: 25,000 bottles

Quality: 🍇🍇🍇   Price: ★★★★

In the course of this century, the former Château Rabaud has twice been divided up into two properties. Nowadays Sigalas is the part that is not Rabaud-Promis. The wines share a similar character, being light and elegant rather than plump and unctuous. Indeed the owner, Comte Emanuel de Lambert, and his winemaker, Jean-Louis Vimeney, happily admit that they pick their grapes relatively early. Chaptalization is, however, rare. The grapes are pressed in a vertical press and the must is fermented in tanks, where it remains for three to six months. Only a portion of the crop goes into *barriques* at any one time, but a quarter of the barrels are new. M. de Lambert does not want pronounced woody flavours in his wines, but seeks freshness and aroma. The wine is bottled fairly young and is not intended to be aged for decades.

None of this sounds very promising, yet I have often found Sigalas immensely pleasurable. Its freshness and lack of structure mean that the sweetness of the grape sugar comes bursting through, together with a lemony acidity that can be racy and bracing. The wines have good length. Among recent vintages I have enjoyed the 1983, 1985, 1987, 1988, 1989 and 1990.

Those who like their Sauternes as aperitif wines rather than as post-prandial blockbusters should look out for Sigalas-Rabaud.

CHÂTEAU SUDUIRAUT

AC Sauternes, *premier cru classé*

Preignac, 33210 Langon

Vineyard: 196 acres (80 per cent Sémillon, 20 per cent Sauvignon)

Production: 200,000 bottles

Quality: 🍇🍇🍇🍇   Price: ★★★★★

This large estate is dominated by the fine château and the attractive park laid out by Le Nôtre. In 1940 it was bought by an industrialist, Léopold Fonquernie, whose daughters now run the estate. The winemaker is Pierre Pascaud, whose ambitions may be slightly constrained by the demands of his numerous employers. Suduiraut became somewhat notorious for its policy of picking grapes relatively early. In some vintages, such as 1982, this paid off, as rain savaged the crop of estates that boldly waited into October. On the other hand, it also means that in vintages such as 1983 Suduiraut's wine is clearly not up to scratch, lacking the rich botrytis one expects from a top property in a top year.

The estate went through a miserable patch in the 1970s, and the wines spent more time ageing in tanks than in barrels. This has all changed, although fermentation still takes place in tanks. The wine now spends up to two years in *barriques*, of which a third are new.

When Suduiraut is on form, as in 1975 and 1989, it is one of the richest Sauternes, with a substantial amount of residual sugar. The 1982 is better than the 1983, while both the 1985 and 1986 are disappointing and ungainly.

Like Coutet and Caillou, Suduiraut produces a Crème de Tête in fine vintages such as 1982, when 4,800 bottles were made, and 1989. These wines are extremely costly and immensely sumptuous.

CHÂTEAU LA TOUR-BLANCHE

AC Sauternes, *premier cru classé*

Bommes, 33210 Langon

Vineyard: 74 acres (78 per cent Sémillon, 19.5 per cent Sauvignon, 2.5 per cent Muscadelle)

Production: 60,000 bottles

Quality: 🍇🍇🍇🍇 (since 1986)   Price: ★★★★★

In 1855 this estate was regarded as outclassed only by Yquem. I have tasted prewar vintages which demonstrated that the property was still making some splendid wines earlier this century. Then something went wrong. In the 1970s and well into the 1980s La Tour-Blanche was truly awful: botrytis was absent, sulphur dioxide was often overwhelming, and the wines were one-dimensional and barely drinkable. In 1909 the proprietor, Daniel Osiris, bequeathed the property to the ministry of agriculture and it became a wine school. Evidently by the 1970s only the least promising students were permitted to make Sauternes.

Then in 1983 Jean-Pierre Jausserand arrived as director, and things began to change. He was determined to restore the estate's tarnished reputation. Yields were halved – in 1983 the yield was the maximum permitted by law – and only grapes with a minimum must weight of 19° were picked. Chaptalization ceased. In 1987 a pneumatic press was installed, and from 1989 the entire crop was fermented in new *barriques*. The wine now spends up to two years in barrels, half new.

The 1986 is very good, the 1988 and 1989 superb. The price has also skyrocketed, though M. Jausserand lowered his prices considerably in 1990. La Tour-Blanche is perhaps the most striking example of how a long-neglected estate can be restored to its full potential with determination, investment and a lucky run of fine vintages.

The second label, largely used for rejected or chaptalized lots, is called Mademoiselle de St-Marc (before 1985 it was known as Cru St-Marc).

CHÂTEAU D'YQUEM

AC Sauternes, *premier grand cru classé*

Sauternes, 33210 Langon

Vineyard: 247 acres (80 per cent Sémillon, 20 per cent Sauvignon)

Production: 60,000–120,000 bottles

Quality: 🍇🍇🍇🍇🍇   Price: ★★★★★

Yquem truly is the supreme Sauternes. Vintage after vintage it demonstrates its magnificence. Every aspect of its viticulture and vinification is impeccable. The vineyards are drained by channels installed in the last century and carefully maintained. The estate's soils are so varied that it would be possible to make four distinct wines from the estate, so the blending of different lots is an essential part of the making of Yquem.

There is a myth that Yquem picks grape by grape, rather than bunch by bunch. There may be occasions when this is so, but it is not a very practical way of harvesting. What is undoubtedly the case is that Yquem goes to unmatched efforts to pick only botrytized grapes with high must weights. The *triage* is so scrupulous that in some vintages the harvest lasts for two months, employing 150 pickers.

The vinification is ultra-traditional: Yquem has vertical presses, and each day's crop is fermented separately in new *barriques*. The wine spends over three years in wood; after about 15 rackings no filtration is necessary. What is particularly impressive at Yquem is the selection of lots. Even in superb vintages such as 1975 and 1976, 20 per cent of the wine was rejected, and in 1985, when botrytis was so elusive, 85 per cent was sold off to merchants as generic Sauternes or employed in the blend for the dry white 'Y'. Quality control is carried to an heroic extreme.

Yquem is traditional but not hidebound. Alexandre de Lur-Saluces, the owner, favours cryo-extraction, for example. The only other change of recent years is the replacement of Pierre Meslier as manager by Francis Mayeur. Guy Latrille is entering his third decade as Yquem's cellarmaster.

In recent years Yquem has not put a foot wrong. Even difficult vintages such as 1981 and 1982 have been superb, while 1975, 1976 and 1983 have been simply sublime. Yquem triumphs with its sheer concentration of flavour, a richness that is sumptuous without ever being vulgar or blowsy, and a massive structure that permits it to improve in bottle over decades.

CLOS HAUT-PEYRAGUEY

AC Sauternes, *premier cru classé*

Bommes, 33210 Langon

Vineyard: 37 acres (80 per cent Sémillon, 18 per cent Sauvignon, 2 per cent Muscadelle)

Production: 40,000 bottles

Quality: 🍇🍇🍇   Price: ★★★★

The Clos formed the upper part of Château Lafaurie-Peyraguey until 1878, when the property was divided. The Clos was acquired in 1914 by the Pauly family. The vineyards are well situated, and one large parcel adjoins Yquem. The average age of the vines is over thirty years.

The wine here ought to be far better than it actually is. Clos Haut-Peyraguey is light, fresh and elegant, without faults and without distinction. Yields are fairly high, and until 1989 the wine was fermented in cement vats. Thereafter 25 per cent of the crop was fermented in new *barriques*, and in 1990 the proportion rose to 30 per cent. The wine is barrel-aged for up to twenty-two months.

Jacques Pauly admits that he is looking for finesse rather than for wines that are *liquoreux* – sweet and fat. I liked the elegant, appley 1983 because it was considerably richer than some other vintages, and Pauly made a good 1985. Clearly the 1990s will see an attempt to make the wine, at present not of *premier cru* quality, worthy of its status.

OTHER SWEET WHITE BORDEAUX

Sauternes is not the only sweet wine of Bordeaux made from Sémillon, Sauvignon and a dash of Muscadelle. Just north of Barsac is the tiny appellation of Cérons, but all the other wines in this style, apart from generic Graves Supérieurs, are made on the other bank of the Garonne. Of the various appellations that cover these wines, Ste-Croix-du-Mont is often considered marginally superior in quality, followed by the generally lighter Loupiac and Cadillac, and the more diffuse Premières Côtes de Bordeaux.

Very old vintages of wines from these areas demonstrate that these vineyards are capable, in top years, of producing wines that approach in quality the best Sauternes. Yet the wines now made there are mostly feeble. These regions met the postwar demand for sweet wines by turning out tanker-loads of the stuff, almost all poorly made, sulphurous and as cheap as the market demanded. Prices remained low, so there was scarcely any new investment in the region. Ancient barrels were replaced not by costly new *barriques* but by cement tanks. Yields were considerably higher than those for Sauternes. *Triage* almost became extinct. No serious attempt was made to wait for botrytis to appear. Growers directed their efforts towards red wine production, and many white vines were grubbed up or not replanted when they aged. Château Fayau at Cadillac, for example, made nothing but white wines in 1948. Today 75 per cent of their production is red wine.

There are signs of improvement, now that these appellations are being dragged in the wake of Sauternes. When the price of Sauternes rose steeply in the late 1980s, consumers began to look to other Bordeaux appellations for more affordable wines. Some producers responded by making improvements in the quality, and succeeded in obtaining higher prices for their wines while, in relation to Sauternes, giving an impression of remaining inexpensive. The wholesale price for wine in Sauternes in 1990 was between 40,000 and 45,000 francs per *tonneau*, whereas in Ste-Croix-du-Mont and Loupiac the price was 16,000 francs, except for a few producers who could obtain 20,000.

Most producers, especially of generic wines, still churn out some truly wretched wines. Even among more ambitious and sophisticated producers, postwar habits have become enshrined as though they were traditional. Thus many proprietors profess a dislike for wood-maturation and continue to age their wines in tanks. My own comparative tastings of wines from cask and tank convince me that careful wood-ageing makes an enormous contribution to a wine's complexity. Yet, for understandable financial reasons, many winemakers still hesitate to purchase barrels, and thus fail to make the most out of the raw materials at their disposal. Moreover, as Claude Armand of Château La Rame at Ste-Croix-du-Mont points out, you need rich musts to age in *barriques*, otherwise the oak will merely dry out the wine, and standard viticultural techniques in these appellations won't deliver the goods.

In a vintage such as 1989, when must weights of 20° were commonplace in the best vineyards, it should have been possible to make truly outstanding wine. With *triage*, low yields, light pressings and *barrique*-ageing there is no reason why these wines should not rival in quality those of the more celebrated left bank. The reason they do not is commercial rather than technical. The Sauternes producer can hope to recoup his costs; the Loupiac or Cérons producer could never get away with charging the prices necessary to justify, for example, halving his yields, which in effect means discarding over half his crop. It is a classic vicious circle: until prices increase, producers cannot afford to make the best wine possible, but until the standard of winemaking improves noticeably it is hard to justify a significant increase in prices.

The appellation of Cérons applies to the communes of Cérons, Podensac and Illats. Growers may choose between declaring their wines as sweet Cérons or as dry white Graves. This is handy, since it means that in years when there is either very little or very late botrytis, growers can harvest grapes intended for use in a sweet wine and can produce instead a dry wine. The production of the sweet wine has been steadily declining. In 1981, 160,000 gallons were produced; by 1985 the quantity was reduced to 69,000, and thereafter remained steady.

The vines are planted on gravel outcrops similar to those found in neighbouring Barsac. Towards the east there is more clay in the soil; to the west more sand. The minimum alcohol level is 12.5°, compared with Sauternes's 13°. Maximum yields are 40 hectolitres per hectare (2.66 tons per acre), though the best producers, such as Jean Perromat, would like to see them brought into line with those of Sauternes, which are 25 hectolitres per hectare (just under 2 tons per acre). This would certainly improve the quality of the wine, but it would reduce the quantity too, as growers know that if they make dry wine instead, yields of 4 tons per acre are feasible. Because of the option of making dry instead of sweet wine, it is hard to quantify the number of Cérons producers, but in 1986 it was about fifty.

There are twice as many producers in Ste-Croix-du-Mont on the opposite bank of the Garonne. Many of them grow vines as a sideline, and there are only thirty full-time growers in the district. Annual production varies from 340,000 to 422,000 gallons. There are considerable differences between the two sides of the river. In Sauternes, the River Ciron provokes the mists which invite botrytis spores to attack the grapes. On the right bank there is no such influence, and fogs and mists are consequently less frequent. The soil is different too. Sauternes, like most of the Graves, is fairly flat. On the right bank, however, cliffs rise up behind the shore. These are composed of limestone, and Ste-Croix is famous for fossil deposits composed mostly of oyster shells. These cliffs rise to a plateau of clay over a limestone subsoil. Other areas are more stony and lack limestone. Wines made from such soils tend to have a more floral aroma and are better suited for drinking young than wines made from grapes grown on limestone soils, which are more reticent but better capable of ageing. Maximum yields here are also 2.66 tons per acre. With limited *triage*, average must weights are lower than in Sauternes, and chaptalization more frequent. In a good year such as 1988, must weights varied from 16° to 19°, whereas in Sauternes a conscientious grower would only have picked grapes with a minimum of 18°.

Loupiac, which adjoins Ste-Croix-du-Mont, has just over 740 acres under vine, and a production ranging between 265,000 and 316,000 gallons. Loupiac is said to be a slightly less rich wine than Ste-Croix, though it is doubtful whether anyone tasting the wines blind could differentiate between the two.

Encircling Loupiac and Ste-Croix is the large district of the Premières Côtes, which includes thirty-seven different communes. This appellation is reserved for sweet wines, while dry wines are sold as plain Bordeaux. The catchment area for the Cadillac appellation, embracing twenty-two communes, is smaller than that for Premières Côtes, but there is a notional quality difference, since only wines sold in bottle may, since 1973, be called Cadillac. There is also a difference in the maximum yield. That for Premières Côtes is 50 hectolitres per hectare (3.3 tons per acre), plus a 20 per cent increase in excellent years; Cadillac's is 40 hectolitres per hectare (2.66 tons per acre). It is virtually impossible to make decent sweet wines from the more generous yields of the Premières Côtes. With very few exceptions, anything labelled Premières Côtes – and in 1986, 660,000 gallons were made – is likely to be inferior to Cadillac, of which 80,000 gallons were made. The final appellation, Graves Supérieurs, is almost as abundant as Premières Côtes and, with one or two exceptions, is just as undistinguished. These wines come from grapes grown in the communes beyond the Sauternes borders such as Pujols and St-Pierre-de-Mons.

It is usually safe to assume that a good Sauternes vintage is, potentially at any rate, a good Loupiac or Cadillac vintage. But the region is quite large, and some vineyards entitled to sweet wine appellations are far from the Garonne and rarely exposed to botrytis.

CHÂTEAU DE CÉRONS

AC Cérons

Cérons, 33720 Podensac
Vineyard: 15 acres (mostly Sémillon)
Production: 16,000 bottles
Quality: 🍇🍇 Price: ★★★

The owner of Château de Cérons, Jean Perromat, is also the mayor of the village and an ardent promoter of its wine. He takes far more care than most in harvesting his grapes, and his yields compare favourably with, say, a good bourgeois growth in Sauternes. In 1988 they were 1.4 tons per acre, and in 1989, which gave an abundant crop in Sauternes too, they were 1.7 tons per acre.

Vintages from the 1970s were pleasant, agreeable wines with few traces of botrytis. They were aged for up to five years in cask, presumably because the wines sold slowly and were only bottled on demand. Since 1988 Perromat has become more adventurous, fermenting a portion of the crop in *barriques*. I compared two samples of the 1989 vintage: one from *barrique*, the other from tank. The *barrique* wine was a full golden colour, very sweet and rich in flavour. The tank sample had a lovely purity of flavour but less richness and complexity. Perromat will blend the two, giving a very good wine, but I cannot help wishing he would bottle the two separately, since the *barrique*-fermented 1989 compares favourably with a number of Sauternes from the same vintage and proves how fine Cérons could be if the wines were made with the same care as good Sauternes.

CHÂTEAU FAYAU

AC Cadillac

33410 Cadillac
Vineyard: 25 acres (100 per cent Sémillon)
Production: 80,000 bottles
Quality: 🍇   Price: ★★

This is the largest estate producing Cadillac. It ought to be the appellation's flagship, but isn't. For some inexplicable reason it has quite a good reputation, but the winemaking is unashamedly commercial. Maximum yields are routinely obtained, *triage* is minimal, chaptalization common. The wine is not wood-aged and is bottled within ten months of the harvest. Fayau wants consistency in its wines – not a concept that would make any sense to a Sauternes producer – and will blend wines of different vintages to achieve that result. The Cadillac sometimes has a certain ripeness, which is attractive, but it can also be excessively alcoholic, sulphury and hard.

CHÂTEAU LA GRAVE

AC Ste-Croix-du-Mont

Ste-Croix-du-Mont, 33410 Cadillac

Vineyard: 33 acres (85 per cent Sémillon, 15 per cent Sauvignon)

Production: 35,000 bottles of Château La Grave; 25,000 bottles of Château Grand-Peyrot

Quality: 👁👁   Price: ★★★

Jean-Marie Tinon makes two sweet wines, one from his own estate of La Grave, the other from a rented estate called Grand-Peyrot. They are always bottled separately. The vines at La Grave are planted on stony soil, and are younger and less favourably exposed than at Grand-Peyrot. Both properties have some very old vines, including a parcel of 85-year-old Sémillon. One of the more progressive winemakers at Ste-Croix-du-Mont, Tinon has installed both a pneumatic press and a cryo-extraction chamber. In addition, he now ages a small proportion of Grand-Peyrot in new and old *barriques* for ten months.

Grand-Peyrot, from a limestone soil, has more finesse than La Grave, though in years such as 1975 and 1988 La Grave too produced some delicious wines. Since 1985 Grand-Peyrot has been consistently good, with a surprisingly lush and evolved 1987. The *barrique*-aged 1986 Grand-Peyrot, in which the oak is nicely judged and not too obtrusive, suggests the fine potential of these well-crafted wines.

CHÂTEAU LOUBENS

AC Ste-Croix-du-Mont

Ste-Croix-du-Mont, 33410 Cadillac

Vineyard: 37 acres (95 per cent Sémillon, 5 per cent Sauvignon)

Production: 20,000–30,000 bottles

Quality: 🍇🍇   Price: ★★★

Château Loubens is the most dramatically located property in Ste-Croix, seated above the famous cliff composed of fossilized oyster shells, the largest such concentration along the river. Tunnelled into the cliffs are seven galleries of cellars, full of barrels that, sadly, are now empty.

Loubens's vineyards are situated on good clay and limestone slopes. The Sauvignon grapes are not always used in the blend. The grapes, picked when possible at a must weight of 18–19°, are pressed in a vertical press and fermented slowly in tanks, using indigenous yeasts. The wines are then aged in tanks for up to three years. Wine considered not good enough for Loubens is sold as Château des Tours.

The quality of fruit achieved at Loubens is clearly outstanding, and the wines have a rich and spicy orange and mango flavour. The proprietor, Antoine de Sèze, wants elegance rather than power, so the wines are never overwhelming. They would benefit enormously from *barrique*-ageing, but de Sèze seems content with the consistent style he is presently producing. The wines age extremely well, and although expensive for the appellation are still quite good value for the quality. The 1989 is exceptionally rich, as the grapes were picked with must weights between 21° and 23°.

CHÂTEAU LOUPIAC-GAUDIET

AC Loupiac

Loupiac, 33410 Cadillac

Vineyard (including Château Pontac): 64 acres (80 per cent Sémillon, 20 per cent Sauvignon)

Production: 75,000 bottles of Château Loupiac-Gaudiet; 25,000 bottles of Château Pontac

Quality: 🍇   Price: ★★

Marc Ducau, the urbane proprietor of this leading estate, also owns a smaller property, Château Pontac, and the two wines are vinified in the identical way. Pontac, located higher up on the slopes of the foothills, has a higher gravel content in the soil. The must is fermented in stainless steel, then aged in tanks for two years or so before bottling. Both wines are cleanly made and always have good acidity and an attractive purity of flavour. What they lack is weight and complexity.

CHÂTEAU LOUSTEAU-VIEIL

AC Ste-Croix-du-Mont

Ste-Croix-du-Mont, 33410 Cadillac

Vineyard: 37 acres (75 per cent Sémillon, 15 per cent Sauvignon, 10 per cent Muscadelle)

Production: 45,000 bottles

Quality: 🍇   Price: ★★

Owned by the Sessacq family since 1843, the many parcels that make up the Lousteau-Vieil vineyards are located on the highest land of the commune and include some ninety-year-old vines. The must is fermented in temperature-controlled vats and aged for a year or so in mostly old barrels. Roland Sessacq, now giving way as winemaker to his son Rémy, favours a powerful alcoholic style that I find heavy-handed. The most attractive vintage I have encountered is the elegant 1975, which is still lean and lively. Many subsequent vintages have been marked by aromas of banana and by coarse, unbalanced flavours. The 1983 is much richer than most Lousteau-Vieil vintages of the 1980s, and the 1989, which has a large dose of aromatic Muscadelle, is atypical but promising.

*

CHÂTEAU LA RAME

AC Ste-Croix-du-Mont

Ste-Croix-du-Mont, 33410 Cadillac

Vineyard: 62 acres (80 per cent Sémillon, 20 per cent Sauvignon)

Production: 65,000 bottles

Quality: 🍇 (Réserve wines 🍇🍇🍇)   Price: ★★

Claude Armand is constantly striving to improve the quality of his wines. He is experimenting with canopy management in his vineyards, has installed a cryo-extraction chamber, and tries to avoid using cultivated yeasts. Before 1986 his wine was aged in a blend of tanks and old barrels. Since then he selects the best wines after fermentation and ages them for a year in *barriques*, of which one third are new. The *barrique*-aged wine is labelled Réserve du Château, and wine not good enough for either of the La Rame labels is sold under the second label of Château La Caussade.

Despite fairly high yields, above 2 tons per acre, La Rame makes fresh, delicate wines that can age well. The 1975 is still elegant and intense, and other good vintages include 1983, 1985 and 1988. The first Réserve vintage, 1986, was over-oaked, but Armand got the balance right in 1988, producing a wine rich and meaty without being heavy and, like the 1975, with extremely good length. La Rame is now making probably the best wines of the appellation.

CHÂTEAU DE RICAUD

AC Loupiac

Loupiac, 33410 Cadillac

Vineyard: 32 acres (100 per cent Sémillon)

Production: 40,000–60,000 bottles
Quality: 🍇 Price: ★★

Many years ago this estate, dominated by its grand neo-Gothic château, produced the finest wine in Loupiac. After 1970 its quality plummeted. In the 1980s the estate was bought by the enterprising Alain Thiénot, who also acquired Château Rahoul (q.v.) in the Graves. A determined effort is being made to improve the quality, and ageing in *barriques*, of which a third are new, is now routine. Recent vintages show a marked improvement, with vibrant orangey fruit; the contribution of the oak is as yet very discreet.

Château de Ricaud also produces an anaemic dry Sémillon.

DOMAINE DU NOBLE

AC Loupiac

Loupiac, 33410 Cadillac
Vineyard: 30 acres (80 per cent Sémillon, 20 per cent Sauvignon)
Production: 30,000 bottles
Quality: 🍇 Price: ★★

This modest estate is run by Patrick Dejean, who on occasion can call on the expertise and the cryo-extraction chamber of his brother Philippe, the winemaker of Château Rabaud-Promis in Sauternes. Dejean insists, rightly, that to make good sweet wine *triage* is essential, and that it is pointless to substitute, as more idle producers do, chaptalization for selective picking. In 1988 he aged one third of the crop in *barriques*, and in 1989 produced two *cuvées*: one oaked, the other not. Unfortunately, no distinction is made on the label between the two, although the two wines are sold in different markets. The unwooded wine has pure tangerine and apricot flavours, which are attractive if simple, while the *barrique*-aged bottling is lightly studded with oak tones. This will be an interesting estate to follow in the 1990s.

GRAND ENCLOS DU CHÂTEAU DE CÉRONS

AC Cérons

Cérons, 33720 Podensac

Vineyard: 64 acres for Cérons and Graves (80 per cent Sémillon, 20 per cent Sauvignon)

Production: 10,000 bottles

Quality: 🍇   Price: ★★★

The Grand Enclos lies within walled vineyards that were originally part of ecclesiastical estates. The property is now owned by Olivier Lataste. He devotes most of his energies to making a white Graves, Château Lamouroux, but also makes a reasonable Cérons. In 1988 he began to use a vertical press to make the sweet wine, and fermented some of the must in *barriques*; in 1989 he aged the entire crop in wood, experimenting in order to find the best woods and best methods for making Cérons. If the results now seem somewhat ungainly, it seems clear that Lataste is ambitious and keen to improve his wines, so this is an estate to watch in the 1990s.

Loire

Sauvignon Blanc is so firmly associated with Sancerre and its neighbouring appellations that it is difficult to believe that the grape is a relative newcomer here, not widely planted until about 1910. A few other grapes are still grown, notably Pinot Noir, Pinot Gris and Chasselas. Until a couple of decades ago the wines had a mostly local reputation. Most growers practised polyculture, and only since the Second World War has specialization in vineyard cultivation become common. Other changes have aided the wines' commercial prospects. The low

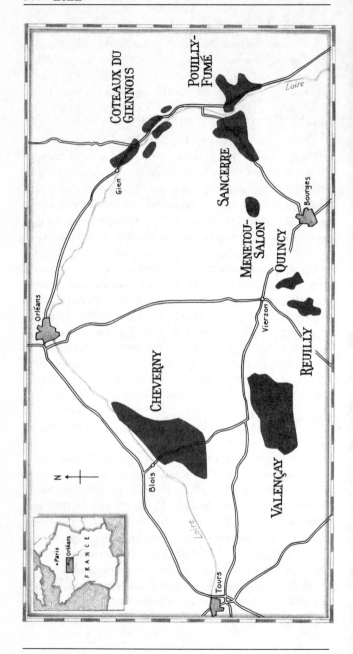

yields of the past – often the consequence of poor vineyard management and disease rather than a reflection of high quality – are now almost unheard of, and regulations that prohibited vinifying grapes until the vines were seven years old have been altered so that three-year-old vines may now be used. Young vines have vigour, but the shallow roots cannot draw up the nutrients that lie deeper in the soil.

A number of clones have been developed at the local agricultural station at Cosne. Some growers are wary of them on the grounds that they are overproductive; others favour them because they are resistant to disease and regular in their yields. The differences in flavour and aroma between different clones are slight, according to Henry Pellé of Menetou-Salon, who has planted a number of them and made controlled vinifications for comparative purposes. Many growers plant four or five different clones, so as to iron out any differences that may develop.

Sauvignon from the Loire is regarded as the quintessential Sauvignon: fresh, racy, fruity, slightly herbaceous, clean, a wine of gooseberry flavours made to be drunk young. The arguments of growers, such as Didier Dagueneau, who believe that Sauvignon should be treated with the same respect and care as Chardonnay have already been elaborated in the Introduction. His ideas are certainly catching on and the number of producers employing *barriques* grows each year. None the less, well-made, crisp, unwooded Loire Sauvignon remains so popular, and rightly so, that it is unlikely to be supplanted by *barrique*-aged versions.

Making unwooded Sauvignon is not especially demanding. The principal difficulties are likely to appear in the vineyard, as the variety ripens late and is susceptible to rot. The harvest usually begins in early October. The best wines usually come from the best vineyards, which have been known for generations, or from producers who ensure that they only harvest fruit of the highest quality. Presses employed are usually of the horizontal type, though the superior pneumatic presses are also found here. Some winemakers favour maceration before pressing; others chill the must after pressing and give it a lengthy *débourbage*. Fermentation in stainless steel or other tanks usually takes place at about 18 °C. Some producers add bentonite during fermentation to give cleaner must. Malolactic fermentation is rare, and in my experience undesirable. Most winemakers who export feel obliged to chill the wines so as to precipitate tartrate deposits. Whether such treatments harm the wine is a matter of dispute. Bottling usually takes place in the spring, but can begin earlier if demand is particularly heavy. An alcohol level of about 12.5° is normal, though in hot vintages 13° is not unusual. High acidity is of course a characteristic of the grape and, for many of us, one of its attractions. Total acidity levels in the wine can easily be more than 6 grams per litre, but many winemakers feel this is too aggressive for the many consumers who prefer a more rounded wine with 5.0–5.5 grams per litre. In general, it is wise to drink unwooded Sauvignons from the Loire fairly young, although a well-made Pouilly-Fumé often benefits from a year or so in bottle.

The Loire is northerly, as wine regions go, and vintages are extremely variable. There are some appalling years, such as 1972 when it rained almost every day. 1981 was a very difficult year, with spring frosts, diseases such as *coulure*, and hail in August, but the few grapes that survived the onslaught made good wine. Extremely ripe years can be problematic, and 1982 and 1985 have sometimes developed marked vegetal flavours that are disagreeable to most wine lovers. The ripeness of 1985 also led to some problems with vinification, and there are wines from 1985, 1989 and 1990 that have a troubling residue of sugar. 1983 was an excellent vintage and a large crop too.

1986 was a good vintage, despite some rot in the vineyards. 1987 was poor, with many grapes failing to ripen; better made examples, however, in their youth were clean and bracing. 1988 was a classic vintage that gave full-flavoured, elegant wines, but 1989 will be problematical. Because of the ripeness of the grapes, acidity was often lower than usual. Many 1989s are flabby and unlikely to improve. On the other hand, many top producers made splendidly fruity wines and the vintage proved ideal to those who employ wood-ageing. 1990 was comparable; picking began on 24 September and had mostly ended by 8 October. Many wines are even more alcoholic than in

1989, with up to 14.5° of natural alcohol. 1989 and 1990 permitted certain adventurous growers to leave some bunches on the vine and use them to make sweet late-harvest wines of remarkable quality. 1991 was the year of the savage April frosts, and crops were reduced by over 50 per cent. Quincy and Reuilly were very badly hit, but the quality in Sancerre and Pouilly was surprisingly good.

MENETOU-SALON

This small appellation covers only 420 acres. Nowadays about 60 per cent of the vines are Sauvignon, and the rest is Pinot Noir. In terms of its climate and soil – mostly Kimmeridgian limestone – the appellation resembles Sancerre, but the aspect is quite different. Whereas Sancerre is dominated by vine-covered slopes, in Menetou-Salon the vines present patches of light greenery among the darker vegetation of woodlands. Until the appellation was created in 1959, the area was known simply as Coteaux de Sancerrois. The maximum authorized yield here is 65 hectolitres per hectare (4.3 tons per acre), though in practice yields of 3 tons are more common, if the local growers are to be believed, as a consequence of frequent hail and frost. As elsewhere in this part of the Loire, it is now legal to pick vines that are only three years old.

Grapes have been grown in the area since at least the thirteenth century, but no one knows which varieties originally flourished here. Since no river flows through Menetou-Salon, and transportation of wines would have been difficult, the theory is that the wines were probably distilled and reduced to a liquor of lesser volume before being sent to nearby Bourges. More recently, producers from Sancerre have woken up to the fact that land here is considerably cheaper and still available for new planting, which is not the case in Sancerre.

Since 1980 the entire harvest has been picked mechanically under the auspices of a cooperative organization called

CUMA. One would imagine that there would be a rush with everybody wanting to use the machines at the same moment, but growers seem satisfied with the system. About one third of the thirty or more growers like to pick early, another third are never in a hurry, and the rest can pick in between.

The cooperative, Les Vignerons Jacques Coeur, is well run. It buys in all its grapes, and produces 130,000 bottles of Sauvignon of middling quality. Its wines are available abroad, as are those of Jean-Paul Gilbert. I mention the latter because of their curiosity value, since M. Gilbert is a great believer in malolactic fermentation and seems proud that his cellars lack any temperature control. I find his wines plodding, but clearly they enjoy a following as he sells 50,000 bottles each year. The wines of the delightfully named Jacky Rat are well known outside France, but I often find them coarse.

DOMAINE DE CHATENOY

AC Menetou-Salon

18510 Menetou-Salon
Vineyard: 42 acres of Sauvignon
Production: 80,000 bottles
Quality: 🍇🍇   Price: ★★

Bernard Clément is the thirteenth generation of his family to produce wine here. At present he grows all his own grapes, but there are plans afoot to buy in grapes from other sources and to double production. Some of the vines are fifty years old. Harvesting is by hand as well as by machine. Vinification is standard, though in the late 1980s Clément experimented with maceration. Clément also uses the label Domaine de la Montaloise. There is no difference between the two wines, which are soundly made.

*

PELLÉ, HENRY

AC Menetou-Salon

18229 Morogues
Vineyard: 37 acres of Sauvignon
Production: 90,000 bottles
Quality: 🍇🍇🍇🍇   Price: ★★

The enthusiastic mayor of Morogues is the best winemaker of the appellation. He produces two *cuvées*, one labelled under the village name, and a single-vineyard wine, Clos des Blanchais. He is gradually expanding his vineyard holdings.

Since 1989 he has used a pneumatic press, but does not favour maceration which, he claims, exaggerates the already pronounced aromas of Sauvignon. Pellé aims for a fruity style that is easy to drink. Acidity is often low, but the wine is always well balanced and has good length.

These attractively priced Sauvignons filled with gooseberry fruit are frequently superior to more expensive Sancerres. The Clos des Blanchais has a touch more spiciness and class than the regular bottling, but both are highly recommended. Pellé also makes a Sancerre from the 12-acre Clos de la Croix au Garde, but the vines are young and I prefer his Menetou-Salon.

ROGER, JEAN-MAX

AC Menetou-Salon

Bué, 18300 Sancerre
Vineyard: 10 acres of Sauvignon
Production: 30,000 bottles
Quality: 🍇🍇–🍇🍇🍇   Price: ★★

Roger is one of a number of Sancerre producers who own vines at Menetou-Salon. From his vineyards at Le Petit Clos,

Morogues, he obtains a vivid, spicy, flowery wine, usually with excellent fruit.

POUILLY-FUMÉ

Because styles of winemaking can vary, and because both Sancerre and Pouilly enjoy a variety of soils, it is often difficult to tell the wines apart. Many growers maintain, however, that Pouilly wines have more body than Sancerre, are slower to develop and consequently are better capable of ageing in bottle. Theoretically, there could be almost 5,000 acres under vine here, but half the vineyards were abandoned after the severe frosts of the 1950s. At present about 1,700 acres are cultivated and the vineyards are located around seven villages. About seventy growers bottle their own wine. Chasselas was the major grape variety here during the last century and still survives under the appellation Pouilly-sur-Loire.

Much of the soil in Pouilly is Kimmeridgian *marne* (marl), which heats up slowly and retards the maturation of the vines, giving relatively rich wines that take a while to develop. There is also a good deal of chalk and *silex* (flint). *Silex* land is particularly impoverished, with very little soil, and gives concentrated and closed wines that require some bottle-age. The best *silex* soils are around St-Andelain, where the mixture of flint and clay gives the wines the gunflint aroma associated with the term *blanc fumé*, as Sauvignon is called here. Faster-evolving and attractively scented wines are made from grapes grown on *caillottes* (known as *criots* locally), which is alluvial limestone soil. This heats up quickly on warm days and accelerates the maturation of the grapes. The flatter land around Tracy has a sandy clay soil, which also gives rapidly evolving wines.

The maximum yields here are 55 hectolitres per hectare (3.6 tons per acre), with a supplement of 20 per cent in certain abundant years. In 1983 and 1987, for example, yields of 4.3 tons per acre were common. A stroll through certain vineyards reveals pruning practices that seem incompatible with such yields, and some growers have planted very prolific clones and produce far more wine than the regulations permit. Such practices do not enhance the reputation of the appellation. About 90 per cent of harvesting is now mechanical, though very young and very old vines are usually picked by hand to avoid damaging them.

An insight into the way Blanc Fumé used to be was given me by the octogenarian M. Chabanne, a former president of the local growers' association. He recalled that half a century ago 2 tons per acre was regarded as a good yield, even if disease rather than a passion for quality was responsible for this state of affairs. From his cellar in Pouilly he fished out a bottle from the 1949 vintage, a full yellow-straw in colour, soft and honeyed on the nose, full-flavoured and concentrated on the palate, though undoubtedly fading and a touch flat. This wine had been neither fined nor filtered.

For Didier Dagueneau, the remaining riches of M. Chabanne's cellar are proof that Pouilly-Fumé is capable of ageing and developing in bottle for decades. Moreover, in 1929 the wine merchants Nicolas were offering ten-year-old Loire Sauvignons at prices comparable to well-known clarets. For Dagueneau and his followers, these are the true Pouilly-Fumés, and all his techniques are directed at reviving this style of wine. These techniques include low yields, skin contact, fermentation of the top wines in new oak, and leaving the wine on the fine lees. Wines made from vines grown on *silex* are particularly appropriate for such an approach, which suits Dagueneau, whereas wines made on limestone soils have more youthful finesse and less body and angularity. Many growers, such as Michel Redde, are furiously opposed to any kind of barrel-ageing, arguing that oak destroys the typicity, the purity of flavour, of Pouilly-Fumé. Certainly, unoaked Pouilly-Fumé can be a brilliant and wholly satisfying wine, and barrel-ageing must be employed with the greatest skill and only in vintages capable of supporting the powerful aromas and flavours it imparts.

The important cooperative is responsible for 20 per cent of the production. Founded in 1948, it consists of 130 growers who press their own grapes and sell the must. The wines are straightforward and rather characterless, although the Vieilles Vignes bottling is more concentrated. In addition to the wines listed below, I have enjoyed bottles from J. C. Dagueneau, Edmond and André Figeat, Didier Pabiot and Roger Pabiot. Michel Redde produces an acceptable commercial style at La Moynerie, but his luxury Cuvée Majorum does not justify its high price.

CHÂTEAU FAVRAY

St-Martin-sur-Nohain, 58150 Pouilly

Vineyard: 26 acres

Production: 85,000 bottles

Quality: 🍇🍇🍇–🍇🍇🍇🍇   Price: ★★★

The first vintage of this revived estate was 1984, and the David family have been highly successful ever since. Their vines are planted on soil with a high limestone content, which gives their wines exceptional aromas and purity and finesse. This is a sharp gooseberry-flavoured wine, full of character, rich fruit and liveliness. In a fine vintage such as 1986 or 1988, Château Favray is all one hopes for from good Pouilly-Fumé: rich yet austere, fruity but elegant.

CHÂTEAU DE NOZET. See Ladoucette

CHÂTEAU DE TRACY

Tracy, 58150 Pouilly

Vineyard: 62 acres

Production: 200,000 bottles

Quality: 🍇🍇   Price: ★★★

This ancient estate is now run by Henri D'Estutt d'Assay, whose family settled here five centuries ago. The wines are quite good but clearly not a full realization of the vineyards' potential. They tend to be rounded rather than racy, and are intended to be drunk young. Since they are among the most expensive wines of Pouilly, they do not offer very good value.

CHÂTELAIN, JEAN-CLAUDE

Les Berthiers, 58150 Pouilly

Vineyard: 44 acres

CUVÉE PRESTIGE

Quality: 🍇🍇🍇🍇   Price: ★★★

OTHERS

Quality: 🍇🍇🍇   Price: ★★

Châtelain produces some of the best wines in Pouilly, made from his own grapes and also from must and wine bought from other growers. There are four labels: Domaine des Chailloux, from low-yielding vines planted on clay and flint soils in St-Andelain; St-Laurent-l'Abbaye, from soils of clay and chalk; Les Chaudoux; and, since 1982, a Cuvée Prestige, made from late-picked vines, some of which are between thirty and fifty years old and grown on one third *silex*, two thirds *marne*.

His cellars are equipped with a pneumatic press and a centrifuge used to clean the must after pressing. The Cuvée Prestige is bottled later than the other wines, in September, and given six months' bottle-age before release. For all his wine he likes an acidity level of 5.0–5.5 grams per litre to give elegance and length of flavour, with no excessively pungent aromas.

I have tasted most of the vintages of Cuvée Prestige (none was made in 1987) and it is a very fine wine: rich, smoky and concentrated. With age it develops a lovely, almost honeyed ripeness. The St-Laurent bottling has been rather sweet, while the Chailloux has the most typically Sauvignon fruit, with spicy gooseberry flavours.

DAGUENEAU, DIDIER

St-Andelain, 58150 Pouilly

Vineyard: 17 acres

Production: 40,000 bottles of Chailloux; 8,000 bottles of
Silex; 4,000 bottles of Pur Sang

CUVÉE SILEX, CUVÉE PUR SANG

Quality: 🍇🍇🍇🍇🍇   Price: ★★★★

OTHERS

Quality: 🍇🍇🍇🍇   Price: ★★★

Given that Dagueneau has only been making wine since 1982,
his impact has been astonishing, especially since it was only in
1985 that he began to employ skin contact and ageing in new
oak on a regular basis. Fanatical about quality, he is as attentive
to his vines as to cellar techniques. Despite his advocacy of
hand-picking, *triage*, yields rarely in excess of 45 hectolitres per
hectare (3 tons per acre), skin contact, long *débourbage*, barrel-
fermentation and *batonnage*, he does not make wine to a formula. Sometimes the grapes are de-stalked, but not always; the
length of the *débourbage* can vary considerably, as can the
maturation of the wine.

His standard wine, Chailloux, is unwooded, ripe and fruity,
impeccably balanced. Silex, made from old vines, is entirely
fermented and aged in new oak. Pur Sang, first made in 1988, is
almost as sumptuous, except that part of the wine is aged in tank
or large new casks. Some of his other labels can be confusing.
Buisson-Menard, not made every year, is a blend of old and
younger vines, given minimal skin contact, but left on the fine
lees and not racked. In the poor vintage of 1987, Dagueneau
made no Silex, but produced a Vieilles Vignes bottling from the
same vines, with only a portion of the crop vinified in wood.

Dagueneau's wines are expensive, but they are hand-crafted
by a man possessed. We must wait another ten years to know
whether the claims he makes for them will be borne out, but

given their youthful concentration and elegance, it is reasonable to give him the benefit of the doubt.

The 1988 vintage is probably the finest of the 1980s for Dagueneau, who also made wonderfully rich 1989s and 1990s from yields of only 2.5 tons per acre. Their wealth of extract compensates for a slight lack of acidity. In 1989 and 1990 he also made small quantities of late-picked wine with 14.5° alcohol and 5° residual sugar.

DAGUENEAU, SERGE

Les Berthiers, 58150 Pouilly
Vineyard: 37 acres
Production: 70,000 bottles
Quality: 🍇🍇–🍇🍇🍇   Price: ★★–★★★

A tasting of the current vintage in Serge Dagueneau's impeccable modern cellars can be exhausting, for each tank is different, reflecting the many different soils on which his vines are planted. He enjoys experimentation, and has produced two *cuvées* of an identical wine, one using indigenous yeasts and the other using cultivated yeasts; apart from the difference in aroma and flavour, the wines were separated by 0.6° in alcohol. His best *cuvée*, Clos des Chaudoux, is made from grapes grown on *marne* soils and given skin contact. Dagueneau favours a rounded style, which makes his wines less exciting than I would expect from a winemaker of his skill and subtlety. But they are very fruity and age well.

LADOUCETTE (CHÂTEAU DE NOZET)

58150 Pouilly
Vineyard: 128 acres
Production: 1.5 million bottles

BARON DE L

Quality: 🍇🍇🍇🍇   Price: ★★★★★

OTHERS

Quality: 🍇🍇   Price: ★★

It was Patrick de Ladoucette who established the modern reputation of Pouilly-Fumé. Only a small portion of the production
derives from his own vineyards at Nozet, which have been in
Ladoucette ownership for two centuries, yet given the quantity
of wine released every year, the quality is quite high. Every
region needs what the French call a *locomotive* to tug the rest of
the appellation behind it, and in Pouilly this vehicle is the
estate-grown luxury *cuvée* 'Baron de L', first made in 1973 and
only produced in good vintages. Precisely why this excellent
concentrated wine is so expensive it is hard to know, but it has
certainly demonstrated that long-lived wine of very high quality
can be made from Sauvignon in the Loire. Indeed, Ladoucette's
ordinary wine has similar properties: a 1953 I sampled in 1987
was buttery and rounded and still very drinkable.

Ladoucette is also a major producer of Sancerre (under the
Comte Lafond label) and Sauvignon de Touraine (under the
Baron Briare label).

MASSON-BLONDELET

58150 Pouilly

Vineyard: 30 acres

Production: 80,000–100,000 bottles; 4,000–8,000 bottles of
  Tradition Cullus

Quality: 🍇🍇🍇–🍇🍇🍇🍇   Price: ★★–★★★

In 1975 Jean-Michel Masson teamed up with his in-laws to
produce wines from their combined properties. These wines

are sold under a number of labels: a generic Pouilly-Fumé; Les Angelots (his father-in-law's vines, mostly old); Villa Paulus; the two single-vineyard *crus* Les Bascoins and Les Criots; and a luxury *cuvée* called Tradition Cullus. The vines at Les Criots are young, whereas Les Bascoins's vines are up to fifty years old. Tradition Cullus is made from old vines and only from the first pressings; first produced in 1985, it has since 1986 been fermented partly in new oak. The 1987 tastes over-oaked, and the 1988 vintage is far superior.

Masson is not keen on skin contact, but leaves the wines on the lees for a few months. He is clearly a dedicated winemaker and an enthusiast for the wines of Pouilly, but a combination of partial malolactic fermentation and excessive use of treatments such as filtration and chilling appears to rob the wines of some of their vigour. Nevertheless, Les Bascoins is often a well-scented and elegant wine, and Tradition has a sweet, oaky richness that is attractive although, like many of Masson's wines, it sometimes lacks persistence of flavour.

SAGET, GUY

58150 Pouilly
Vineyard: 44 acres
Production: 2.5 million bottles
Quality: 🍇–🍇🍇 Price: **

Saget are the major *négociant* of Pouilly, and only a tiny percentage of their wines derives from their own vineyards. Numerous labels are used, and a blend of wines from selected sites is sold as Les Roches. The Saget wines are clearly commercial and lack character, especially on the nose. They are rounded and will offend no one. Les Roches is distinctly better than the ordinary bottlings.

QUINCY AND REUILLY

Quincy is a small appellation with 270 acres of vines, all of it Sauvignon, planted on gravelly and sandy soil close to the River Cher. The climate is cooler than in Sancerre or Pouilly, so grapes take longer to ripen and occasionally fail to do so properly. In my experience the wines are lacklustre. Pierre Mardon and the large Domaine de Maison Blanche produce acceptable rounded wines, but neither is outstanding and both seem to lack verve.

Reuilly, with only 148 acres under vine, of which 60 per cent are planted with Sauvignon, is even smaller. Like Pouilly and Quincy, Reuilly is prone to frost damage, so production can be variable. The vineyards are ranged along the banks of the rivers Cher, Arnon and Théols. I have encountered few white wines from Reuilly that are not mediocre or clumsy. Leading producers include Gérard Cordier and Jean-Michel Sorbe, who markets a small quantity of Sauvignon fermented and aged in new oak: an attractive wine, though lacking in varietal character. Claude Lafond is probably the best winemaker in the appellation.

SANCERRE

The best known of the Loire Sauvignon regions, Sancerre is also the largest and most picturesque. The almost 4,000 acres of vineyards are spread among fourteen communes on a variety of soils, and divided among about 300 growers. The principal communes are Sancerre itself, Bué, Crézancy, Ménétréol, St-Satur, Ste-Gemme, Sury-en-Vaux and Verdigny. Vines are also found in Bannay, Menetou-Ratel, Montigny, Thauveney, Veaugues and Vinon. The vineyards are 80 per cent Sauvignon, the remainder Pinot Noir. Because of the commercial importance of Sauvignon here, Sancerre is in the peculiar position of having most of its best sites occupied by Sauvignon rather than the aristocratic Pinot.

The following soil types are prevalent: *marne argileuse*, the heaviest and most widespread soil (also known as *terres blanches*); *caillottes*, a chalk and gravel soil; to the west *silex* (flint). Often wines made from different soils are blended, but many of the best producers also make single-vineyard wines that demonstrate the subtleties of specific *terroirs*. Sury and Verdigny, for example, are dominated by *marne*, while Chavignol and Bué are *caillottes* communes. There is slightly more limestone in Bué than Chavignol, and consequently the latter wines have a better reputation for longevity. (Chavignol is also the source of a famous goat cheese, *crottin*, which happens to be matched deliciously by Sancerre.) Flint soils give backward wines that need at least a year in bottle, while the faster-maturing *caillottes* wines have the greatest aromatic charm and finesse. The soil is less deep than in Pouilly and some growers fear that over-exploitation may exhaust some of the best sites, even though between 1955 and 1985 the AC region of Sancerre has increased threefold.

Growers with holdings in the best vineyards used to be able to specify them on their labels. *Négociants* abused the practice, which is now outlawed. Consequently producers of impeccable reputation such as Jean-Max Roger and Henri Bourgeois may only indicate single-vineyard bottlings by initials such as 'MD' for Monts Damnés. This hardly helps the consumer, who cannot be expected to know that 'CM' means Chêne Marchand.

From the ramparts of Sancerre itself there are excellent views of the undulating countryside. Many of the best vineyards are remarkably steep, and around Bué, for example, you can see wide-flanked hills that plunge into deep valleys. The most racy and elegant wines often come from higher up the slopes. The steepness accounts for the fact that machine-harvesting is less prevalent here than in Pouilly.

Sancerre is still a region of small family-owned properties. In 1979, when a census was last made, the average property was no more than 5.88 acres. The local cooperative and *négociants* mop up much of the production from small growers, but innumerable individual growers know that with the relatively high prices that can be obtained for Sancerre it makes sense for them to control production at all stages. As in Pouilly, a number of leading growers, including Pierre Archambault, Henri Bourgeois, Alphonse Mellot and Joseph Balland-Chapuis, have been experimenting with barrel-fermentation and oak-ageing.

In addition to the wines listed below, I have enjoyed wines from other producers such as J. L. Bonnin, Bernard Crochet, Domaine Pastou, André Dezat, Raimbault-Pineau and Jean Reverdy.

ARCHAMBAULT, PIERRE

Verdigny, 18300 Sancerre
Vineyard: 60 acres of Sauvignon
Quality: 🍇🍇🍇 (Carte d'Or 🍇🍇🍇🍇)　　　Price: ★★

The headquarters of Pierre Archambault's complex operation is the Cave de la Perrière, a huge natural cave which he has successfully transformed into a tourist attraction where, not surprisingly, his own wines may be tasted and bought. He produces Sancerre under a number of labels, including the single-vineyard Domaine de Bannon, Clos La Perrière (a fifteen-acre vineyard) and a luxury *cuvée* called Carte d'Or, made from hand-picked grapes from certain steep slopes in Crézancy. Archambault supplements his own production by buying in grapes, must and, on occasion, wine.

Archambault favours a very light maceration and slow fermentation that can last up to one month. The Clos La Perrière can be a fairly abrasive wine, grassy and bracing. Carte d'Or, as one would expect, has more weight and richness of fruit, and is a very good wine indeed.

*

BALLAND-CHAPUIS, JOSEPH

Bué, 18300 Sancerre

Vineyard: 32 acres of Sauvignon

Production: 100,000 bottles

CUVÉE PIERRE

Quality: 🍇🍇🍇🍇   Price: ★★★★

OTHERS

Quality: 🍇🍇🍇   Price: ★★

From his vineyards in Bué and four other communes, Balland produces a generic Sancerre, Le Chatillet, as well as Le Vallon. The grapes from the celebrated Chêne Marchand vineyard are vinified in *barriques*, of which half are new, as are Vendange Tardive (late harvest) wines in appropriate years such as 1989 and 1990. These are called Cuvée Pierre, and are only made from overripe late-picked grapes. Yields are astonishingly low, at 1 ton per acre, and the must is fermented in new Allier *barriques* and barrel-aged for eight months. The wines are massively structured and very rich. The wines seem to have sufficient concentration of flavour to support the new oak, though only time will tell.

Cuvée Thibault is a Vieilles Vignes wine of fine concentration. Balland-Chapuis also offers wines from Pouilly and a Sauvignon from Coteaux de Giennois, including a most peculiar *barrique*-aged Vendange Tardive called Cuvée Marguerite-Marceau.

BOURGEOIS, HENRI

Chavignol, 18300 Sancerre

Vineyard: 100 acres of Sauvignon

Production: 700,000 bottles

Quality: 🍇🍇🍇–🍇🍇🍇🍇 (La Bourgeoise 🍇🍇🍇🍇🍇)

Price: ★★–★★★

This family firm is now in its tenth generation. In addition to its own excellent vineyards, Bourgeois buy in grapes and must on a regular contract basis. Vigne Blanche is their basic Sancerre; grown on *caillottes* soil it is tart and racy and best drunk young. Grande Réserve, also known as Les Baronnes, is selected from particular sites that give the balance they seek in this wine. Monts Damnés in Verdigny is a celebrated south-facing single vineyard. La Porte de l'Abbaye is made from vines grown on flinty soils, and has a strong mineral flavour I particularly like. La Bourgeoise is their finest wine, made from fifty-year-old vines with low yields grown on south-west facing slopes. Bourgeois also produce a wine called Étienne Henri, a *cuvée* of La Bourgeoise aged in oak barrels, some of which are new. I find the oakiness of this wine less exciting than the rich, firmly focused brilliance of La Bourgeoise.

Most of the crop is machine-picked, centrifuged, then fermented very slowly. Malolactic fermentation is avoided. La Bourgeoise can be aged for some years without problems. Grand Réserve is less rich and concentrated, but perhaps has more typically exuberant Sauvignon fruit.

CAVE DES VINS DE SANCERRE

18300 Sancerre

Production: 1.4 million bottles

Quality: 🍇   Price: ★★

No fewer than 165 growers now participate in this well-equipped cooperative, and 85 per cent of the production is of Sauvignon. The cooperative rather than the growers takes care of most of the vinification. A number of different labels are used, with the Duc de Tarente brand at the top of the range. Many importers such as British supermarkets purchase the wine under their own labels; the code 'Bottled by 18–42' is the only way in which the source the wine is identifiable. Unfortunately the cooperative indulges in the practice of using the grower's name on the label if the grower has supplied all the grapes or wine and the product is treated separately. This gives the purchaser the impression that he or she is buying a grower's wine when this is not the case.

CROCHET, LUCIEN

Bué, 18300 Sancerre
Vineyard: 56 acres of Sauvignon
Quality: 🍇🍇🍇   Price: ★★

Although Crochet buys in grapes and must from other sources, his best wines come from his own hand-picked vineyards at Chêne Marchand (12 acres) and Grand Chemarin. His Clos du Chêne Marchand is one of the most complex and refined Sancerres available, and his Cuvée Prestige LC, a rich, creamy wine, is made from the oldest vines, which yield just over 2 tons per acre. His wines are made in steel tanks and bottled in the late spring.

LAPORTE

St-Satur, 18300 Sancerre
Vineyard: 35 acres of Sauvignon
Production: 200,000 bottles
Quality: 🍇🍇🍇 (Domaine du Rochoy 🍇🍇🍇🍇)
Price: ★★

This domaine, owned until 1987 by René Laporte, has been acquired by Henri Bourgeois. The holdings generate three different wines: Domaine de la Cresle, Domaine du Rochoy and, at Chavignol, Clos de la Comtesse. La Cresle is made partly from bought-in grapes. For my taste, Rochoy is the best wine thanks to the perfect location of this flinty vineyard. Recent vintages suggest that Bourgeois will maintain and possibly surpass Laporte's own high standards.

MELLOT, ALPHONSE

> 18300 Sancerre
>
> Vineyard: 100 acres of Sauvignon
>
> Production: 230,000 bottles, including 50,000 Cuvée Edmond
>
> CUVÉE EDMOND
>
> Quality: 🍇🍇🍇🍇   Price: ★★★
>
> OTHERS
>
> Quality: 🍇🍇🍇   Price: ★★

Alphonse Mellot is a meticulous and impassioned winemaker, committed to keeping yields low and to picking his grapes by hand. His estate Sancerre, La Moussière, is full-bodied and flavoury, but a touch loose-limbed.

Since 1987 Mellot has produced an oak-aged wine called Cuvée Edmond. This is made from forty-year-old vines and half the must is fermented and aged in new oak. Whereas yields for his ordinary Sancerre are around 4 tons per acre, those for Cuvée Edmond are only 2.5. In rich years such as 1988, 1989 and 1990 the wine maintains its Sauvignon typicity, and the oak gives the wine structure and complexity rather than a woody character.

MELLOT, JOSEPH

> 18 rue Saint Martin, 18300 Sancerre
>
> Vineyard: 62 acres of Sauvignon

LA CHÂTELAINE
Quality: 🍇🍇🍇   Price: ★★★
OTHERS
Quality: 🍇🍇   Price: ★★

Joseph Mellot is both grower and *négociant*, buying in grapes to supply 65 per cent of his production. His Menetou-Salon (a good example) and Quincy are both made from bought-in grapes, but his Pouilly-Fumé is made from the 17 acres of vineyards he owns in that appellation. Three Sancerres are made: La Gravelière, La Châtellenie from twenty-year-old vines, and the prestige *cuvée* of La Châtelaine de Joseph Mellot. La Châtelaine is the best wine, made from vines twenty-five years old; 30 per cent is aged in new oak and from 1990 onwards that same proportion will also be fermented in new oak. The wine has weight and richness, but not at the expense of vigour and varietal character.

MILLÉRIOUX, PAUL

Champtin, Crézancy, 18300 Sancerre
Vineyard: 27 acres of Sauvignon
Production: 72,000 bottles
Quality: 🍇🍇   Price: ★★

Millérioux runs a small up-to-date commercial winery to reliable standards. His best vineyard is the Clos du Roy, 5 acres of limestone soil; his other single-vineyard wine is Côtes de Champtin, higher ground that produces more robust, fatter wines. Clos du Roy is a dependable wine, though it often develops vegetal flavours with bottle-age, and the acidity is relatively low.

PRIEUR (PAUL) ET FILS

Verdigny, 18300 Sancerre

Vineyard: 16 acres of Sauvignon

Production: 50,000 bottles

Quality: 🍇   Price: ★★

This family estate is now run by Didier and Philippe Prieur.
The soil is 60 per cent *caillottes* and 40 per cent *marne*. The best
holdings are on Monts Damnés, and much of the harvesting is
done by hand. The Prieurs seem particularly successful in less
good vintages such as 1984 and 1987, and even a 1972,
although past its best, had not lost its fruit fifteen years later.
The wines lack some concentration, possibly because of the
generous yields.

REVERDY, BERNARD

Chaudoux, Verdigny, 18300 Sancerre

Vineyard: 17 acres of Sauvignon

Production: 50,000 bottles

Quality: 🍇   Price: ★★

Reverdy and his son Noël make two good Sancerres: a generic
wine and the single-vineyard La Perrière. The harvesting is
manual and there is never any malolactic fermentation, not
even in high-acidity vintages such as 1972. The wines are light
and clean and well made.

RIFFAULT, PIERRE ET ÉTIENNE

Domaine des Trois Pressoirs, Chaudoux, Verdigny, 18300
Sancerre

Vineyard: 25 acres of Sauvignon

Production: 80,000 bottles

Quality: 🍇🍇   Price: ★★

The vineyards of this small family estate are spread around a number of communes, with *caillottes* soil at Verdigny and *silex* at St-Satur and Ménétréol. All harvesting is still done by hand. Vinification is standard for Sancerre – no skin contact, *débourbage*, tank fermentation at 15 °C, bentonite fining during fermentation, no malolactic fermentation – and the Riffaults aim for a wine that is not too high in acidity and drinkable young. The wines are flavoury but lack a little excitement.

ROGER, JEAN-MAX

Bué, 18300 Sancerre

Vineyard: 42 acres of Sauvignon

Production: 200,000 bottles

Quality: 🍇🍇   Price: ★★

Roger, who also makes a good Menetou-Salon, produces Sancerre in a number of different bottlings such as Les Caillottes, Grand Chemarin (GC) and Chêne Marchand (CM). He also makes 5,000 bottles of Vieilles Vignes, his most concentrated, and expensive, wine. His Chêne Marchand is very good too. Roger's wines are exuberant and often racy, yet there is something neutral about them, as though the fruitiness of Sauvignon were being deliberately suppressed. Roger is devoted to fermentation at low temperatures and to heavy bentonite fining, both of which might well contribute to his wines' lack of character and of aromatic complexity. On the other hand, they age well.

*

VACHERON

> 18300 Sancerre
> Vineyard: 45 acres of Sauvignon
> Production: 200,000 bottles
> Quality: 🍇🍇–🍇🍇🍇   Price: ★★

At this well-known property, Denis Vacheron takes care of the vineyards and his brother Jean-Louis works in the cellars. All their wines come from their own vineyards, which are planted on two soils: limestone and flint. The grapes are hand-picked. The wines appear under a variety of labels, but they signify nothing and are no more than the favoured marketing devices of different clients. Vacheron make an elegant, medium-bodied, rather soft Sancerre which is good rather than first-class.

VATAN, ANDRÉ

> Chaudoux, Verdigny, 18300 Sancerre
> Vineyard: 16 acres of Sauvignon
> Production: 60,000 bottles
> Quality: 🍇🍇🍇   Price: ★★

André Vatan is one of ten sons of Jean Vatan, himself a veteran winemaker now in retirement. Although the vines are planted in all the major soil types of Sancerre, the lots are always blended. The harvest is manual, and the only variation in the standard Sauvignon vinification is that Vatan prefers a slightly higher fermentation temperature than most of his fellow winemakers. The wines are lively and tangy, and though as yet they seem to lack the sheer fruity exuberance of his father's wines, they may well reach that exemplary standard soon.

OTHER SAUVIGNON BLANC FROM THE LOIRE

In recent years the Sauvignon grape has crept westwards from Sancerre and Pouilly and been planted extensively in 2,800 acres of eastern Touraine, where it thrives under its own appellation as Sauvignon de Touraine and constitutes 60 per cent of all white wine from the region. Yields are higher here than in Sancerre, and the wines tend to be more dilute. They are also much less expensive, and many wine lovers would rather pay a modest sum for a modest but fresh and lively wine than almost twice the price for a wine that may often be only marginally better. The basic yield for Sauvignon de Touraine is 60 hectolitres per hectare (4 tons per acre), but officially sanctioned increases have led in recent vintages to an average yield of 69 hectolitres per hectare. Sub-regions are developing within the Touraine, with the area around Oisly believed to produce the most elegant wines, and the region along the River Cher around Meusnes giving weightier wines from flint soils. Cooperatives are quite powerful and *négociants* find the area a source of inexpensive Sauvignon, but the Touraine is still dominated by small, unpretentious properties.

In addition to the estates given entries below, there are also good wines to be found at Domaine des Acacias at Chemery, where Charles Guerbois succeeded in 1989 in producing a piquant late-harvest Sauvignon with 55 grams per litre residual sugar. At Meusnes, Jacky and Philippe Augis make a spicy, rounded, but heavy-handed Sauvignon, sold either as Touraine or Valençay, for rapid consumption. Thierry Michaud, Hubert Sinson at Meusnes, Joel Delaunay, Jacques Delaunay (Domaine de Sablons at Pouillé), and Guy Mardon (Domaine du Pré Baron at Oisly) are other good producers.

Other appellations with significant plantations of Sauvignon include Cheverny, Coteaux du Giennois, Haut-Poitou, Valençay, and the more amorphous Vin de Pays du Jardin de France and Vin de Pays du Cher. Valençay, with a mere 100 acres of vines, is virtually indistinguishable from Sauvignon de Touraine, as the borders of the appellations meet. Coteaux du Giennois stretches from Cosne, close to Pouilly, to Gien itself further north. Only 250 acres are planted, some of them with Sauvignon, but I have never tasted one that cried out to be recommended. Tiny Cheverny, in eastern Touraine, is potentially more interesting, although the leading white grape here is Romorantin rather than Sauvignon. An excellent producer is Domaine des Huards at Cour-Cheverny.

The Haut-Poitou appellation is the virtual monopoly of the excellent local cooperative. Jardin de France is the jolly name given to the *vin de pays* of the entire region, and the wines sold under that name or as Vin de Pays du Cher will be simple indeed. One of the few outstanding Jardin de France wines comes from Domaine des Saulaies at Faye in the Anjou, where Philippe Leblanc makes a light, clean and vigorously grassy Sauvignon. Finally, Sauvignon is grown at St-Pourçain, well to the south of Pouilly, but the wine is often blended with Chardonnay or with the local Tresallier grape.

BARBOU, MAURICE

AC Sauvignon de Touraine

Domaine des Corbillières, 41700 Oisly
Vineyard: 30 acres of Sauvignon
Production: 80,000 bottles
Quality: 👿   Price: ★

Maurice Barbou's grandfather Fabel achieved local fame as the first person to plant Sauvignon in eastern Touraine. His wines became so popular that other growers soon followed suit. All the same, until 1961 he was the only grower to sell Sauvignon in bottle to his customers.

The soil here, sand over clay, is fairly light, giving straightforward fruity wines. The wines are attractively modest in alcohol, at about 11.5°, yet have a vibrant acidity. The Barbous are aiming for wines that are fruity and rounded and not especially aromatic. I find the wines well made, zesty and very good value.

BUISSE, PAUL

AC Sauvignon de Touraine

41400 Montrichard

Production: 24,000 bottles of Cristal

CRISTAL

Quality: 🍇   Price: ★

Buisse is a leading Loire *négociant* who now sells 1.5 million bottles each year. He makes three brands of Sauvignon: a generic wine, a Cuvée Prestige and Sélection Cristal. The first two are blends of bought-in wines and not of especial interest; Cristal is vinified by Buisse's team from must bought from contract growers in Oisly. The wine is aged *sur lie* for some months before bottling. Buisse is producing lean, elegant wines that can be drunk rapidly. Cristal is easily his best wine: dependable, medium-bodied, cleanly made if far from sensational.

CAVE COOPÉRATIVE DU HAUT-POITOU

AC Haut-Poitou

86170 Neuville-de-Poitou

Quality: 🍇🍇   Price: ★

The Haut-Poitou is about 15 miles north of Poitiers, and is dominated by the excellent cooperative, which is responsible for about 95 per cent of the production. Until recently a VDQS region, it was promoted in 1989 to full AC status. Over

1,800 acres are entitled to the appellation, and Chardonnay and Sauvignon are extensively cultivated. For many years the Sauvignon has been an inexpensive yet very dependable wine. In style it is pungent, and it has a tangy, almost tart acidity reminiscent of grapefruit. The 1989, sweeter and spicier than most, is atypical. Those used to more rounded styles may find this wine somewhat extreme.

CONFRÉRIE DES VIGNERONS DE OISLY ET THESÉE

AC Sauvignon de Touraine

Oisly, 41700 Contres

Production: 450,000 bottles

Quality: 🍇–🍇🍇🍇 Price: ★

At this outstanding cooperative, founded in 1960, fifty-two members cultivate 765 acres on both sides of the River Cher. About 40 per cent of the production consists of Sauvignon, and the proportion has been rising constantly. Half the wine is vinified by the growers and half by the cooperative, but the entire process is closely monitored by the technical directors. The growers participate in quality-control tastings of their own wines, so it is theoretically possible for a grower to reject his own wine.

There are four grades of Sauvignon, and many of them appear under a variety of labels. Since the cooperative is very wary of identifying which *cuvée* is bottled under which label, it is impossible to make critical judgements about the production in any detail. Nevertheless, my tastings clearly establish that the overall quality is very good, and that the top grade, under whatever guise it leaves the winery, is deliciously fruity and a serious rival to Sancerre.

GIRARD, CHRISTIAN ET ANNIE

AC Sauvignon de Touraine

Phages, Thenay, 41400 Montrichard
Vineyard: 12 acres of Sauvignon
Production: 35,000 bottles
Quality: 🍇🍇   Price: ★

This is a small family property that despite its rustic aspect produces fruity wines of considerable character. There are advantages to cellars that lack all the latest technology; Girard's wines are not stripped of all their character by excessive filtration and other treatments. Although the wines are light they do have good acidity, even in hot vintages such as 1989.

MARIONNET, HENRY

AC Sauvignon de Touraine

Domaine de la Charmoise, Soings, 41230 Mur-de-Sologne
Production: 80,000 bottles
Quality: 🍇🍇   Price: ★

Marionnet is one of the few growers in the Touraine who picks his grapes manually, even though his vineyards are laid out in a way that would make mechanical harvesting simple enough. Yields are low, largely because of the poor sand and gravel soil, and he picks as late as possible so as to avoid pungent catty aromas. Half his crop receives a whole-grape maceration for three days in order to extract aromas. Only indigenous yeasts are used, and there is no fining or chilling of the wine, which is bottled early and intended to be drunk young. Although the fruit is excellent, this rounded Sauvignon does lack a little excitement.

In 1988 Marionnet made a late-harvest wine from selected bunches, and the wine was fermented to dryness.

OCTAVIE, DOMAINE

AC Sauvignon de Touraine

Marcé, 41700 Oisly

Vineyard: 18 acres of Sauvignon

Production: 50,000 bottles

Quality: 👑👑   Price: ★

This family property is run by Jean-Claude Barbeillon, who looks for good maturity in the grapes and uses indigenous yeasts only. The wine spends a month or so *sur lie*. The result of this careful vinification is a well-balanced, rounded, vigorous wine with good fruit.

VIGNERONS DE LA VALLÉE DU CHER

AC Sauvignon de Touraine

Production: 200,000 bottles of Chervignon

Quality: 👑👑   Price: ★

This well-known cooperative buys in 90 per cent of its production as wine, and the remaining 10 per cent as grapes. Its Sauvignon is marketed under the name Chervignon, and it is a very light, racy, but decidedly fruity wine, ideal as an aperitif. It should be drunk very young.

Other Regions

Sauvignon Blanc, and to a lesser extent Sémillon, are widely planted in other French regions. South of Bergerac, the Côtes de Duras has a similar white-grape mix to Entre-Deux-Mers.

The cooperative, under its brand name Berticot, produces a pure Sauvignon as well as a more traditional blend. The Domaine de Durand and Domaine de Ferrant have a good reputation for Sauvignon, and I have enjoyed simple lemony Sauvignons from Château La Pilar. The Australian-trained winemaker Hugh Ryman is active at a number of small estates in south-west France, such as Domaine du Colombet and Domaine de Petitot in Côtes de Duras, and the results are fresh, lively, modestly priced wines of above average quality. The Côtes de Duras also produces lightly sweet wines from Sémillon and Muscadelle, but I have not encountered them. White wines are in the majority in this region, while further south in Gascony the Buzet appellation, which has a similar grape mix, only produces a small quantity of simple Sauvignon-based whites. The Vignerons de Buzet cooperative produces attractive examples.

Quite a few *vins de pays* are made from pure Sauvignon. I have come across acceptable but undistinguished examples from around Toulouse with the regional appellation Vin de Pays du Comte Tolosan. As new technology reaches southern France, more and more Sauvignons – simple but well made and not always identified as Sauvignon – are being marketed. In Provence more and more estates are planting Sauvignon, but it is usually blended with grapes such as Clairette and Ugni. The progressive organic estate of Terres Blanches in the Les Baux area within the Coteaux d'Aix appellation experimented in 1989 with fermenting overripe Sauvignon in mostly new *barriques*. The proprietors marketed 1,500 bottles as Cuvée Anais, and did not take offence when I found the wine less than enjoyable.

A more significant production is found midway between Chablis and Sancerre in the region entitled to the Sauvignon de St-Bris VDQS appellation. The principal villages are St-Bris itself, Chitry and Irancy. The climate is more extreme than in the Loire, with hotter summers and colder winters. Even before phylloxera, Sauvignon vines were planted here, but they only acquired commercial importance after the Second World War. Even so, the plantation, with about 200 acres in production, is small. The vineyards are divided among about fifty growers, many of whom sell to *négociants*. Average yields are at least 4 tons per acre. Despite its somewhat anomalous identity as the only Sauvignon permitted within Burgundy, the wine is popular, especially in export markets. Nevertheless growers would rather plant Aligoté, which can also be used, unlike Sauvignon, in the production of sparkling wine.

Among recent vintages, 1988 and 1989 were both excellent; many 1990s are less satisfactory because of low acidity. Because many producers practise malolactic fermentation to produce softer styles, few examples age gracefully in bottle. In general the wines are attractive and lively, though many are dilute in flavour and anonymous in character. I have encountered good examples from Bersan, J. M. Brocard, Serge Goissot, E. Lavallée, Michel Sorin, Philippe Sorin and J. P. Tabit.

ISRAEL

Israelis do not consume much wine, so perhaps it is not surprising that many Israeli winemakers and consumers simply do not realize how appalling most of their wines are. There is a good deal of Sauvignon planted, mostly in totally unsuitable locations. The large Carmel winery, for instance, operates from coastal vineyards that are high-yielding and extremely hot, thus guaranteeing low acidity. Even Carmel's superior grade, its Selected Sauvignon Blanc, is dire.

Some years ago, however, a group of kibbutzim were inspired to plant vineyards in the remote Golan Heights, where the climate can be positively wintry. The first wine sold, in 1983, was a Sauvignon Blanc, and subsequent vintages proved that Israel was indeed capable of making good wines. The Golan Heights Winery hired Californian oenologists and winemakers, so the wines do have Californian echoes. The Sauvignon receives skin contact, is cool-fermented, and ages in *barriques*. The long, cool, growing season gives the wine a tartness quite lacking in the coastal wines, but it can also give a grapefruit character that may be too much of a good thing when combined with the slight bitterness imparted by the oak-ageing. In the Israeli context, the Golan Heights Sauvignon is excellent, but other New World-style Sauvignons continue to offer better quality and value.

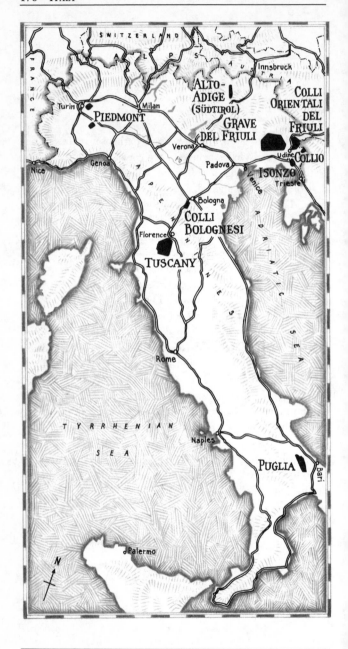

ITALY

In terms of its wine culture, Italy has become a nation of strategists. Italy has wonderful native grape varieties, yet many growers feel compelled to cultivate the more familiar noble varieties. The consequence has been a nationwide rash of Cabernet Sauvignons and Chardonnays, and very fine some of them are. There are also occasional outcrops of Sauvignon Blanc. Sauvignon has been planted for decades in certain northern areas such as the Alto-Adige and Friuli, but it is a newcomer to Tuscany and Piedmont.

In the Alto-Adige (or Südtirol, as the German-speaking locals call it) Sauvignon was first planted in the 1950s, and the best results have been obtained around Terlan. But the quantities are tiny. Only 42 acres are planted with Sauvignon, with 27 of them in Terlan, and only eight producers vinify the grape. Cooperatives, notably that of Terlan itself, make 60 per cent of the wine, and their share of the market is growing thanks to the generous subsidies they receive. Private wineries find it difficult to compete with the cooperatives' prices, especially as Sauvignon is easily the most expensive grape variety of the Alto-Adige. Many of the cooperatives' Sauvignons lack character and seem to have a dash of added acidity I find disagreeable. In addition to the growers listed below, Herbert Tiefenbrunner makes a firm, full-flavoured Sauvignon that lacks a little vigour.

The best wines can age reasonably well. The 1985s tend to be low in acidity. 1986 was good but not exceptional, and 1987 was a fine year for whites. 1988 was probably the best vintage of the 1980s, but 1989 was no better than the 1986. 1990 was good.

In Emilia-Romagna, the Vallania family's Terre Rosse estate has established a reputation for Sauvignon produced within the DOC Colli Bolognesi. It is a good, cleanly made, grassy wine with medium length, but hardly outstanding. Gian Matteo Baldi at Castellucio di Modigliano has since 1981 been making a Sauvignon called Ronco del Re which is aged in Limousin *barriques* for up to a year. It is a big, heavy, oaky wine, lacking in finesse, produced in infinitesimal quantities and absurdly overpriced.

In Friuli, in north-eastern Italy, Sauvignon is found under a number of appellations: Colli Orientali, Collio, Isonzo and Grave del Friuli. Although many of the wines from Grave del Friuli are routine efforts with little varietal character or concentration of fruit, the best wines from the other zones are the finest Sauvignons of Italy: flavoury, aromatic, and with a steely backbone. With very few exceptions they are unwooded and none the worse for it, allowing the crisp fruit and firm acidity to express themselves. Since 1984 Friuli has enjoyed a number of successful vintages, though 1987 was disappointing in Collio. The 1990 is exceptionally rich and fat, the 1991 leaner but more elegant.

In addition to the producers given entries below, I have found well-made Sauvignons (DOC Isonzo) with plenty of charm and light, zippy fruit from Angoris, both under their own label and under the Le Marne label. Very good wines are made by Livio Felluga, who have 50 acres of Sauvignon. Tangy gooseberryish versions, vigorous if lacking concentration, are made by Le Fredis and Pighin (both DOC Grave del Friuli). From Collio come a crisp, herbaceous Sauvignon by Gradnik, unmistakably varietal but lacking depth of flavour; spicy, slightly anonymous Sauvignon from Russiz Superiore; and a pungent unoaked Sauvignon from Venica that I prefer to their costly *barrique*-aged Cero.

Very little Sauvignon is planted in Piedmont. The tiny estate of Colle Manora near Monferrato makes 6,000 bottles of fresh, lively, unwooded wine with exemplary varietal character. Production will eventually be doubled. Angelo Gaja, Piedmont's most celebrated winemaker, has planted 2.5 acres with a few Bordeaux clones of Sauvignon, but has not yet released the wine, even though it has been made since 1986. The style is Graves-like, with maceration, barrel-fermentation and barrel-ageing for three months. One third of the *barriques* are new, the remainder one year old.

In Tuscany, home of Italy's oenological avant-garde, a few growers dabble with Sauvignon. Fattoria di Ama first made one in 1988 from sixteen-year-old vines that were grafted over in 1986. It is an unwooded wine, spicy with quite good length. In Montepulciano, Avignonesi grafted some vines over to Sauvignon in 1986; production will eventually reach 25,000 bottles. Initially unwooded the wine, La Vignola, was more expensive than their *barrique*-aged Chardonnay. It is now a barrel-fermented wine of considerable complexity, but remains overpriced.

The great Italian winemaker Maurizio Castelli (who is responsible for Torniello from Castello di Volpaia (q.v.)) has been making a mere 3,750 bottles of Spartito, a lightish Sauvignon blended with 8 per cent Trebbiano, at the Chianti estate of Castellare. Another Chianti estate, Ricasoli, has launched a wine called Nebbiano, a blend of 60 per cent Sauvignon Blanc and 40 per cent Riesling Italico. I have not tasted it, but it sounds bizarre. Further south in Montalcino, Villa Banfi have since 1987 been producing a Sauvignon called Fumaio, aged for four months in French *barriques*. I find it far too oaky and lacking in freshness and varietal character.

In the Veneto, Sauvignon is usually vinified in a very commercial style, giving thin, hard, dilute wines that lack varietal definition. Typical examples come from houses such as Ca' Donini and Pasqua and are hard to recommend.

In Umbria, Antinori use 60 per cent Sauvignon in their Borro della Sala wine (200,000 bottles) from Orvieto, blended with Trebbiano and Pinot Blanc. The Sauvignon is quite prominent on the nose, but on the palate the wine lacks vigour and structure. Antinori also use some Sauvignon in their botrytized Muffato, a charming, creamy wine that spends one year in oak.

In Puglia, a very hot region, a number of producers such as Vallone have planted Sauvignon. Andria's Vigna al Monte Sauvignon is smartly packaged but oily and hot on the palate.

*

BORGO CONVENTI

DOC Isonzo

> 34070 Farra d'Isonzo, Gorizia
> Production: 12,000 bottles
> Quality: 🍇🍇🍇   Price: ★★

This estate, revived in 1976 by the severe Gianni Vescovo, is not always regarded as being in the top flight, but the Sauvignon, from a local massal selection, is first-rate. Yields are fairly high at 4–5 tons per acre, yet good fruit is obtained. The wine is fermented at fairly high temperatures, up to 22 °C, and is unwooded. The 1988 was especially fine, with stylish aromas, good weight on the palate and very good length.

CASTELLO DI VOLPAIA

Torniello, Vino da Tavola

> 53017 Radda in Chianti, Siena, Tuscany
> Blend: 70 per cent Sauvignon, 30 per cent Sémillon
> Production: 8,000 bottles
> Quality: 🍇🍇🍇   Price: ★★★

Volpaia, advised by Maurizio Castelli, produces fine Chiantis and one of the few good Tuscan whites. The vines are imports from France – the Sauvignon from Sancerre, and the Sémillon, apparently, from Yquem – and have been planted on the highest sites on the estate. Since 1987 the wine has been *barrique*-fermented. It is left on the fine lees for about four months and regularly stirred. The wine improves from vintage to vintage. The 1988 was very oaky, beautifully textured and supple, and seemed likely to improve with some bottle-age. Unusually for Italian oaked Sauvignon, Torniello has real finesse.

FRESCOBALDI

Vergena, Predicato del Selvante

Via S. Spirito 11, 50125 Florence
Quality: 🍇🍇🍇   Price: ★★★

Vergena is the name of a high, south-facing tufa vineyard at Castelgiocondo near Montalcino planted solely with Sauvignon, first vinified in 1984. The must is cold-fermented and aged for a month or so in French *barriques*, and then aged in bottle for eight months. Sometimes the wine has an overripe flavour, but its weight blends well with the spiciness imparted by the light oak-ageing. But Vergena is overpriced.

LA GIUSTINIANA

Piedmont, Vino da Tavola

Fraz. Rovereto, 15066 Gavi
Vineyard: 7.5 acres of Sauvignon
Production: 3,500–7,000 bottles
Best vintages: 1986, 1988, 1989
Quality: 🍇🍇🍇🍇   Price: ★★★

La Giustiniana is best known for its high-quality Gavi wine, but decades ago a small plot of Sauvignon was planted to supply the personal needs of the former princely owners of the estate. The new owners, to their credit, have restored the vineyard and released the wine since 1984. Labelled Campoghero, it is made only from late-harvested grapes picked in November. The yields are no more than 1 ton per acre. The wine spends a month or so in Nevers oak but is only bottled after two years, then aged in bottle for a year before release. It has 14–15° alcohol, and 2° residual sugar. The bouquet is highly con-centrated, rich, toasty, and firm with a hint of wood. On the palate it is very intense, chewy, pungent and austere, with the sweetness scarcely apparent at all. A remarkable wine.

GRAVNER, FRANCESCO

DOC Collio

Via Lenzuolo Bianco, Oslavia, 34070 Gorizia
Quality: 🍇 Price: ★★

Gravner, whose vineyards straddle the Yugoslav border in north-eastern Friuli, is one of the most controversial, as well as highly talented and single-minded, winemakers of the region. Although Friuli is known for its clean, firm whites – the Italian counterparts to Alsatian wines – these qualities alone do not interest Gravner. He seeks complexity, and is unimpressed by the fresh, aromatic wines of his competitors. 'They drink with their nose,' he told me. He wants to make Sauvignon with structure and body, and blends *barrique*-aged wine with wines ageing in stainless steel tanks. The wines are massive and very high in alcohol: the 1988 vintage had 14°, and in 1985 he had a *cuvée* with 15.5° (unchaptalized), even though his grapes are planted on a north-east slope. He planted a number of Sauvignon clones in 1975 from French cuttings. Yields rarely exceed 2 tons per acre and fermentation is at temperatures that would make a Californian winemaker turn pale. The results? Very rich, sometimes dangerous white wines, intensely flavoured and highly individual.

HOFSTATTER, JOSEF

DOC Alto-Adige

Rathausplatz 5, 39040 Tramin
Quality: 🍇🍇🍇 Price: ★★

In a comparative tasting of every Sauvignon produced in the Alto-Adige in 1989, Hofstatter's stood out as the most aggressive. I was delighted with its piquant acidity and fierce attack on the palate, balanced against a satisfying richness of fruit, but many wine lovers may find this style too much of a good thing.

JERMANN

Collio, Vino da Tavola

Via Monte Fortino 17, 34070 Villanova di Farra

Quality: 🍇🍇🍇   Price: ★★★

You only have to step into Silvio Jermann's offices and winery to know that at this estate style is a very important notion. This brilliant winemaker is exactly in tune with modern tastes, producing wines that are uncomplicated yet rich in flavour, beautifully packaged yet strong in content too. They are all sold as Vini da Tavola to give him maximum flexibility. Yields are about 3 tons per acre. Sauvignon is not his best wine, yet it is typical of his style: very fresh, packed with ripe fruit, quite alcoholic, and creamily textured even though the wine sees no wood.

LAGEDER, ALOIS

DOC Alto-Adige

Drususstrasse 235, 39100 Bozen

Vineyard: 3 acres of Sauvignon

Production: 13,000 bottles of Sauvignon; 7,000 bottles of Lehenhof

SAUVIGNON

Quality: 🍇🍇   Price: ★★★

LEHENHOF

Quality: 🍇🍇🍇-🍇🍇🍇🍇   Price: ★★★★

Best vintages: 1983, 1987, 1988, 1989

Lageder, one of the very best producers of the Südtirol, has been making Sauvignon since the early 1970s. His best grapes come from Lehenhof, a steep south-facing vineyard that looms 500 metres over the valley, and for some years its wine has been bottled separately. Yields never exceed 4 tons per acre. The soil is volcanic with porphyry, and in dry years irrigation is necessary. Other Sauvignon grapes come from leased vineyards.

The grapes are hand-picked and receive only a few hours' skin contact. Lageder ferments both in stainless steel and in *barriques*. After malolactic fermentation the wine is aged up to five months in large old casks, bottled in June, and then aged in bottle for six months before release.

The wines exhibit a complex, full-bodied style with considerable length of flavour; the bouquet is quite rich, although Lageder does not seek a wine that is especially aromatic. With age some vintages develop a vegetal nose, but most vintages benefit from being kept for a few years. An experimental batch of 1988 Lehenhof that was entirely barrel-fermented was superb, so Lageder's Sauvignon is likely to evolve in promising directions.

ORNELLAIA

Poggio alle Gazze, Vino da Tavola

57020 Bolgheri

Vineyard: 15 acres (82 per cent Sauvignon, 18 per cent Sémillon)

Production: 44,000 bottles

Quality: 🍇🍇   Price: ★★

Various clones were planted here in 1983 on a south-west facing site selected with the help of the Californian oenologist André Tchelistcheff. The soil is a mixture of clay and flinty pebbles of marine origin. Winemaker Federico Studerini favours whole-cluster fermentation at a cool temperature for about two weeks. There is no wood-ageing and the wine is bottled in February. The 1987 was not successful, but 1988 has a fresh, light, Sauvignon nose and a clean, spicy flavour with good acidity. The 1989 is less assertive, but weightier and more elegant.

PUIATTI

DOC Collio

Via Dante 69, 34070 Farra d'Isonzo, Gorizia

Production: 48,000 bottles

ENOFRIULIA

Quality: 🍇🍇🍇 Price: ★★

OTHERS

Quality: 🍇🍇🍇🍇 Price: ★★★–★★★★

Vittorio Puiatti and his son Giovanni own no vineyards but have long-term contracts with some of the region's best growers. To ensure the best-quality fruit, they pay a 20 per cent premium on grapes, to the irritation of other Collio producers, but the results show in the bottle. Vinification is straight-forward. There is no skin contact, the presses are pneumatic, the must is fermented at a relatively high temperature but there is no malolactic fermentation; the wine is aged in tank for up to eight months before bottling. The aim is harmoniousness, with complexity of aroma and no heaviness on the palate.

The Puiattis believe strongly that Sauvignon is capable of evolving in bottle, and they also market a range called Arche-tipi, which are simply wines that have been bottled a few months later than the ordinary *cuvée*, then cellared for a few years before release.

Wines not considered worthy of the Puiatti label are sold under the Enofriulia label. These wines are by no means second-rate. On the contrary, they are often utterly delicious, strongly varietal in character and reasonably priced.

I find all these wines reliable, even in doubtful vintages such as 1987, and richly vinous. The great Veneto winemaker Nino Franceschetti believes the Puiattis are the best white wine technicians in Italy. He may well be right.

SCHIOPETTO

DOC Collio

> 34070 Capriva del Friuli, Gorizia
> Vineyard: 4.5 acres of Sauvignon
> Production: 15,000 bottles
> Quality: 🍇🍇🍇🍇 Price: ★★★

Many regard Mario Schiopetto as the greatest winemaker of the Friuli. Puiatti, Jermann and Gravner are snapping at his heels, but Schiopetto's wines are unquestionably of very high quality. I admire them for their unshakeable vigour and purity of fruit. His Sauvignon, from twelve-year-old vines, is stylish, very fresh, sprightly and clean. It is also highly aromatic without being obviously assertive. Sauvignon is one of four varieties used by Schiopetto in his blend called Blanc di Rosis. The only criticism one could make is that the wine seems very high-priced given that it is unoaked.

NEW ZEALAND

It is hard to believe that until 1981 no Sauvignon Blanc was sold commercially in New Zealand. So thoroughly has the country demonstrated its skill with this variety that one would imagine that there was a long-standing tradition of making Sauvignon in New Zealand. Not a bit of it. The first plantings were made in the 1970s by the Matua Valley vineyard. One of the largest wineries, Montana, planted Sauvignon in Marlborough on South Island, which has since established itself as the sunniest and best region for the cultivation of this variety. During the 1980s other regions were planted with Sauvignon: Auckland, Gisborne and Hawke's Bay on North Island, and Nelson on South Island. By 1989, 845 acres were under vine with Sauvignon; the 29 acres planted in Auckland, 50 in the Waikato region, 151 in Gisborne, 217 in Hawke's Bay, 355 in Marlborough and 11 in Nelson being the major concentrations. This represented only 8 per cent of New Zealand's vineyards, but new plantations ensured that by 1991 the proportion had risen to 10.6 per cent.

Marlborough Sauvignons, grown on very stony loam, are distinguished by their crisp, almost citric herbaceousness, pungent without being aggressive, and in good vintages full-flavoured on the palate without a trace of heaviness. New Zealand enjoys a long, cool growing season not unlike that of the Loire, allowing the grapes to ripen slowly so that they avoid the coarse, over-alcoholic quality of many other New World Sauvignons. Hawke's Bay has a variety of soils, from sandy loam to shingle; drip irrigation is permitted to combat particularly dry summers. It is dangerous to generalize, but the Sauvignon in Hawke's Bay tends to be richer than in Marlborough, which is why this is probably the best region in New Zealand for Chardonnay. Auckland, however, seems less suitable for

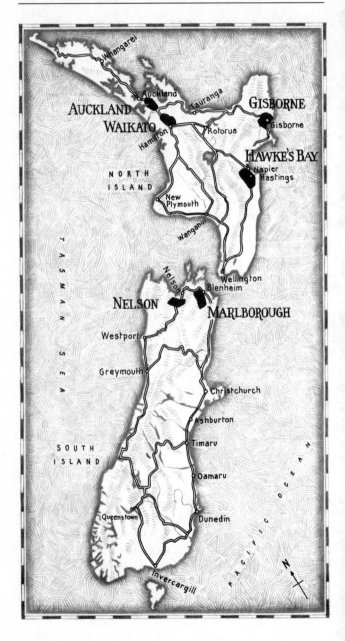

Sauvignon, since the climate is considerably wetter and the grapes are more prone to disease and rot – and to excessive production.

Most New Zealand Sauvignons are unoaked, or very lightly oaked to give the wine some roundness and structure without imprinting it with oaky vanilla flavours. It is these wines, with their clean, vibrant, racy fruit, their purity of flavour, that have so impressed lovers of Sauvignon. More recently, however, some producers have grown ambitious and cast an eye at the Graves. These are early days, but as yet I do not find most oaked New Zealand Sauvignons particularly succesful. Not because they are poor wines, but because they appear to be imitations of a French style rather than a pure expression of the grape. There is nothing wrong with simplicity if you have fruit of the quality of the best Marlborough or Hawke's Bay Sauvignon.

Sémillon is also encountered in New Zealand, though it shares many of the herbaceous characteristics of Sauvignon. The coolness of the climate robs Sémillon of the richness and high must weights present in the grape in the hotter climates of Bordeaux or Australia's Hunter Valley. Botrytized wines are made from Sémillon when conditions are appropriate, and from Sauvignon too, but these wines are rarely seen outside the country.

Despite their enormous success, New Zealand winemakers are not resting on their laurels. New Zealand is a leading centre for research, and viticulturalists such as Dr Richard Smart, now living in Australia, have acquired a worldwide reputation for their work on site selection and canopy management.

New Zealand Sauvignon is not a wine to be aged in bottle. Even the celebrated Cloudy Bay wine, which does spend a short time in oak, begins to decline after about two years. The outstanding vintage of recent years is the 1989, thanks to an exceptionally warm and dry growing season. The 1986 and 1988 vintages were better in Marlborough than Hawke's Bay; in 1987 the reverse was true. In 1990 frost during the harvest seriously marred Marlborough Sauvignon. Rain followed the frost and grapes were picked in mediocre condition. Growers who picked early had sound fruit, but many of these grapes may not have been fully ripe and will give green wines. The excellent 1991 vintage is particularly successful in Marlborough.

Other producers, not discussed in detail below, include De Redcliffe (North Island). Their Sémillon–Chardonnay blend is sweet and rounded, and the oak-aged Sémillon–Sauvignon blend is sumptuous but lacking in zest and bite. Mission, New Zealand's oldest winery, makes a serviceable Sauvignon and a rounded, oaky Sémillon–Sauvignon blend. Ngatarawa's Hawke's Bay Sauvignon has been inconsistent, with delicious wines in 1986 and 1989. Vidal, on North Island, produce a Fumé and a very good unwooded Hawke's Bay Sauvignon. In Nelson on South Island, Weingut Seifried produce a highly regarded wood-aged Sauvignon that I have never found to my taste. Merlen, Neudorf, the sensibly priced Tui Vale and the ambitious new Vavasour winery all make attractive, zesty Sauvignon.

BABICH

Babich Road, Henderson, Auckland

Quality: 🍇   Price: ★★

This large winery is also one of the oldest in the country. Most of the grapes are bought in. Their Sauvignon is characterized by a ripe fruitiness that can seem rather soft. This is not one of the most bracing of New Zealand Sauvignons. I often find it lacking in vigour and bite, though there is no denying the richness of the fruit.

Babich also produce a blend of 75 per cent Sémillon and 25 per cent Chardonnay. The 1985 and 1986 vintages from Hawke's Bay fruit were a touch tart at first, although fresh and clean, but with two years in the bottle they had become more sweet and supple. More recently the grapes have come from Gisborne, giving a clean but slightly confected style. All these wines are unoaked.

CLOUDY BAY

Jackson's Road, Blenheim

Vineyard: 56 acres (90 per cent Sauvignon, 10 per cent Sémillon)

Production: 120,000 bottles

Quality: 🍷🍷🍷🍷-🍷🍷🍷🍷🍷   Price: ★★★

This South Island winery is the brainchild of Cape Mentelle, David Hohnen's acclaimed Western Australian estate. He set up Cloudy Bay in 1985, and made his first vintage of Sauvignon with bought-in fruit from Stoneleigh. Its impact on the wine-drinking world must have surpassed even Hohnen's expectations. It soon acquired cult status in Britain. For once, the fuss is justified. This is a marvellous Sauvignon, and its gorgeous fruit and impeccable balance have shone through in blind tastings I have organized.

Hohnen, and his winemaker Kevin Judd, give the must skin contact overnight. They blend in up to 20 per cent of Sémillon and 15 per cent of the Sauvignon is barrel-fermented and aged four months in oak. It is very difficult to detect the oak, but it gives the wine body and complexity without adding tannin and obtrusive vanilla flavours. In the 1988 and 1989 vintages I detected a touch of residual sugar that gave the wine a more commercial appeal than the relatively assertive earlier vintages. Even though half the grapes are bought in and the remainder are machine-picked, quality remains very high. With an increase in production that still falls short of demand, there may be some dilution in the intensity of the fruit, but this wine remains a Sauvignon to make any Loire winemaker tremble.

COOKS

Paddy's Road, Te Kauwhata, South Auckland

Vineyard: 147 acres (75 per cent Sauvignon, 25 per cent Sémillon)

Production: 1 million bottles

SAUVIGNON BLANC

Quality: 🍇–🍇🍇   Price: ★★

Although only established in 1969 Cooks are now the second-largest wine producer in the country. They make a range of wines from Hawke's Bay and Marlborough. Half the grapes come from their own estates, and the wines are marketed under five labels, including Stoneleigh (q.v.). The 1988 Hawke's Bay Sauvignon was quite herbaceous, and had a green edge to it that was not altogether pleasing. The superior 1989 vintage was better, with a lively gooseberry flavour, but it was also rather sweet and lacking in concentration. From Marlborough comes a Sémillon that is given some ageing in new oak. The wine is rounded and soft and rather dull.

COOPER'S CREEK

Main Road, Huapai, Auckland

FUMÉ BLANC

Quality: 🍇🍇   Price: ★★

MARLBOROUGH SAUVIGNON BLANC

Quality: 🍇🍇🍇   Price: ★★

Most of the grapes for this North Island winery are bought in, so there is some inconsistency in the range. I have not been a fan of the oaked Fumé Blanc, which has good rich fruit that seems ill at ease with the slight bitterness of the oak. But this is a serious wine with considerable depth of flavour. Better is the

Marlborough Sauvignon, which in 1989 produced a highly aromatic wine, a touch overripe on the palate but with excellent persistence of flavour. Unfortunately it began to fall apart and develop coarse edges after a year in bottle.

DELEGAT'S

Hepburn Road, Henderson, Auckland
Vineyard: 55 acres of Sauvignon
Production: 60,000–70,000 bottles
Quality: 🍇🍇–🍇🍇🍇   Price: ★★

This well-established winery, founded in 1947, buys in about 70 per cent of its grapes, and favours skin contact for Sauvignon. I have conflicting notes on their Hawke's Bay Sauvignon. Some vintages, such as 1986, have struck me as broad, almost blowsy; others, such as 1987, were piquant and had atypical tropical fruit, pineapple flavours. I was thrilled by the 1989 when I tasted it in February 1990; less impressed when I tasted it blind six months later. Whether the wine was becoming pallid and losing its zest with age, or whether my palate was inconsistent, it is hard to say. Fairly high yields and the practice of leaving a little residual sugar in the wine leads to a rather commercial style. None the less, this is a well-made, lively, gooseberryish Sauvignon, never less than good, sometimes exemplary.

ESK VALLEY

Main Road, Bay View, Napier
Vineyard: 15 acres of Sauvignon
Production: 48,000 bottles
Quality: 🍇🍇🍇   Price: ★★

The winery was bought in 1987 by Villa Maria and winemaker Tony Hooper produces a fresh, exciting, unwooded Sauvignon from bought-in Hawke's Bay grapes. The acidity is marked but well balanced by delicious fruit. Whether Esk Valley can continue to make wines as good as its 1989 vintage remains to be seen.

HUNTER'S

Rapaura Road, Blenheim

Vineyard: 9 acres

Production: 72,000 bottles

OAK-AGED SAUVIGNON BLANC

Quality: ♦♦♦　　Price: ★★

MARLBOROUGH SAUVIGNON BLANC

Quality: ♦♦♦♦♦　　Price: ★★

This expanding South Island winery, founded in 1981, is rapidly establishing a reputation as one of the very finest producers of Sauvignon. Half the grapes are bought in from contracted growers. The 1989 Marlborough Sauvignon is outstanding: a racy, tangy wine with bags of ripe fruit and lovely length of flavour. Hunter also produce an oak-aged Sauvignon (with a dash of Sémillon), which is 25 per cent barrel-fermented and then aged for four to six months in Nevers *barriques*. The assertiveness of the unwooded wine is toned down here and replaced by a richer, fatter style that lacks some definition. This is one of the best oaked New Zealand Sauvignons, in which the oak alters the character of the wine while respecting its varietal flavours.

KUMEU RIVER

> 2 Highway 16, Kumeu, Auckland
> SAUVIGNON BLANC
> Quality: 🍇🍇   Price: ★★
> NOBLE DRY SAUVIGNON BLANC
> Quality: 🍇   Price: ★★★

This North Island winery is owned by the Brajkovich family, and they have produced Sauvignon in a variety of styles. A Fumé Blanc bottling struck me as broad and inelegant, with disturbing vegetal notes. More straightforward Sauvignon bottlings have also been somewhat vegetal, although the 1989 vintage was a great improvement. Kumeu River has attracted considerable attention by producing occasional Noble Dry Sauvignon Blancs from grapes that are partially botrytized but fermented to dryness. The wine, which is barrel-fermented, has an enthusiastic following, but I find its overripe honeyed flavours heavy and awkward.

Kumeu River employs a second label under the Brajkovich name for wines made primarily from bought-in grapes. The 1989 Sauvignon was fruity and spicy but rather aggressive.

MATUA VALLEY

> PO Box 100, Kumeu, Auckland
> RESERVE SAUVIGNON BLANC
> Quality: 🍇   Price: ★★
> BROWNLIE VINEYARD SAUVIGNON BLANC
> Quality: 🍇🍇🍇   Price: ★★★

Matua Valley produce two styles of Sauvignon: an unoaked version from Brownlie Vineyard in Hawke's Bay, and an oaked Reserve from grapes grown at Waimaku near Auckland and at Brownlie. These grapes are picked a week later than those for the unwooded wine, fermented in Nevers and Vosges *barriques*, and aged for up to three months in wood. In 1989 half the wine went through malolactic fermentation. I have always liked the unwooded wine: it has abundant fruit and acidity, tasting rich and spicy with plenty of vivid gooseberry flavours. I wish I could be as enthusiastic about the Reserve, which I find heavy, pungently oaky, and sweet on the finish. Perhaps with a little bottle-age the wine may become more harmonious and elegant, but I prefer the varietal freshness of the unoaked wine.

MONTANA

PO Box 18–293, Auckland

Vineyard: 225 acres (85 per cent Sauvignon, 15 per cent Sémillon)

Production: 850,000 bottles

Quality: ♥♥♥–♥♥♥♥   Price: ★

If Cloudy Bay proved that New Zealand Sauvignon rivalled the best from the Loire, it was Montana that brought the wine to the masses. Nor was it a copycat operation, for Montana was a pioneer in planting Sauvignon at its Brancott estate in Marlborough as long ago as 1973. Today 30 per cent of the grapes are bought in. The wine is consistently excellent, and very reasonably priced; in quality alone it often surpasses wines from smaller wineries at twice the price. The style is aggressive, packed with intense gooseberry fruit and a dashing acidity. It delivers its message directly and pungently. In my experience it should be drunk as young as possible, for after a year in bottle it can acquire vegetal, almost cabbagey, tones. Montana also produce a sweetish blend of Sauvignon and Chenin Blanc, and a barrel-fermented style that has yet to be exported.

MORTON

RD 2, Katikati, Bay of Plenty
Quality: 🍇🍇🍇🍇   Price: ★★

The Morton Estate was founded in 1982, and from the beginning the Australian winemaker John Hancock has been responsible for its very high standards. The Australian connection was strengthened in 1988, when Mildara bought the estate. Most of the estate vineyards are in Hawke's Bay; grapes are also bought in. The Hawke's Bay Sauvignon is consistently fine and stylish. The 1986 was quite superb, complete in every respect, and the 1989, a great vintage, was equally good when young, but with bottle-age the presence of late-picked grapes in the blend imparted an odd, almost stewed flavour that detracted from the usual purity of the style. (Morton also make an oak-aged Black Label Fumé Blanc and a Late Harvest Sauvignon, which I have never encountered.)

NOBILO

Station Road, Huapai, West Auckland
Production: 240,000 bottles
FUMÉ STYLE SAUVIGNON BLANC
Quality: 🍇   Price: ★★
MARLBOROUGH SAUVIGNON BLANC
Quality: 🍇🍇–🍇🍇🍇   Price: ★★

This North Island winery makes two Sauvignons: a Hawke's Bay Fumé Style and, since 1989, a Marlborough Sauvignon from a newly planted vineyard. The Fumé is fermented in new French and German *barriques* and aged for eight weeks. The oak flavour is restrained but imparts a rounded quality that diminishes the wine's varietal power; nor do I care for the often melony flavours reminiscent of anonymous California Fumé styles. Much better is the Marlborough wine, which is intensely aromatic, richly fruity and long in flavour.

SELAK'S

> PO Box 34, Kumeu
> Quality: 👁👁 Price: ★★★

An old family-run winery on North Island, Selak's make lively, grassy Sauvignon and an oaked 60 per cent Sauvignon, 40 per cent Sémillon blend. I find the wines good but inconsistent. The pricy Sauvignon is sometimes excessively herbaceous, and although the 1986 Sauvignon–Sémillon was delicious when young, subsequent vintages have been less impressive. The Sémillon is barrel-fermented, blended with tank-fermented Sauvignon and then oak-aged for three months in German and Nevers barrels. Selak's also produce a dry, barrel-fermented Sémillon.

STONELEIGH

> Great North Road, Henderson, Auckland
> Quality: 👁👁👁👁 Price: ★★

Stoneleigh, like Cooks, is part of the Corbans empire. The corporate structure does not sound promising, but the Stoneleigh Marlborough Sauvignon is excellent. The fruit, from vineyards next to Cloudy Bay, is more rounded, less assertive, than one would expect from Marlborough vines, and the wine, although unwooded, sometimes tastes oaked. Most vintages contain a dose of about 5 grams per litre residual sugar, but the acidity is sufficiently elevated to keep the wine in balance. It should be drunk young.

TE MATA

> Te Mata Road, Havelock North
> Production: 80,000 bottles
> Quality: 🍇🍇🍇🍇   Price: ★★★

Te Mata is the creation of John Buck, who set his stylistic mark on the striking architecture of the estate as well as on his excellent range of wines. Peter Cowley is the winemaker. The Castle Hill Sauvignon is a lovely piquant wine with a strong gooseberry character; only the 1988 was somewhat lacklustre. The must is cold-fermented slowly, then left on the fine lees in tank, which may well account for the wine's powerful aromas. Te Mata is a prestigious estate so the wines are expensive, and the unwooded Sauvignon is overpriced.

VILLA MARIA

> PO Box 43046, Mangere, Auckland
> Production: 300,000 bottles
> Quality: 🍇🍇🍇   Price: ★★

At this North Island winery, founded in 1961, Kym Milne makes a reliable unwooded Private Bin Sauvignon from bought-in Hawke's Bay and Gisborne grapes, as well as other bottlings derived from wines not up to private bin standards. Villa Maria are planting vines in the Marlborough region, a source that dominates its 1990 Private Bin. This latter wine is crisp and tart, spry and lean, with intense gooseberry flavours. It lacks some complexity and must be drunk young. In exceptional years a barrel-fermented Reserve Sauvignon is made in small quantities.

SOUTH AFRICA

Sauvignon Blanc is widely planted in South Africa, and over 9,000 acres of Sémillon can also be found, though the grape is less frequently vinified on its own. My experience of these wines is limited since, like many other wine writers, I was reluctant to taste and discuss the wines produced under the apartheid system. By 1991 it seemed clear that a major change was under way in South Africa, and I began to take up opportunities to taste the wines. The styles of winemaking vary greatly, with unwooded versions outnumbering oaked versions. Almost all the wines I have encountered are well made in a fresh, uncomplicated style and are clearly intended for early consumption. Most of the unwooded versions do have varietal character, though quite a few were dull.

Although my experience is patchy, I have admired Sauvignon from Boschendal (rather more than their oak-fermented yet neutral Sauvignon-dominated Grand Vin Blanc), Buitenverwachtung's racy, grassy version, Neil Ellis's fresh, impeccably balanced Whitehall Sauvignon Blanc, Fairview's rich, oaky Charles Gerard White Reserve (where Sauvignon is blended with Chenin Blanc), Franschhoek Vineyards' rich and spicy La Cotte bottling, Uiterwyk's balanced and complex wine, and Zonnebloem's spicy version. The few Sémillons I have encountered have tended to be somewhat neutral, though I enjoyed the well-made if one-dimensional version under Franschhoek's La Cotte label. All in all there seems little doubt that certain regions are well suited to the production of elegant, fruity Sauvignon.

Of recent vintages, 1990 is considered better than 1989, although many of the South African winemakers I have spoken to found few marked differences between vintages for Sauvignon.

SPAIN

Except in the Rueda, Sauvignon Blanc is little grown in Spain. Miguel Torres, predictably, grows Sauvignon in Penedès, and blends it with Parellada to make his oak-aged Gran Viña Sol.

Rueda is dominated by the Verdejo grape, but since 1985 Sauvignon has been permitted as an experimental variety. Both the climate, which is continental with Atlantic influences, and the soil, which is sandy and stony, are suitable for its cultivation. However, it has only been planted by some of the better wineries in the region. Cooperatives such as the one at La Seca have no plans to market a Sauvignon. Bodegas Castilla La Vieja have planted 52 acres with Sauvignon, as well as a smaller area of Sémillon, but at time of writing the first vintage was not yet on the market.

RISCAL, MARQUÉS DE

DO Rueda

> Ctra Nacional IV, km 172.6, Rueda, Valladolid
> Vineyard: 98 acres of Sauvignon
> Production: 50,000 bottles
> Quality: 🍇🍇🍇   Price: ★

Marqués de Riscal are a leading Rioja producer, but they have chosen to make their white wine out in Rueda at a winery that goes by the name of Vinos Blancos de Castilla. They produce three whites: a regular bottling from mostly Verdejo, a Reserve Limousin from Verdejo, and Sauvignon. Their first vintage of

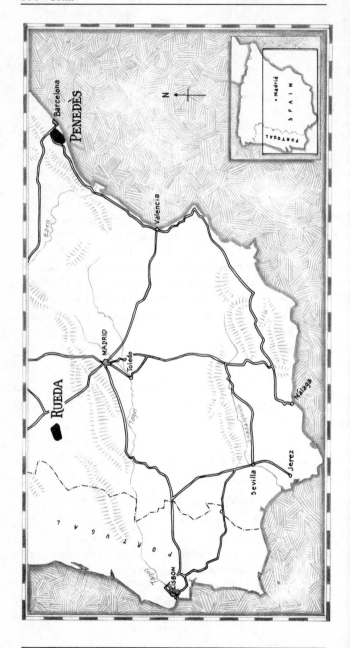

Sauvignon was 1975. It is very well made: not bursting with varietal character perhaps, but slightly grassy and with an assertive personality of its own, and good length of flavour.

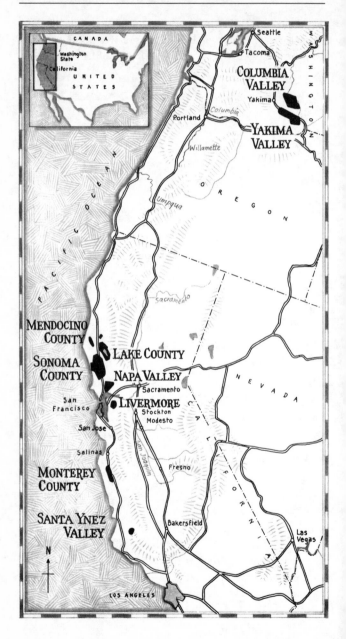

USA

California

It seems strange that a region that has produced, with seem-ingly effortless confidence and expertise, world-class wines from Chardonnay and Cabernet Sauvignon should experience such difficulties with Sauvignon Blanc. Part of the reason lies in the lack of care given in previous decades to site selection. The New Zealanders, with their maritime climate, located exactly the right soils for their Sauvignon, but the Californians tended to plant vines in any old place and hope for the best. With Chardonnay and Cabernet the climate made up for the defi-ciencies of the site – and of course some of the sites, such as the Rutherford Bench, were superb.

With Sauvignon, and even more with Sémillon, the soil was less forgiving. The first cuttings were brought here from Yquem in 1878 and planted at the Wente vineyards in the Livermore Valley. Thereafter young vines were often planted in rich, deep soils in warm microclimates, and the result was abundant fruit of mediocre quality. The position was further complicated by the density patterns of Californian plantation. To facilitate accessibility to tractors and mechanical harvesters, and because land was cheap, only 454 vines per acre were planted. This led to excessive vigour and an abundance of foliage, which then needed to be curbed. (In the 1980s some growers began to plant new vineyards with density patterns closer to the French norm.) Not even the wizardries of Davis-trained Californian winemakers could turn tons of bloated Sauvignon grapes into distinguished wine.

Overproductive vines often gave fruit with a pronounced herbaceous character. Californians found the grassiness of the

Loire Sauvignons attractive, but were disinclined to tolerate the same character in their own wines. Some winemakers, such as Robert Pecota, believe that this grassiness also derives from the clones commonly planted in California, notably the Wente clone. The best clone may well be Sauvignon Musqué, also known as the Ventana clone, which ampelographers maintain is closest to French Sauvignon and least likely to develop vegetal aromas and flavours. Two thousand acres have been planted with this clone.

Whatever the source of the vegetal flavours, the consumers didn't like them. The solution to this problem was found by Robert Mondavi. He exploited the chic image of Pouilly-Fumé by producing a wine called Fumé Blanc. It was, and remains, a very good wine, but it bore very little relation to its French model. The Mondavi wine was oaked, and in the case of the Reserve bottling, heavily oaked. The wine was a hit, and almost every other California winery with Sauvignon vines followed his example. (The name Fumé Blanc does not, however, guarantee an oaked wine.)

When I read the American wine press, I am always puzzled to come across the following, typical, tasting notes for Sauvignons: 'Layers of nectarine, peach and herb overtones . . . ripe melony fruit . . . a rich, toasty, herbaceous, honeyed melon and fig bouquet . . . layers of herb, vanilla, pear and spicy flavors'. They may be describing delicious wines, but they are evidently remote at every level from their French or New Zealand counterparts.

The problem with most California Sauvignons is their dullness. Even Mike Lee of Kenwood, a leading producer of the variety, finds most of them boring. Yields are excessive, and it cannot be easy to produce intensely flavoured wines from vines yielding, as they routinely do here, 6 tons per acre. Yet Craig Williams of Phelps recalls high-yielding vintages such as 1982 and 1985 that gave good Sauvignons because, in his view, there was a better balance between the root system and the foliage. Moreover, the increasing use of virus-free rootstocks also generates a larger crop without, arguably, diminishing quality. Even if we discount this factor, and I do not, there are other factors at work: the climate, for instance, encourages high must weights. It is perfectly possible to make a balanced Sauvignon with 13°, but only if the fruit is perfectly ripe. In the hotter zones of California the grapes reach technical ripeness before they are fully mature, especially in terms of aromatic development. The result is wines high in alcohol yet lacking in varietal character and fruitiness. The solution ought to have been a re-examination of viticultural practices, but instead it was decided to pretend that the grapes were Chardonnay.

Not that oak-ageing is to be scorned. After all, the greatest Graves wines receive a great deal of it. But the tendency in California, with producers unable to charge high prices for Sauvignon and Sémillon, is to ferment these varieties in tank, and then soup them up later with barrel-ageing. A handful of wineries, who believe in these varieties and are prepared to take some trouble over them, opt for costly barrel-fermentation. Jeff Baker of Carmenet, one of the few wineries with subterranean cellars ideal for barrel-maturation, believes that barrel-fermentation brings out Sauvignon's varietal character.

I cannot prove it, but I suspect that the almost universal use of a single cultivated yeast – prise de mousse – is partially responsible for the uniformity of so much California Sauvignon. Prise de mousse is very effective, ensuring a fairly high level of alcohol, which is just what California wines don't require. Cultivated yeasts, of course, offer the winemaker security, as there is no risk of a stuck fermentation.

The usual result of all these viticultural and vinification practices is that confection of toast and melon and fig that passes for California Sauvignon. It seems to suit the American palate. American consumers do not want austerity in a wine, especially white wine. Many winemakers compound their already considerable offences by leaving a dollop of residual sugar in the wine to give it a gentle rounded flavour. Some New Zealanders also leave a few grams of residual sugar in Sauvignon, but there the acidity is at least 7 grams per litre, a level at which it is difficult to detect a touch of sweetness. Moreover, American consumers are not accustomed to ageing their wines, even oaked wines with ample structure, and winemakers feel obliged to produce Sauvignons that are ready to drink on the day of purchase. Since the average length of time that a purchased wine is aged is less than a week, this is not an idle consideration.

Fifteen thousand acres of Sauvignon are found in many different regions of California. In Napa (3,750 acres) it tends to be planted on the valley floor, probably the worst place for it. However, cultivation of mountain sites with low-yielding 'stressed soil' is costly, and since Sauvignon does not have sufficient prestige to bear a high price tag, it is difficult for a conscientious mountain vineyard producer to recoup his costs. Dan Duckhorn used to buy Sauvignon from a low-yielding mountain vineyard – until the grower did his sums and promptly grafted the vines over to Merlot, which fetches twice the price of Sauvignon. In some Napa mountain sites, moreover, Pierce disease, an infection of tiny grasshoppers, is rampant. Sonoma Valley (2,025 acres) has a number of cooler slopes more suitable for Sauvignon. To the north-east of Napa lies Lake County, and here 900 of the 3,000 acres of vineyards are planted with Sauvignon on sandy and volcanic soils. Nights are cool here, slowing the maturation process and giving well-balanced fruit. Good-quality Sauvignon is also grown in Potter Valley in Mendocino County.

The problems encountered with Sauvignon are compounded with Sémillon. California has 2,725 acres planted with Sémillon, 270 in Napa, 280 in Sonoma and 510 in Monterey County. Hardly anybody has a good word to say for it. Dan Duckhorn remarks that when planted in rich soils, as it usually is, it produces grapes the size of water melons – perhaps a slight exaggeration. In any case, from such grapes no good wine can be made. This losing combination of the wrong soil, inappropriate climate and poor clones gives California Sémillon a woeful neutrality of flavour. Its abysmal reputation discourages most winemakers from even attempting to make good wine from it.

However, Sémillon does have its defenders. Clos du Val in Napa Valley produce a varietal Sémillon. Jeff Baker at Carmenet agrees that the grape is basically neutral, but says that it develops interestingly in bottle, adding complexity to a Sauvignon-based wine. Unfortunately, few wine buyers have the patience to allow that development to take place. My tastings of wines such as Lyeth White and Chevrier and Chevriot–Sauvignon–Sémillon blends, some of which are no longer made, so unenthusiastic has been their commercial reception – confirm that even California Sémillon can, when blended, produce a complex wine. In addition, the susceptibility of Sémillon to attacks of botrytis is not neglected by Californian winemakers, who have produced superb sweet wines from this grape.

The late 1980s saw a string of good vintages, with, of course, climatic variations in different parts of this enormous state. A warm summer in 1987 and a cool September gave particularly well-balanced white grapes in northern California. In 1989 there was heavy rain, especially in parts of Napa and Sonoma, and rot was widespread. Wineries that picked early were better able to make successful wines. Sauvignon was usually picked before the rain, but was not always fully ripe. Difficult weather, mostly heavy spring rains, halved yields in 1990, especially in Sonoma, so the crop was small, but quality good.

In addition to the estates with full entries, I have relished many other wines. From Napa, I have enjoyed a pleasant sweetish Sauvignon (blended with 14 per cent Chardonnay) from Caymus. Monticello made Sauvignon and Sémillon from 1982 to 1986, then stopped; their best wine was Château M, a resplendent botrytized Sauvignon. Raymond make a rounded, spicy, occasionally flabby Sauvignon, and in 1989 produced a late-harvest Sémillon. Spring Mountain's Sauvignon is firm, fruity and reliable; Rutherford Hill's is more lively. Sterling's Sauvignons, which contain 20 per cent Sémillon, are usually disappointing, and only modestly fruity. Merryvale produce a Graves-style blend, barrel-fermented in new oak, which shows great promise.

From Sonoma, Chalk Hill made a series of indifferent Sauvignons (and some zesty late-harvest wines), but the hiring in 1990 of winemaker David Ramey should herald a huge leap in quality. Dry Creek Vineyard has a good reputation for *barrique*-aged Fumé Blanc and an estate-grown Reserve aged *sur lie*, but I have found the wines sound but unexciting. In 1990 in the Santa Ynez Valley, Firestone, not previously known for brilliant Sauvignon, produced a deliciously crisp bottle. Further south, Ojai's serious barrel-fermented Graves-style blends strike me as heavy and awkward, but Vita Nova's 'Chien Méchant', named in honour of Didier Dagueneau, is an exceptionally stylish Sauvignon–Sémillon blend.

BERINGER

Napa Valley

> 2000 Main Street, St Helena, CA 94574
>
> Production: 110,000 bottles of Napa Fumé Blanc; 720,000 bottles of Knight's Valley Sauvignon Blanc
>
> NAPA FUMÉ BLANC
>
> Quality: 🍇🍇   Price: ★★
>
> KNIGHT'S VALLEY SAUVIGNON BLANC
>
> Quality: 🍇🍇   Price: ★★★
>
> BOTRYTIZED SAUVIGNON BLANC AND SÉMILLON
>
> Quality: 🍇–🍇🍇🍇🍇   Price: ★★★★

Beringer, one of the giants of Napa Valley, is a major producer of Sauvignon. There are two principal wines: a Napa Fumé, made from Sauvignon planted in deep loam south of Yountville, and a Sauvignon–Sémillon blend from Knight's Valley, a very cool area with stony and alluvial soil. The Fumé is tank-fermented, then aged for two months in oak. Three quarters of the Knight's Valley must is barrel-fermented and blended with the tank wine in Nevers and Limousin oak, in which it is aged for six months. Some of the wine goes through malolactic fermentation.

One of Beringer's specialities is a botrytized wine from either Sauvignon or Sémillon grown near Yountville. Myron and Alice Nightingale pioneered at Beringer the technique of inducing botrytis after picking rather than waiting for its random arrival in the vineyard. This enabled them to produce minute quantities of oak-aged botrytized wines almost every year. They are very intense, but oddly one-dimensional. I prefer the Sémillon to the more lemony Sauvignon.

As for the two regular wines I find the use of oak heavy-handed, and the Napa Fumé can be too alcoholic. The Knight's Valley wine is far more complex and the fruit supports the oak more firmly.

CAKEBREAD

Napa Valley

8300 Highway 29, Rutherford, CA 94573

Production: 130,000 bottles of Sauvignon

RUTHERFORD GOLD

Quality: 🍇🍇🍇🍇🍇   Price: ★★★★★

OTHERS

Quality: 🍇🍇🍇–🍇🍇🍇🍇   Price: ★★★

Best vintages: 1985, 1988

Cakebread grow 65 per cent of their Sauvignon grapes, and their first commercial vintage was in 1976. The Cakebreads have been experimenting with different kinds of trellising and leaf-thinning to reduce the vigour of the vines on this rich clay soil. After fermentation in tank about 80 per cent of the wine is aged in Limousin and Nevers *barriques*, of which 20 per cent are new, for up to four months. Given the richness of the soil the wine has surprising fragrance and good depth of flavour, with a touch of smokiness from the oak.

In 1982 botrytized Sauvignon was picked at 48 Brix, a very high concentration of sugar, and produced a sensationally rich wine, Rutherford Gold, which was aged for two years in oak. In 1990 it still tasted very youthful, as its very high acidity balanced the lush sweet fruit.

CARMENET

Sonoma Valley

> 1700 Moon Mountain Drive, Sonoma, CA 95476
>
> Production: 80,000 bottles of Sonoma Sauvignon Blanc, 30,000 bottles of Reserve Sauvignon Blanc
>
> SONOMA SAUVIGNON BLANC
>
> Quality: 🍇🍇🍇   Price: ★★
>
> EDNA VALLEY SAUVIGNON BLANC
>
> Quality: 🍇🍇🍇🍇   Price: ★★★
>
> Best vintages: 1984, 1988

This fine estate is located high on Mt Pisgah, but neither the Sauvignon nor Sémillon is estate-grown. There are two bottlings: an Edna Valley wine from grapes grown in the Paragon Vineyard, and a Sonoma Valley wine from grapes bought from a number of carefully monitored growers. Yields are 3–4 tons per acre and grapes are picked very ripe. Since 1988 the Edna Valley wine, which accounts for 75 per cent of Sauvignon–Sémillon production, has been labelled as Carmenet's Reserve Wine. This Reserve also contains 30 per cent Sémillon.

Both wines are barrel-fermented, but more new oak is used for the Reserve. The cellars here are carved into volcanic tufa rock, providing ideal conditions for barrel storage. The wine is stirred on the fine lees for seven months. The aim is a Graves-style wine capable of evolving in bottle, hence the presence of Sémillon. The winemaker, Jeff Baker, finds malolactic fermentation desirable, but doesn't fret if some parcels are resistant. One admirable practice here is the bottle-ageing of the Sonoma wine for one year and the Reserve for about two years before release.

Both wines age well, although some vintages, such as 1987, have developed vegetal tones. With the 1988 vintage Baker achieved the style he wanted, and the Reserve is outstanding: lush and spicy and unashamedly oaky, a fine Californian adaptation of the Graves style.

CHÂTEAU ST JEAN

Sonoma Valley

8555 Sonoma Highway, Kenwood, CA 95452

Production: 180,000–240,000 bottles of Sonoma Sauvignon Blanc; 60,000–120,000 bottles of Petite Étoile Sauvignon Blanc

SÉMILLON D'OR

Quality: 🍇🍇🍇🍇-🍇🍇🍇🍇🍇   Price: ★★★★★

OTHERS

Quality: 🍇🍇-🍇🍇🍇   Price: ★★★

Best vintages: 1981, 1986

Single-vineyard Fumé Blancs from Château St Jean were my introduction to California Sauvignon, and I was overwhelmed. They were immense wines, and I loved their power and concentration and abundant fruit. I am less certain that I would like them today. At any rate, they are a thing of the past. The Forrest Crimmins Ranch that produced some of those wines is now an apartment complex in Healdsburg. The only single vineyard remaining is the 44-acre Petite Étoile in Windsor, formerly leased but bought by Château St Jean in 1989. The grapes are hand-picked and yields are 3–4 tons per acre. The Sonoma Sauvignon comes from various parts of the county.

The Sonoma wine contains a dash of Sémillon, but Petite Étoile is all Sauvignon, barrel-fermented and aged in mostly American oak for up to seven months. The Sonoma wine is 15 per cent barrel-fermented and 10 per cent wood-aged. There is no malolactic fermentation. With every year that passes, the wine seems to become lighter, more anaemic, less interesting. Whether this has to do with the requirements of the new Japanese owners, Suntory, one can only speculate.

Château St Jean still makes some glorious sweet wines. The Sémillon d'Or (made in 1983, 1984, 1985, 1986 and 1989) is a Sauternes-style wine of great succulence and complexity, and a

1985 Select Late Harvest Johnson Vineyard Sauvignon, picked at 31.5 Brix, is equally fine.

DUCKHORN

Napa Valley

> 3027 Silverado Trail, St Helena, CA 94574
>
> Vineyard: 7 acres (70 per cent Sauvignon, 30 per cent Sémillon)
>
> Production: 100,000 bottles of Sauvignon
>
> Quality: ♥♥♥   Price: ★★
>
> Best vintages: 1983, 1986, 1987, 1988, 1989

Duckhorn are best known for their Merlot, but a very attractive Sauvignon is also produced from vines planted in 1981 on sandy loam soil, supplemented by fruit bought in from north of Yountville and Calistoga. Yields are high and only very ripe grapes are picked. The wine contains 25 per cent Sémillon. There is no skin contact and both grape varieties are 40 per cent barrel-fermented. The wood-fermented lots are aged for two to three months in 70 per cent new *barriques* from Limousin and Nevers. There is no malolactic fermentation. Duckhorn seek both a wine that is ready to drink on release and a wine with viscosity and weight. As it ages, its ripe grapefruit flavours become more honeyed.

Surplus Sémillon is used to make a lightly oaked wine called Decoy Sémillon: a soft, clean, easygoing style.

FAR NIENTE

Napa Valley

> Off Oakville Grade, Oakville, CA 94562
>
> Production: 7,500 bottles

DOLCE

Quality: 🍇🍇🍇   Price: ★★★★★

This luxurious estate has for some years aspired to make a sweet wine modelled on Yquem. The grapes are bought in from Napa vineyards, though in the future the winemaker, Dirk Hampson, hopes that estate-grown grapes will be suitable. Dolce has only been made in 1985, 1986 and 1989. The 1989 is the first Dolce to be released. The blend contains about 60 per cent Sémillon and is aged, like Yquem, for about three years in new oak. Since the wine is more expensive than any Sauternes other than Yquem, one is justified in expecting a truly special wine. Dolce is a good, rather citric wine with powerful flavours of oak and dried apricots, but it does not have the intensity and length of the finest Sauternes.

FERRARI-CARANO

Sonoma Valley

8761 Dry Creek Road, Healdsburg, CA 95448

Quality: 🍇🍇🍇🍇   Price: ★★

This winery's Fumé Blanc is a blend of grapes from Alexander Valley and Dry Creek. The wine is partially barrel-fermented, aged in French *barriques* for a few months and blended with a dash of Sémillon. It is a copybook Sonoma Sauvignon: very fresh, with ripe, lightly herbaceous melony flavours and a touch of sweetness on the finish. In 1986 and 1989 botrytized Sauvignon was bottled as Eldorado Gold Late Harvest.

FLORA SPRINGS

Napa Valley

1978 W. Zinfandel Lane, St Helena, CA 94574

Production: 8,000 bottles of Soliloquy

SAUVIGNON

Quality: 🍇🍇🍇   Price: ★★★

SOLILOQUY

Quality: 🍇🍇🍇🍇   Price: ★★★★

This classy winery seeks to make Sauvignon in a Graves style and has been fairly successful, despite idiosyncratic methods. The grapes are fermented in steel, then matured in a mixture of French and American *barriques*, and larger oak casks. Since 1989 selected lots from fifteen-year-old vines have been left on the lees for six months in large German oval casks. The result, when bottled, was California's highest-priced dry Sauvignon, but the wine was exceptionally fragrant and refined, far more classic than the fruity, pear-drop, regular Sauvignon. Production of Soliloquy is gradually expanding.

FROG'S LEAP

Napa Valley

3358 St Helena Highway, St Helena, CA 94574

Production: 110,000 bottles of Sauvignon; 1,200 bottles of Late Leap

SAUVIGNON

Quality: 🍇🍇🍇   Price: ★★

LATE LEAP

Quality: 🍇🍇🍇   Price: ★★★★

There is frivolity in the air at Frog's Leap – the corks are marked 'ribbit' in imitation of frog-squawk – but the wines are lovely. Most of the Sauvignon is bought in from dry-farmed vineyards in Pope Valley, Oakville and Yountville. Ninety per cent of the must is tank-fermented using indigenous yeasts, and all the wine is aged in large casks. There is no malolactic fermentation. The resulting wine lacks weight, but its herbaceous, grapefruity flavours are refreshing in comparison with the usual heavyweight Napa Sauvignon. It is best drunk young.

Even better is the Late Harvest wine, called Late Leap. In 1986 the grapes were picked at 39 Brix and barrel-fermented. The results were out of balance: too much alcohol, insufficient residual sugar. So John Williams, the winemaker, added Sémillon Süssreserve to repair the balance. A delicious honeyed, oaky wine, though lacking the concentration of a fine Sauternes.

GALLO, E. & J.

Central Valley

600 Yosemite Boulevard, Modesto, CA 95353
Quality: 🍇   Price: ★

One does not expect great things from an industrial winemaker as large and as commercial as Gallo, but their Sauvignon is perfectly acceptable: light to be sure, even thin, but with fresh, crisp fruit. The wine is priced in line with its merits.

GRGICH HILLS

Napa Valley

1829 St Helena Highway, Rutherford, CA 94573
Production: 95,000 bottles
Quality: 🍇🍇🍇–🍇🍇🍇🍇   Price: ★★★

Mike Grgich's skilfully crafted Fumé Blanc from the estate's Olive Hills vineyard always retains its fruit, despite a spell of five months in Limousin *barriques*. The oak is apparent in the smoky bouquet too, as well as in the spiciness of the palate, which is unusually complex. Grgich often adds a dash of Muscat, which seems to do the wine no harm at all and probably contributes to its fragrance.

INGLENOOK

Napa Valley

> 1991 St Helena Highway, Rutherford, CA 94573
> Vineyard: 25 acres of Sauvignon
> Quality: 🍇–🍇🍇   Price: ★★

This large, long-established winery produces a Sauvignon, a Sémillon and a blend called Gravion. The Sauvignon is rounded out with 25 per cent Sémillon, tank-fermented, then aged in Limousin *barriques* for six months. Despite the oak-ageing, this tends to be a simple, somewhat vegetal wine. The Sémillon, from Yountville grapes, is unwooded, pleasantly dry, but nondescript.

The best of the three is Gravion, a half-and-half blend, barrel-fermented in Limousin, then aged *sur lie* for six months. Again, it is less rich than the high alcohol – over 13° – and oak-ageing would suggest, but it is cleanly made and attractive in an undemanding way.

IRON HORSE

Sonoma Valley

> 9786 Ross Station Road, Sebastopol, CA 95472
> Vineyard: 20 acres of Sauvignon
> Production: 60,000 bottles
> Quality: 🍇🍇🍇   Price: ★★★
> Best vintages: 1983, 1985, 1986, 1988

Iron Horse produce their Sauvignon entirely from estate-grown grapes, a single clone planted in the foothills of the Alexander Valley. The winemaker, Forrest Tancer, seeks to make a wine neither Loire-like nor Graves-like, but a Sonoma wine. The vineyards are cool, with enormous swings of temperature in summer, which conserves acidity. The grapes are hand-picked and skin contact has been abandoned. Since 1985 the wine has been barrel-fermented and aged *sur lie* for five months, although there is no *bâtonnage*. The wine has 13–13.5° alcohol and a bracing 7.5 grams per litre acidity, and benefits from some ageing in bottle. The melony flavours, harmonizing with oak, are very Californian, but a trifle dull.

KENDALL-JACKSON

Lake County

> 600 Matthews Road, Lakeport, CA 95453
>
> Production: 700,000 bottles of Lake County Sauvignon Blanc; 2,400 bottles of Sémillon
>
> SÉMILLON
>
> Quality: 🍇🍇 Price: ★★
>
> SAUVIGNON BLANC
>
> Quality: 🍇🍇 Price: ★★★
>
> SELECT LATE HARVEST SAUVIGNON BLANC
>
> Quality: 🍇🍇🍇🍇 Price: ★★★★★
>
> Best vintages: 1985, 1986, 1988

Under the supervision of Jed Steele this large winery produces two Sauvignons from a region that is becoming increasingly important for the variety. The estate wine is made from hand-picked Jackson Vineyard grapes which give yields of 5 tons per acre. The Lake County wine is made mostly from bought-in grapes, either from lakeside vineyards or from vines planted on more volcanic soils away from the shore. Steele often adds about 5 per cent Chardonnay to soften the wine, and some Sémillon Süssreserve to give the wine some all too discernible residual sugar.

There is no skin contact and no malolactic fermentation, if

Steele can help it. Half the Lake County wine is oak-aged for two months; the estate wine is barrel-fermented and aged in Burgundian oak. Until 1986 Kendall-Jackson made a Sauvignon–Sémillon blend called Chevriot that aged beautifully; unfortunately, production has been discontinued. Steele aims for wines that are neither heavy nor alcoholic, for early consumption. They are certainly well made but rather bland, sustained by a faint buzz of carbon dioxide.

In 1983, 1985 and 1989 Kendall-Jackson made delicious botrytis wines from 80 per cent Sauvignon, the remainder being Chardonnay and Riesling. The wine is barrel-fermented and aged for a few months in new oak.

KENWOOD

Sonoma County

9592 Sonoma Highway, Kenwood, CA 95452

Vineyard: 40 acres of Sauvignon

Production: 650,000 bottles of Sauvignon

Quality: 🍇🍇🍇   Price: ★★

Best vintages: 1985, 1987, 1988

Kenwood is one of the largest producers of Sauvignon in California, and it accounts for about 25 per cent of their turnover. Contract growers provide 70 per cent of the grapes. Skin contact was abandoned in the early 1980s and the must is tank-fermented. About 60 per cent of the wine is aged in French *barriques* (one third are new) for about four months; 20 per cent goes into large oak casks, and the remainder stays in tank. There is no malolactic fermentation, so the wine is high in acidity. This is a thoroughly reliable Sauvignon: fresh, clean, medium-bodied, grassy, stylish, with plentiful fruit. It also ages surprisingly well, developing riper, more honeyed aromas.

LONG

Napa Valley

1535 Sage Canyon Road, St Helena, CA 94574
Production: 7,000 bottles
Quality: 🍇🍇🍇🍇   Price: ★★★

Until 1988 this tiny hillside winery made Sauvignon from grapes that came from Chalk Hill in Sonoma. The winemaker, Sandy Belcher, achieved a distinctive style by blending in 18 per cent Chardonnay. From 1989 they have been buying Sauvignon from the Hyde Vineyard in Carneros. The grapes are picked early to preserve freshness and acidity, and to avoid high alcohol. The must is fermented in old barrels and aged for up to nine months. There is no maceration and no malolactic fermentation. It is one of the few California Sauvignons intended to be bottle-aged for about five years. I have only tasted the Chalk Hill wine, which was floral and lemony on the nose and had splendid depth of flavour and concentration. Despite its severity, the wine had abundant fruit.

MATANZAS CREEK

Sonoma Valley

6097 Bennett Valley Road, Santa Rosa, CA 95404
Production: 95,000 bottles
Quality: 🍇🍇🍇🍇   Price: ★★★

For many years Matanzas have produced one of the very best Sauvignons in California. All the grapes are bought in. Half the must is barrel-fermented in one-third new oak, but the tank-fermented batch receives the same time, about five months, in oak. The wine shows impeccable balance, with rich, ripe fruit, oak and acidity all in harmony. Because it is not made in the usual overpowering Californian style it has real elegance too. The wine evolves very slowly in bottle, a tribute to the winemaking skills of David Ramey and his successor Susan Reed.

MERLION

Napa Valley

> 880 Vallejo Street, Napa, CA 94559
> BLANC DOUX
> Quality: ♦♦♦♦   Price: ★★★★★
> OTHERS
> Quality: ♦–♦♦   Price: ★★

The owners of Merlion, which produced their first wine in 1985, came from Vichon, a winery that had made outstanding Graves-style blends. George Vierra and winemaker John McKay pursued the same policy at Merlion. Their Sauvrier is a fifty-fifty blend with a hefty waxy, Sémillon nose; its heaviness and lack of concentration suggest that the Sémillon is making an excessive impact. The same problem afflicts the somewhat dour Chevrier, a varietal Sémillon. A rich sweet wine called Blanc Doux has been made from 71 per cent Sémillon and 29 per cent Sauvignon, and has 13° residual sugar. There is plenty of spicy oak on the nose, and the wine is rich and lively on the palate, lacking only in intensity of flavour. All the wines age well.

MONDAVI

Napa Valley

7801 St Helena Highway, Oakville, CA 94562

WOODBRIDGE

Quality: 🍇   Price: ★

FUMÉ BLANC

Quality: 🍇🍇   Price: ★★

FUMÉ BLANC RESERVE

Quality: 🍇🍇🍇🍇   Price: ★★★

BOTRYTIS SAUVIGNON

Quality: 🍇🍇🍇🍇   Price: ★★★★★

Best vintages: 1981, 1983, 1986, 1987, 1988

Robert Mondavi has a lot to answer for. He coined the term Fumé Blanc for his 1966 Sauvignon, and it has spread throughout the New World to denote – well, that's the problem. There is no consistency in usage, though for Mondavi the term has always meant an oaked style. The hand-picked grapes come from Oakville's Tokalon Vineyards and from Oak Knoll in the Stag's Leap area. Tokalon is mostly dry-farmed and the soil is clay loam with gravel; with yields kept down to 3–4 tons per acre it gives Sauvignon with fine floral aromas. Oak Knoll is cooler and gives more citric, green-apple aromas. Some Tokalon vines are over forty-five years old and are used to make the Reserve Fumé. About 10 per cent Sémillon is usually blended in after barrel-ageing is complete.

Since the wines tended to be rather heavy, in the early 1980s Mondavi abandoned maceration and malolactic fermentation and experimented with *sur lie* ageing to produce a livelier wine. Only a tiny portion of the must is barrel-fermented, but the wine is aged in older oak barrels for up to eight months. The Reserve, however, is almost all barrel-fermented and is aged in one- and two-year-old Nevers *barriques*.

In 1988 Mondavi began producing a simple but most

agreeable Woodbridge White, using Sauvignon from Santa Barbara, San Luis Obispo and the North Coast.

In 1981 and 1983 very sweet, intense Botrytis Sauvignon wines were made. They had tangy botrytis and tropical fruit flavours but lacked complexity and depth.

The Fumé is sometimes a disappointment, especially in recent years, but the Reserve remains rich, oaky and generous.

NEWTON

Napa Valley

> 2555 Madrona Avenue, St Helena, CA 94574
>
> Production: 24,000–60,000 bottles
>
> Quality: 🍇🍇🍇🍇   Price: ★★
>
> Best vintages: 1984, 1985, 1986, 1987

Peter and Su Hua Newton made Sauvignon at Sterling before they created this magnificent mountain estate. Here their ambition was to make a Graves-style blend, entirely barrel-fermented, half in new oak. The first vintage was 1983, and the last 1987, as the Newtons could not obtain sufficiently high prices to recoup the considerable production costs. The blend was 75 per cent Sauvignon, 25 per cent Sémillon; yields were very low, no more than 3 tons per acre. The wine stayed *sur lie* for nine months and was only released about thirty months after the harvest. It is sad that there was no room in a market crowded with overpriced Chardonnays for this exemplary blend.

PHELPS, JOSEPH

Napa Valley

> 200 Taplin Road, St Helena, CA 94574
>
> Production: 140,000–180,000   bottles   of   Sauvignon;
> 2,400–6,000 bottles of Délice du Sémillon

SAUVIGNON

Quality: 🍇   Price: ★★

DÉLICE DU SÉMILLON

Quality: 🍇🍇🍇   Price: ★★★★

For some reason Phelps has never made impressive Sauvignon. The wine, which completes fermentation in large oak casks, is simply dull. In appropriate years (1983, 1985, 1986, 1989) winemaker Craig Williams also makes a late-harvest wine called Délice du Sémillon, which is barrel-fermented in mostly new Nevers *barriques* and blended with a little Sauvignon, which is picked at 25 Brix but is not botrytized, and which provides the acidity usually lacking in Sémillon. The wine is sweet, appley and soft, lush and toasty in some vintages, but it does lack concentration, since the yields are a surprisingly high 2.5 tons per acre.

PRESTON

Sonoma Valley

9282 W. Dry Creek Road, Healdsburg, CA 95448

Vineyard: 26 acres (84 per cent Sauvignon, 16 per cent Sémillon)

CUVÉE DE FUMÉ

Quality: 🍇   Price: ★★

ESTATE RESERVE SAUVIGNON

Quality: 🍇🍇🍇   Price: ★★

Best vintages: 1986, 1988

Using almost solely estate-grown grapes Preston produce two Sauvignons. Cuvée de Fumé (75 per cent Sauvignon, 16 per cent Chenin, 9 per cent Sémillon) is tank-fermented and aged *sur lie* for six weeks in French *barriques*, of which half are new. The Estate Reserve is 80–85 per cent Sauvignon, and the balance is Sémillon. It is barrel-fermented, often in new *barriques*, then aged for three months in oak, half of which is new. The Fumé grapes tend to come from heavier soils, giving more grassy aromas, while the Reserve grapes are riper, giving the melon and pear flavours so beloved of California Sauvignon fanciers. The grapes are hand-picked and yields vary from 3.5 to a generous 5.5 tons per acre. Lots are vinified separately, so each wine is carefully blended by the winemaker, Kevin Hammel.

The Cuvée de Fumé easily develops vegetal tones and should be drunk young. It is a straightforward wine, blending Dry Creek acidity with a rounded style. The Reserve is much better, with richer, almost tropical, fruit and very good length. Sadly, the Reserve was phased out in 1990.

SILVERADO

Napa Valley

6121 Silverado Trail, Napa, CA 94558
Vineyard: 24 acres of Sauvignon
Production: 180,000 bottles
Quality: 🍇🍇🍇   Price: ★★

At this expanding Yountville winery Jack Stuart makes Sauvignon that is rounded and ripe but has fresh, crisp acidity and good length. Grapes are hand-picked and average yields are just over 5 tons per acre. After tank-fermentation, the wine is aged for two to three months in French *barriques*, some of which are new. The 1989 wine is excessively light and grapefruity.

SIMI

Sonoma Valley

16275 Healdsburg Avenue, Healdsburg, CA 95448

Production: 120,000 bottles of Sauvignon; 3,600 bottles of Sémillon

SÉMILLON

Quality: 🍇   Price: ★★

SAUVIGNON

Quality: 🍇🍇–🍇🍇🍇   Price: ★★★

Best vintages: 1984, 1987

Simi buy their Sauvignon grapes from Chalk Hill vineyards, but an increasing percentage come from their own estate. Since 1987, 45 per cent of the must has been barrel-fermented, then blended with tank-fermented wines and aged *sur lie* for three to four months in French *barriques*, of which 10 per cent are new. In recent years there has been a change of style, with lower acidity and higher alcohol, giving the richer, more melony wines that suit the Californian palate. I preferred the earlier style, and find wines made after 1988 too fat and confected.

The Sémillon is a curiosity, a single-vineyard wine that since 1986 is usually barrel-fermented. In some vintages it is blended in with the Sauvignon. When bottled on its own it needs a few years to develop its character.

In 1989 Simi experimented by fermenting their best must entirely in new oak. It was so immensely superior to any of the bottled wines that it left me wondering about the kinds of compromise winemakers must make to fall into line with consumers' expectations, not least with regard to price.

SPOTTSWOODE

Napa Valley

> 1401 Hudson Avenue, St Helena, CA 94574
>
> Vineyard: 10 acres (80 per cent Sauvignon, 20 per cent Sémillon)
>
> Production: 15,000–28,000 bottles
>
> Quality: 🍇🍇🍇🍇   Price: ★★★

Spottswoode's winemaking is in the hands of the brilliant Tony Soter who, unlike most California winemakers, devotes as much attention to the vineyard as to the winery. He thins the vines to keep yields down to 4–4.5 tons per acre and seeks ripeness without excessive sugar, which would give high alcohol to the wine. At least half the Sauvignon is fermented in new oak and aged for three months in wood, whereas the tank-fermented portion spends only one month in oak. The final blend contains 20 per cent Sémillon. The wine is bottled young as Soter wants a delicate style. This he achieves, and the wine is very distinctive, with a combination of richness of fruit with lacy, oaky elegance.

STAG'S LEAP

Napa Valley

> 5766 Silverado Trail, Napa, CA 94558
>
> Production: 80,000 bottles
>
> HAWK CREST
>
> Quality: 🍇🍇   Price: ★★
>
> STAG'S LEAP
>
> Quality: 🍇🍇–🍇🍇🍇   Price: ★★★

All the grapes for Stag's Leap Sauvignon are bought in from Wooden Valley vineyards on slopes east of Napa. Sémillon, which contributes 15 per cent to the blend, comes from gravelly soil beneath the slopes. The grapes are hand-picked early, and yields are about 5.5 tons per acre. Three quarters of the must is barrel-fermented and aged in one-year-old Allier *barriques* for four months. One fifth of the wine undergoes malolactic fermentation to increase its complexity. The winemaker John Gibson hopes eventually to barrel-ferment all the wine. Recent vintages, labelled Rancho Chimiles, are crisp and lively, with more elegance than depth of flavour. The 1989 was more broad and fruity, but well balanced.

Stag's Leap's other range, Hawk Crest, is mostly tank-fermented and receives only a touch of oak-ageing. The wine is looser in structure than Stag's Leap but is clean and attractive and more refreshing than many baggier California Sauvignons.

TOGNI, PHILIP

Napa Valley

3780 Spring Mountain Road, St Helena, CA 94574
Vineyard: 3 acres of Sauvignon
Production: 1,600–7,500 bottles
Quality: 🍇🍇🍇 Price: ★★★

Philip Togni retains his English accent and manner despite three decades of experience as a Californian winemaker. Since 1981 he has worked this tiny 10-acre estate accountable to no one but himself and his enthusiastic customers. Even though his dry-farmed Sauvignon vines (Wente clones) are 2,000 feet up in the mountains, he finds it hard to restrain their vigour and has adopted some of Richard Smart's canopy-management techniques.

Togni's idea of a good Sauvignon is a wine that complements oysters. Thus his Sauvignon is unwooded but serious. The grapes are picked early, cold-fermented, and after fining and a single filtration bottled very young, but aged for a year before release. It is a splendid wine, with bracing acidity and full-flavoured piquancy.

TOPAZ

Napa Valley

> St Helena
> Production: 4,000–8,000 bottles
> Quality: 🍇🍇🍇🍇   Price: ★★★★
> Best vintages: 1986, 1989

When in 1985 Macauley's owner Ann Watson found that she had 2 acres of overripe Sauvignon, she asked itinerant winemaker Jeff Sowell to produce a sweet wine. He did so. After Watson's death in a car crash Sowell continued making sweet wines, released under the name of Topaz. In 1986 the wine blended 60 per cent Sauvignon, picked at 43 Brix, with Sémillon bought in from Yountville and harvested at 31 Brix. The wine was fermented in mostly new French *barriques* and aged for eighteen months. The next wine, 60 per cent Sauvignon and 40 per cent Sémillon from Monticello's vineyards, was made in 1989 and also aged for eighteen months in *barriques*. These wines are citric, even astringent, in their youth, such is their concentration and oak tannin, but with time they should be superb. In 1989 Sowell also used Monticello fruit to make Dulcinea, a Sémillon-dominated wine, for the Villa Helena winery.

VICHON

Napa Valley

> 1595 Oakville Grade, Oakville, CA 94562
> Production: 240,000 bottles of Chevrignon; 500 half-bottles of Botrytis Sémillon

CHEVRIGNON

Quality: 🍇🍇🍇   Price: ★★★

BOTRYTIS SÉMILLON

Quality: 🍇🍇🍇🍇   Price: ★★★★

Best vintages: 1985, 1987, 1988, 1989

This winery was founded in 1980 by George Vierra and John McKay but bought by Mondavi in 1985, whereupon the previous owners set up Merlion (q.v.). The current winemakers are Karen Culler and Michael Weis. Vichon have specialized in a long-lived Sauvignon–Sémillon blend called Chevrignon, usually with a touch more Sauvignon than Sémillon. Chevrignon survived the change of ownership, and remains a very good wine. The grapes, picked early to give modest alcohol levels that do not obscure the firm fruit, are bought in from ten different low-yielding Napa vineyards. The must is fermented in old French *barriques* and aged *sur lie* for six months. There is no skin contact and no malolactic fermentation.

In 1987 Vichon made a splendid Botrytis Sémillon from grapes picked at 38 Brix: the botrytis was apparent on the nose and the palate showed a rich salad of honey, peaches and lemon, and an acidity that should keep the wine alive and developing for a decade or more.

WENTE

Alameda County

5565 Tesla Road, Livermore, CA 94550

Vineyard: 269 acres (70 per cent Sauvignon, 30 per cent Sémillon)

Production: 180,000 bottles of Sauvignon; 36,000 bottles of Sémillon

Quality: 🍇🍇   Price: ★★

This large Livermore winery was the home of the original plantations of Sauvignon in the last century. The vines in the nursery here, known as the Wente clones, have supplied countless Californian vineyards with cuttings. Wente's vineyards are cool, with a long growing season; yields are kept low, to about 3 tons per acre. The grapes are pressed in whole clusters, fermented in steel tanks and aged in American oak for up to six months. The wines are well made but lack complexity and stylishness.

Wente also produce, when the fruit is suitable, Late Harvest wines from either a single variety or a Sauvignon–Sémillon blend. These are not dessert wines but wines with between 8 and 12 grams of residual sugar.

Texas

Texas would seem an unlikely spot to find Sauvignon, but some successful wines have emerged from the Lone Star State. Many of the best vineyards are high up in the Panhandle where nights are cool and the growing season fairly long. Llano Estacado, outside Lubbock, were among the pioneers in the Panhandle and their early Sauvignons were aromatic and austere and vigorous. The winery also produced a Fumé wine, which I found less impressive. At the Pheasant Ridge winery, also close to Lubbock, Bobby Cox makes a light, herbaceous Sauvignon of no great personality. Other wineries, such as Fall Creek and Cypress Valley, also produce Sauvignon.

An interesting development in recent years has been the purchase of 1,000 acres by the Bordeaux firm of Cordier. The vines are planted on chalky clay soil 3,000 feet up between the Rio Grande and Pecos rivers. As in the Panhandle, the height ensures cool nights and good acidity levels. The grapes receive twenty-four hours' skin contact before being cool-fermented in tanks and aged in French *barriques*.

Washington State

While Californian winemakers struggle against unsuitable growing conditions and climate in their attempt to make good Sauvignon, 800 miles to the north, in Washington State, growers enjoy almost ideal conditions, which they have not been slow to exploit. There are a few insignificant vineyards around Seattle, but the largest and best sites lie to the east, beyond the Cascade Mountains. Seattle and the Cascades are notorious for their heavy rainfall, but the region to the east, in contrast, is officially classified as semi-arid. The average annual rainfall here is only 8 inches, so the Columbia River must be tapped for irrigation. Cool nights prolong the growing season, helping the grapes to achieve the right balance of sugar and acidity. Washington has an additional advantage in that in summer there are often two hours' more daylight than, say, in Napa. The only major problem encountered in Washington is severe frost. Pests such as phylloxera are unknown, thanks to the mostly sandy soil in which the destructive louse cannot thrive.

Vineyard regions have developed around the major rivers: the Columbia, the Snake and the Yakima. Columbia Valley is a touch warmer than Yakima, but there are considerable differences between individual sites. Within this major region there are sub-regions, such as the breezy Wahluke Slope near the Tri-Cities, where over the past twenty years the volcanic loam soils have produced consistently fine fruit. Irrigation is essential, though there are some dry-farmed vineyards located on clay soils that retain moisture better than sandy soils.

Such conditions clearly suit the Sauvignon vine, and by 1988 some 792 acres were planted with it, accounting for 8 per cent of all vineyards. But the Columbia basin is also highly suitable for Sémillon, which is almost as widely planted, with 667 acres under vine in 1988. Whereas Sémillon in California can be embarrassingly overproductive, in Washington it is more restrained, giving more concentrated, firmer flavours, with distinctive herbaceousness. Sémillon needs years in bottle to develop its richness of flavour, rather like Hunter Valley Sémillon, though the American version never attains the complexity of the Australian wine. As for Sauvignon, the characteristic that makes it so exciting in Washington – its high acidity – is precisely the characteristic that most American wine lovers don't care for. So in Washington, as in California, the acidity is moderated either by wood-ageing or by leaving residual sugar in the wine. None the less, Washington Sauvignon is better able to withstand such manipulations than its Californian cousin.

Almost every one of Washington's seventy-five wineries produces Sauvignon, so the following entries are necessarily selective. It is worth mentioning a few other wineries that make good Sauvignon. The new Cascade Crest winery is still finding its feet; its Sauvignon is not good, but the unwooded Sémillon can be very fine. At Staton Hills too, the well-balanced subtle Sémillon is distinctly superior to the uninteresting Sauvignon; unfortunately the Sémillon, which proved hard to sell, is being phased out. Rob Griffin, the former winemaker at Preston and Hogue, has set up his own Barnard Griffin winery, and first releases of his Fumé style, oak-fermented and aged *sur lie*, have shown forceful melony aromas and flavours, and delicious fruitiness.

Stable climatic conditions mean that there are not enormous variations between vintages. In 1990 cold weather during flowering, and a month-long heatwave, did not affect quality, but reduced the crop by at least 30 per cent.

ARBOR CREST

Columbia River

4705 Fruithill Road, Spokane, WA 99207
Production: 170,000 bottles of Sauvignon
Quality: 🍇🍇🍇   Price: ★★

Arbor Crest has, since its first release in 1982, been one of the most successful producers of Sauvignon. Both Sauvignon and Sémillon are grown on the Wahluke Slope. Although the vines are young and vigorous, deliberate thinning of bunches keeps yields down to 3 tons per acre. The grapes are hand-picked and fermented in stainless steel; there is no malolactic fermentation. The wine is aged in Allier *barriques* for up to three months, the Reserve wine for longer. Fifteen per cent Sémillon is blended in. Like most Washington Sauvignons, Arbor Crest has a little residual sugar, although it is not easily perceptible on the palate. It is a very typical Washington Sauvignon: fresh, piquant, with a touch of spiciness from the light oak-ageing. What it lacks in complexity it makes up for in vigour.

BLACKWOOD CANYON

Yakima Valley

Kiona, WA 99320
Production: 15,000 bottles of Sémillon
Quality: 🍇🍇–🍇🍇🍇🍇   Price: ★★★

This is the most eccentric of Washington estates. Mike Moore is in permanent revolt against the squeaky-clean school of winemaking typified by Davis graduates. His wines are hand-crafted, and each vintage is handled differently, depending on the quality of the fruit and his whim. The vines are planted on well-drained sandy loam soil, and the winery, which resembles an old garage, looks chaotic. Moore is more excited by Sémillon than Sauvignon, and he acquires his grapes from a number of local vineyards. Yields are up to 6 tons per acre, but Moore maintains that these vineyards are capable of producing much higher yields without any loss in quality.

There is no skin contact, and after pressing the wine is fermented in old American whisky barrels, which he finds more neutral than French *barriques*. The wine remains *sur lie* for at least ten months, sometimes eighteen months, during which it undergoes malolactic fermentation. Moore has none of the reductive winemaker's fear of oxygen, and he uses no sulphur dioxide at all and leaves the bungs loose in the barrels. The wine is left alone to find its own levels of alcohol and acidity. Occasionally, as in 1986, he produces a single-vineyard bottling from Judkins Vineyard, and, as in 1987, a Botrytis Sémillon (not commercially available as the quantities are minute).

Blackwood Canyon Sémillon is assertive, very herbaceous, high in alcohol, slightly dour and nutty, but it does have tremendous extract and depth of flavour. The headiness and pungency of this Sémillon make it unique, but very much an acquired taste.

CHÂTEAU STE MICHELLE

Columbia River

> Stimson Lane, Woodinville, WA 98072
>
> COLUMBIA CREST RANGE
>
> Quality: 🍇   Price: ★
>
> FUMÉ BLANC, SÉMILLON
>
> Quality: 🍇🍇   Price: ★★
>
> SÉMILLON RESERVE
>
> Quality: 🍇🍇🍇   Price: ★★★

This very large winery has long been advised by the Californian oenologist André Tchelistcheff, and quality has always been high. The Sauvignon and Sémillon come from cool vineyards in River Ridge in the Columbia Basin. Grapes are also bought in.

The winery's range is impressive. The Sémillon is a dry wine aged for three months in large oak casks. Sémillon Blanc is an unwooded wine with about 8 grams per litre of residual sugar. In very good vintages a barrel-aged Sémillon Reserve is also produced. The Fumé Blanc was launched in 1976 in a fairly herbaceous style, and six years later the winery launched a Sauvignon Blanc, which is more mellow and oaky. Both these wines are aged in *barriques* and large oak casks.

The Sémillon is a pleasant, somewhat neutral wine with a touch of tartness. The Sémillon Blanc has a sweetness I find jarring, but it is clearly commercially successful. The Fumé is both sleek and firm but can vary from vintage to vintage, whereas the Sauvignon Blanc is spicy but always slightly sweet. The best wine is the Sémillon Reserve: gently oaky, rich, compact, with an attractive austerity and excellent capacity for ageing in bottle.

Under the same ownership is the Columbia Crest range, made at a separate winery. I find all the wines simple and confected, but they are inexpensive and have proved very popular.

CHINOOK

Yakima Valley

> PO Box 387, Prosser, WA 99350
>
> Production: 4,000 bottles of Sauvignon
>
> SAUVIGNON
>
> Quality: 🍇🍇–🍇🍇🍇   Price: ★★
>
> SÉMILLON
>
> Quality: 🍇🍇🍇   Price: ★★

Kay Simon and Clay Mackey, both formerly of Château Ste Michelle, released their first vintage here in 1983. Grapes are bought in, and the Sauvignon often comes from Clipsun Vineyard near Benton City, a warm area with light sandy soil. Yields are a modest 3 tons per acre. Up to 20 per cent Sémillon is blended into the Sauvignon, but from 1987 onwards the Sémillon has been a single varietal wine, marketed under the name Topaz.

The grapes are pressed in whole clusters, and fermentation begins in stainless steel but is completed in barrels; the wine ages *sur lie* for about ten months in French and American oak. Sometimes, as in 1988, there is a malolactic fermentation. In the finished wine acidity can be high and there is minimal residual sugar.

I find the woody flavours too pronounced in the Sauvignon, as the varietal character tends to be smothered by the extended oak-ageing. I prefer the rich, fatter Sémillon, which has greater depth of flavour.

COLUMBIA

Columbia River

1445 120th Avenue, N. E. Bellevue, WA 98005

Production: 120,000 bottles of Sémillon

Quality: 🍇🍇–🍇🍇🍇   Price: ★★

This large winery, founded in 1962 as Associated Vintners, has been run since 1979 by Englishman David Lake and his oenologist Bruce Watson. The name was changed to Columbia in 1982.

Their Sémillon is made from grapes bought from five growers in Sagemoor and Yakima. The must is tank-fermented and occasionally malolactic fermentation is encouraged to lower the acidity. The aim is to produce a light, unwooded style with no more than 12° alcohol and an acidity of 6–6.5 grams per litre, which will be an ideal accompaniment to the abundant seafood of the Pacific coast. The wine is well made but sometimes lacks character. It has a nutty, spicy tone that keeps the flavours interesting in the mouth. I have had ten-year-old examples that are still drinking well, but the wine does not greatly benefit from extended bottle-ageing.

COLUMBIA CREST. *See* Château Ste Michelle

HOGUE

Yakima Valley

PO Box 31, Prosser, WA 99350

Production: 300,000 bottles of Fumé Blanc

SÉMILLON

Quality: 🍇🍇🍇   Price: ★

FUMÉ BLANC

Quality: 🍇🍇🍇   Price: ★★

Hogue's first vintage was in 1982, and since then the winery has become one of the most acclaimed in Washington. Half the grapes are bought in from growers near Pasco, but Sémillon grapes come from Hogue's vineyards in Sunnyside, planted on sandy loam. The young vines are machine-picked and yields are 4–5 tons per acre.

There is no skin contact and the must is tank-fermented; there is no malolactic fermentation. A proportion of the wine, 15–20 per cent, is aged in American oak for two to three months and is then blended with the remainder. This Fumé Blanc, which contains 25 per cent Sémillon, has a few grams of residual sugar and is intended to be drunk young. Until 1986 the Sémillon was also aged in American oak, but from 1989 onwards this wine was made in an unwooded, and less expensive, style.

The Fumé is rounded and lent some body by the oak-ageing, yet the fruit retains its fresh grassiness. Some vintages, such as 1987, have been a touch confected, but the 1988 is a very good wine. The unwooded Sémillon is delicious, spicy and firm, though it could use more intensity of flavour.

PRESTON

Yakima Valley

> 502 E. Vineyard Drive, Pasco, WA 99301
> Production: 30,000 bottles of Fumé Blanc
> FUMÉ BLANC
> Quality: 🍇   Price: ★
> LATE HARVEST SAUVIGNON BLANC
> Quality: 🍇   Price: ★★★

Sprawling across the sandy loam plain in the southern Columbia Basin are the 180 acres of Preston vineyards, first planted in 1972. Irrigation gives abundant crops, so Bill Preston thins the bunches to keep yields below 6 tons per acre. The grapes have been machine-picked since 1988. The must is tank-fermented and malolactic fermentation is encouraged to soften the wine, which is aged for at least six months in Limousin and American oak. This extended barrel-ageing gives a rounded style and plays down the crisp assertiveness of Sauvignon despite its high acidity. The result is a well-made but intrinsically unexciting wine, lacking in aroma and varietal character. In certain years such as 1978 and 1985 a Late Harvest Sauvignon is made, exhibiting ripe pineapple flavours.

SNOQUALMIE

Columbia River

> 1000 Winery Road, Snoqualmie, WA 98065
> Production: 65,000 bottles of Fumé Blanc; 55,000 bottles of Sémillon
> Quality: 🍇🍇   Price: ★★

All the Sauvignon and Sémillon grapes for this large but financially troubled winery are bought in from growers, mostly from the Wahluke Slope. Yields are a substantial 6 tons per acre. The must is fermented in tank and there is no malolactic fermentation. The Fumé contains a dash of Sémillon, the Sémillon a dash of Sauvignon. The Sémillon is unwooded, but the Fumé spends up to six weeks in oak. The Fumé has aromas of honeydew melon, and tastes ripe and full-flavoured despite its high acidity. The Sémillon is much more austere and needs some bottle-age to show its complexity. Both wines are sensibly priced. A second range of wines, even less expensive and intended to be drunk when released, is available from the associated Saddle Mountain winery.

STEWART

Yakima Valley

1381 W. Riverside Drive, Sunnyside, WA 98944

Production: 50,000–60,000 bottles of Sauvignon

Quality: 🍇🍇–🍇🍇🍇🍇   Price: ★★

The Stewarts, having originally been grape-growers, set up their own winery in 1983. Both Sauvignon and Sémillon have been planted on the Wahluke Slope, but the grapes only came into production in the early 1990s. Previous vintages were made from fruit bought in from the Grandview vineyards in Yakima Valley. The must is tank-fermented, there is no malolactic fermentation and the wine is aged for two months in French oak. The Stewart Sauvignon, now being made by Scott Benham, is bone-dry, so the high acidity comes through racily on the palate and gives the wine exemplary length. There is a hint of smokiness from the oak, but this wine is refreshingly different from the rounded, creamy styles favoured by most Sauvignon winemakers in North America. This is the most Sancerre-like of Washington Sauvignons, and a thoroughly appropriate way to treat cool-climate grapes.

WOODWARD CANYON

Columbia River

Route 1, Lowden, WA 99360
Production: 2,400 bottles of Charbonneau
Quality: 🍇   Price: ★★★★

Most Washington wineries make relatively straightforward wines at a competitive price. Not Rick Small at Woodward Canyon, whose Sémillon is an unabashed attempt to make a serious Graves-style wine. His Sémillon (which contains a little Sauvignon too) is called Charbonneau, named after the Snake River vineyard where the grapes are grown. The soil is shallow and the yields low, giving the fruit considerable concentration of flavour. The grapes are pressed in an old vertical press, and the Sémillon receives skin contact, a rarity in Washington. The must is barrel-fermented in new oak and goes through malolactic fermentation. The wine is stirred on the fine lees for about seven months. The only vintages so far produced have been 1985 and 1988. Charbonneau has been rapturously received, but I found the 1988 wine clumsy and far from harmonious.

YUGOSLAVIA

Sauvignon is widely planted in Yugoslavia, but only the most commercial examples are seen in export markets. Sauvignon is found in Slovenia, where it is sometimes made into an off-dry or late-harvest wine. It is growing in favour in Croatia, especially among private growers who can obtain good prices for the wines. But it is in north-eastern Yugoslavia, in Vojvodina, that larger plantations of Sauvignon are grown. The sub-region of Fruska Gora and Vojvodina alone account for almost 1,200 acres. Serbian Sauvignon is used mostly as a blending wine, and the same is true of this variety in Kosovo.

Sémillon is a less important variety. In Vojvodina, 750 acres are planted, but it is often used as blending wine. The same is true of dispersed plantations in other parts of Serbia, though it is also made into a single-varietal wine. Whereas Sauvignon is relatively unimportant in Kosovo, over 600 acres are planted with Sémillon here, and the wine known as Kosovki Semijon contains a proportion of Sauvignon.

INDEX